ANTONY BRADE.

Τὸ Ἔαρ.

. . . .

Πορφυρέη μείδησε φερανθέος ἄνθεος ὥρη·
Γαῖα δὲ κυανέη χλοερὴν ἐστέψατο ποίην. κ.τ.λ.

[Here] smiles the purple spring's bloom-bearing time;
And swart earth does her glossy green hair trim;
Decks with fresh leaflets every bursting limb.
Here drink the pure and quickening dew of morn
The laughing meads; and the soft rose is born.

. . . .

The shipmen, lithe, plough the wide-foaming seas,
Bellying their sails with frolic Zephyr's breeze.

. . . .

And, aye, the brisk-tongued bird-race plies its song;
Kingfishers seaward; swallows, roofs among.

MELEAGROS, Idyll. *To Spring.*

Antony Brade.

BY

ROBERT LOWELL,

AUTHOR OF "THE NEW PRIEST IN CONCEPTION BAY," ETC.

BOSTON:
ROBERTS BROTHERS.
1874.

CAMBRIDGE:
PRESS OF JOHN WILSON AND SON.

CONTENTS.

ANTONY BRADE.

CHAPTER I.

ST. BARTHOLOMEW'S SCHOOL AND EASTHAM.

Although our story lies at least as much among grown-up people as among boys, yet we begin it among these, because our hero happens to be one of them.

Saint Bartholomew's School in Eastham, or St. Bart's, as it is called for shortness, or Bartlemas, as the boys call it in kindly nickname, stands, or ought to stand, on high ground of easy climbing, surrounded by higher ground on all the colder sides. Below, between it and the town, lies a pretty lake, three-quarters of a mile or a mile across, shored with in-and-out grassy or wooded slopes, green in summer, almost or quite to the water's edge, on all sides but the eastern. On that shore is a shelving beach of sand and gravel. Near that side lies the highway going up northward, white against the high bank of the lake. There is a green and pretty winding lane at the western side; and on the northern bank, approached by an irregular path from the school-buildings above, are two or three boat-houses, two of which are surmounted by flag-staffs.

The school buildings, which are a good mass of brick, make a pretty broad show, and are already kindly taken into fellowship by great Nature, although at first foreign; for her friendly grass has drawn up close to their feet, and She is encouraging woodbine and ivy to play, as they do, gracefully and freely on the brick walls, while awnings over windows, here and there, match, with their green or blue stripes, the earth or sky.

The house is somewhat impressive in the daytime by its size; and in the earlier hours of night glowing with bright light through a long row of windows in the lower story, and here and there above.

What may be called a lawn — for it is a good stretch of green, though broken by scattered trees and shrubs, and clumps of trees and shrubs — spreads outwards and downwards to the bank of the lake.

About these school-buildings of St. Bart's there is a story, — a story not indeed so long as that of St. Martin's Church in the Strand, or University College, Oxford, or the Round Mill at Newport even, and yet a story which might, with pains enough taken, be worked up into romance.

These ample buildings the local memory reports to have been first thrust up into the air, boldly and ambitiously, among the standing and living things of the universe, for a "hat manufactory;" and in that capacity to have "made a failure of it," as the neighbors express themselves. They were still standing up, empty and desolate, among the other things of the universe, when the infatuation about "The Midland Summer House" went through that part of the country.

Under the influence of this epidemic, which rose and spread like any fever, one or two retired city-men, and three or four brisk men still in business in the city, but lodging and spending their spare time among the fields and trees, had put in their few thousands apiece; a country merchant or two had been moved to do as much; and two or three scores of saving farmers and other country people had put in their hundred, or their fifty, or their less; and so altogether they had turned the big building into a hotel and boarding-house. The huge rooms had been cut up with partitions into dining-hall, dance-hall, parlors, and chambers; a wing, two-thirds as long as the main building, and one story lower, had been pushed back from the western end, and filled, like a beehive, with small cells, called bedrooms, on both sides of a long, narrow passage on each floor; verandas had been run along the front and wing; and a consistent cupola, above every thing, caught the fresh breezes and surveyed the broad country.

"The Midland Summer House," when finished, was a joy to the neighborhood, and a hope and expectation to the shrewd investors, and the no less shrewd holders-off; for it was to bring society to the city-men's families, easy and profitable practice to the medical men, a market for the country-people, employment to all the washerwomen, chore-women, masons, carpenters, painters, and whom not?

Besides all this, it was to add one-half to the worth of every foot of ground within five miles from that centre, or, in other words, within a circle of ten miles diameter.

Mr. Thomas Parmenter, of Eastham, was very energetic and public-spirited about it. Mr. Parmenter, once a country merchant, had now for some years had a handsome place in the city, where (without a sign) he dealt in choice foreign fruits and flowers, including, somehow, the specialties of "Aqua-rose" and "Melitrech." He had been twice married, and twice a widower. His experience, as we see, had been large and varied.

He, like the others, had invested his money; and, for his own good and theirs, was busy in all the planning and building; and then had a chief voice in securing one Mr. Sharon Andrews, a bright-colored, pleasant-spoken man, who was understood to have been making money in keeping "The Great European Casino" at the corner of Utopia and Back-bay Streets in Boston, and was willing to come for a year or two to "set the enterprise on its legs."

With this successful gentleman, things lived and flourished at the Summer House through one season of free invitations, and of neighborhood assessments of milk, butter, and vegetables, in which Mr. Parmenter, and some of his rich city-men, bore their shares.

During this time its passages and doorways and piazzas swarmed with guests; the roads of Eastham flashed, and were lively with carriages and saddle-horses, and scarfs and ribbons; the passages of the house were redolent with "Parmenter's Aqua-rose," and all the tables bright with crystal vases of "Parmenter's Melitrech." It had its "hops" and balls, and concerts, sacred and others; it had its private theatricals, and almost its oratorio, which two members of the Handel and Haydn Society nearly succeeded in getting up; it had its moonlight serenades, and pic-nics, and chowders, and clam-bakes, on the lake and its shores, and its ramblers and strollers in the woods. In short, it had all the forms of elegance and intelligence which are usually exhibited by a good many (not perhaps first-rate) fashionable young men and women, and a few "fast" young men and some foolish young women, when they are enjoying themselves and showing themselves off in the sight of rustics. It wound up the season with dinners of "The Agricultural Union," of which Dr. Evans was president, and of "The Farmers' Reserves," of which Mr. Waite, manufacturer at Weston, was president. It had paragraphs in the papers. It had done something toward making a name.

The second year it advertised early, and opened a little late, with the launch of the yacht "Iris" on the lake, and a reunion of "The Three Counties' Medical Association;" languished through three rainy weeks; and then — Mr. Parmenter, having called a meeting of all the persons interested, and then having furnished them with a reasonable feeding of cold chicken and pickles in the dining-room of the hotel, addressed them all as fellow-investors with himself; proposed a plan by which Mr. Sharon Andrews — who had been absent for a few days — should accept an extraordinary opening just offered him in Chicago, and a committee of their own appointing should wind up the affairs of the Summer House, and secure the buildings and property to the common benefit of those concerned. One of the city-men moved the appointment of three gentlemen whom he named, — a farmer, the merchant of the place, and Mr. Parmenter; and, after the going over several times of the whole matter, the committee was appointed. Almost everybody grumbled, especially those who "had always said so when they first put in their money." Mr. Parmenter undertook to "run the house" for the two and a half months remaining, in connection with its clerk; he carried it through; lost only eleven hundred dollars, he said, where he had expected to lose, at the least, thirty-five hundred; the buildings and furniture, after a year or two, were sold by auction, in lots to suit purchasers; Mr. Parmenter had bought the land and buildings, and the bulk of the household stuff; and, within a month after that, Mr. Parmenter had got together a set of gentlemen, of different professions and more or less note, as a Board of Trustees for a school. Within three months they had secured an Act of Incorporation for St. Bartholomew's School, Eastham.

On the Board there were two ex-judges, — Allen and Pearson, — of one court or other; one law lecturer, Pethrick; the Rev. Dr. Cruden Baxter, one of the editors of "The Supplementary Cyclopedia of the Bible," now abroad; the Rev. Dr. Farwell, a member of several Committees and Boards; Dr. Button, whose name we will spell, if we have occasion to use it, with two *n*'s, to show that the accent falls upon the last syllable (Dr. Buttonn was once accountant in a boot-factory, and now for many years a priest); the Rev. Mr. Manson, rector of the little parish in Eastham, and editor of "The Church Post," which he pleasantly called a pillar of the church; the Rev. Mr. Merrill, a long, sober-looking clergyman, member of half as many Boards and Committees as Dr. Farwell; the enterprising Mr. Thomas Parmenter; Mr. Isaiah Don, who, though a man of business, a director in a savings bank, last year a compromise member of the legislature, was after all most notable for being an admirer of Mr. Parmenter and his success, and Mr. Pettie, a man with a face like one of the lesser quadrupeds, but who had become of some account on 'Change by shrewd management of an unexpected legacy. He was the eleventh member of the Board.

As indicating the individual standing of the members and their importance in the community, the Rev. Dr. Farwell, one of them, a man of very moderate size, but of large manner, after studying the written list for some time, remarked to Mr. Manson, a strong, hearty, and hale man, who was a brother clergyman and brother trustee, —

"Among these
Eleven Trustees
Are three LL.- and three D.D.'s."

To this the other added, —

"Two *un*-Doctored parsons, or chicka-D.D.'s.

"We must bring in two more, — Mr. Parmenter and Mr. Don. Well, we can bring them both in, in some such fashion as this, I suppose : —

"And a couple of men representing I D's."

"There's ten," said Dr. Farwell. "Who's left out?" Mr. Manson looked at the list. "Mr. Pettie," said he.

"Well," answered Dr. Farwell, with a solemn jocosity of manner, "we can't make poetry of him."

There was the Board of Trustees of St. Bartholomew's School.

The change in the buildings from the Midland Summer House to St. Bart's School was easily made. The long rows of little bedrooms were thrown open to the long passages between, and then hung with curtains instead of doors; and in this way made as good alcoves for a boys' dormitory as if at first planned for them. Larger rooms were kept here and there for tutors, and for household purposes; some parlors became recitation-rooms; the dining-room stayed much as it was; the ball-room became a school-room; a handsome share of the main house was given to family use; and the cupola became an astronomical observatory, to be furnished when the time should come. The thing was done, and well done; and, what was more, the buildings looked well, and answered their purpose.

Thereafter the liveliness of boys, and the public and private spendings of a large establishment, and the success of a great institution, were to take the place of the fashion and show which had so soon and so utterly fleeted with the second season of the Midland Summer House.

The town of Eastham, in which St. Bart's School stands, and is the chief thing, is as pretty as almost any country place with neat houses and some fine trees, and that which gives it its greatest beauty, — its lake.

As we shall have many readers who are very studious and scholarly persons, and as some of them have already got map in hand to fix their memory of our geography, and as a lake is one of the best things in any landscape, and people know it, we must be a little precise here about this great treasure of St. Bart's and Eastham, and show how it comes that there is a conflict of names in maps and in people's mouths.

Now, all learned readers are, of course, aware of the way in which the human race always makes its additions to the stock of names bestowed by Adam. In all essential respects that way was followed by those members of the race who took upon them the naming of this lake at the seventeenth meeting of "The St. Bart's Boat Club."

Two classical factions in the school laid claim to the privilege of giving it a Greek and a Roman name respectively: the one, on the ground that the Greeks were the finest men that ever lived, and the Greek language was the finest language that ever existed, the Caput said so; the other, because it was a self-evident proposition that the Romans had whipped the Greeks. At length it was reluctantly arranged between the leaders — Gaston, then in the third form, and Burgess, in the fourth, — and accepted with acclamations by the multitude on both sides, who were heartily tired of the discussion, that the water should bear a "Græco-Roman" name, by the combination of the two proposed, which were "Copais," from a lake in Bœotia, the largest that the Phil-Hellenes could find in Greece, and "Trasymenus," from a pond in Etruria. "Copais-Trasymene" it was to be for ever called; Gaston, the Hellene, having secured that ending, which he said was musical and poetical; and a committee, consisting of the aforesaid leaders, was appointed to convey the results of this important deliberation to the map-makers and writers of gazetteers throughout the land, and throughout the world.

The committee, having divided the labor between them, sent carefully written, and of course carefully worded, notes in abundance to the Messrs. Thompson and Mr. Sharpe, and to Mr. Lock, and to Mr. Ledwaite, and to all the rest of the map and atlas men, and in the end achieved this success: one of those publishers got it printed "Eastham P.," and underneath, in parenthesis, ("L. C. T."); three of them returned answer that "they would attend to it when they made new plates" (which Gaston, who was a learned fellow, said was putting off to the Greek Kalends); one got it down as "Copious P.," and in explanation wrote that he "thought the rest was only boys' fooling."

A party in the school strongly set about nicknaming it "Cop;" another tried to call it "Trasy;" and the school settled down upon "Lake Thrash," and there it is this day with that name belonging to it; and the boys of St. Bart's are resolutely determined never to buy map or atlas made by any one of those men.

CHAPTER II.

MYSTERY ABOUT ANTONY BRADE.

Young Antony Brade had come to St. Bart's only that fall, and, as has been seen, the boys soon found, or fancied a mystery about him. It would have been difficult, perhaps, to trace the prevailing opinion to any definite source; but it had spread through the school, and had stayed there, more or less strong and active, according as it was fed, more or less often, from without and within, by fresh supplies of conjecture. He was generally thought to belong to some very important family abroad; he either might be the heir-apparent of royalty, for some reason sent off and concealed a great way from home, or he might be a son of some family lower than royalty, who, for whatever reason (as above), had been sent away to be educated in this country; most likely because this country was the greatest in the world; and sent to the Rector of St. Bart's because "the Caput" was one of the most illustrious scholars and teachers in the world. It was not settled in this community whether the Rector was in the secret of Antony's origin, or partly in the secret, or not at all in the secret; but it was a thing of course to the boys that the lad's guardian in the city knew nothing further than that the boy was to be watched over carefully, and that there was plenty of money appropriated to his bringing-up.

Outside the school, among the families that called themselves "society" in Eastham, an opinion of a somewhat definite character had found a place, — that young Brade was a Russian of high extraction and very great expectations.

This started from some unknown source; but gained its chief circulation from the lively interest taken in it for several days together by Mr. Greenwood, who talked with as many people, and said as many things, as anybody in Eastham. He had got most of his education at Harvard, and a degree in law from Michigan, and was now occupied, as it was understood, with "railroad business," which allowed of his living quietly here, and being one of the liveliest, if not most useful, members of Eastham society, and of his having all the daytime and evening to himself, and working only at such convenient times as would not interfere with his own pleasure, or that of others.

Mr. Greenwood had repeatedly discussed this subject with much interest, never absolutely pronouncing for or against the opinion; but, as he said, "A story, starting from an unknown source in this way, and which cannot be referred to any author, is precisely the material of all early history in every country, — in Greece, in Persia, in Rome, in Germany, in Scandinavia, in England, in Peru, — and nobody can remember how many other countries."

This consideration weighed strongly with many intelligent persons.

At St. Bart's, in spite of the greatness of this mystery, or because of the mysteriousness of Antony's greatness, the boys took him among them pretty quietly, much like any other boy; yet there had been not a few silent on-lookers, when his trunk was unpacked, who expected to see a crown roll out, or a purple robe unfolded, or some strange implement or other fall to the floor. All these were disappointed; for young Brade's clothes (though of better quality than usual perhaps) were much like the clothes of other young boys, — so many jackets and trousers, so many shirts, so many pairs of socks, so many drawers, so many flannel waistcoats. To be sure, a crown stamped in gilding was indeed spied upon his prayer-book; but, as it surmounted a stamped cross, almost every one agreed that it marked no definite distinction between Antony Brade and other Christians, although one — Will Hirsett — held out as long as he could that there was "just a little mite of difference — he could see it well enough, though he could not point it out — between that crown and others."

When the Russian theory made its way within the school limits, the boys were not long in applying their quick wit and broad intelligence to the investigation in the new direction. Hutchins, or Towne, or some one, started the thought of putting in Brade's way a thing which was especially national, and so would be a touchstone that would bring the secret out at once. Such a thing exactly, the boys thought, was the famous "Russian Imperial Kezan Soap" of Mr. Diogenes Smith, Pharmacopeist. Half a dozen cakes of this "inimitable article" they procured, through Mr. Parmenter going to the city, at wholesale price; and one or more of these, in flaming labels, they put in the supposed young Russian's way, but all without appreciable result.

Boys are not slow or scrupulous, within certain limits, short of what seems to them unkind or rude, about seeking to make their fellows satisfy curiosity; and so the mysterious new-comer had, from time to time, been questioned, but as he had, the first time the subject of his family was directly inquired into, galloped off with a laugh, and said, "Oh, yes! I'm a very great man, of course;" and the next time had told his curious young friends that he had neither father nor mother, and was embarrassed and pained whenever it was approached,—the result was supposed to have confirmed the mysteriousness of his origin; and if the curiosity was not so sharp after a little while as at the outset, the only reason probably was that curiosity will, like other things, lose its edge and become dull when tried upon something too hard for it. That he was an excellent scholar, and as willing to work as he was quick at learning, no one could help seeing, and no one could deny that he was a very kind-hearted, obliging young fellow. So he was a leading scholar in the Third Form, though one of the youngest boys in it, and bade fair to be a distinguished member of the school, as time went on.

Several things which bore upon the question, the boys had observed about him. No parent or other relation had visited him at the school; his letters at first had come addressed by his guardian on the outside, although more than one boy was sure of having seen a lady's delicate writing enclosed, which, from Antony's eagerness to read it, and tenderness after reading it, was concluded to be his mother's. Latterly — some said, since this woman in black came — he had received no letters and wrote none; and it was observed that, when others were writing or reading letters, he generally kept away. This at least was the rumor among the younger boys with whom he most associated.

Now, however convenient this might be to somebody

(perhaps his father and mother, who might be pretending to be dead), or whatever purpose it might answer, yet practically it deprived the young fellow of a home, or made him homeless. All this had been often enough discussed, and public opinion at St. Bart's held itself in suspense.

This last circumstance — the loneliness of young Antony, in spite of his supposed lofty extraction — occasioned a pretty general feeling of compassion for him, until it was found that he needed nothing of that sort; and then, as he was very likable in himself, all the boys of the school held him in more or less of tender regard, as no other boy at the time was held. He was nicknamed sometimes "King," sometimes "Duke," sometimes "Royalty," sometimes "Your Highness;" but boys' nicknames are never meant to hurt each other, and are given and taken with equal indifference, and in this case Antony answered to any of these names as readily and as gravely as he would have answered to the name of his family, or to that given him in baptism.

CHAPTER III.

TALK AT THE BONFIRE.

THE time at which our story begins was the early October, and the day was going down cloudless. If any good eyes were scanning the heavens, and had known where to look, they might perhaps have seen a faint smoke rising from somewhere between the school buildings and the horizon. The observer, then, if he had gone till he came to it, would have found a group of boys gathered about a fire, and in all sorts of attitudes, — lying, sitting, leaning, standing, and, for the most part, silent, as we are apt to be (even boys) in declining day, and about a dying fire. A man in plain working clothes, whom they addressed as "Mr. Stout," had just passed by, stopping to look at the state of things, and taking, unmoved, while he stopped, a scattering volley of teasings for leave to break up all sorts of things for fuel.

Of course the little party had had its subjects of conversation before this time, and just now only one — a curly-headed, black-eyed young fellow — is speaking, leaning on his elbow, with his chin in his hand.

"That's her goin' along West Road, now" —

"Where, Hutchins? Where?" asked several voices, as most of the company turned and looked. He went on: —

"In black clo'es: she brings that swell girl with her to church, that never looks at any of the fellahs. I s'pose her mother tells her not to. They ain't what you may call exactly ladies. Some o' the fellahs were with Brade t'other day when he met her, and she only jest looked sideways at him (I don' know whether she *did* look at him), and he turned all over first red, and then as pale as a ghost. I shouldn't wonder if she was a watch over him. They do have such things, — I've read of 'em, — 'dianas' they call 'em, — to watch over girls, and see that they don't get married, in Spain and Italy, and all those places. I suppose Peters can tell us how it used to be in those times of his knights and maidens and things he's so proud of."

A fair-haired, large-eyed, thoughtful-looking boy, on whom the flame into which he had been gazing shone brightly, at the moment, looked up at this appeal, but seemed not to think it worth while to answer, although at first his lips parted, and a voice seemed about to come forth.

Hutchins's story had gone on swimmingly so far, and his conjectures would, no doubt, have been equally successful, if one of the company — a thin, straight-nosed, nervous-looking fellow — had not spied here a weak spot.

"Diana was a goddess. They don't call 'em '*dianas*,' I know. I forget what they do call 'em; but I know it ain't that." But here the rest of the company, who had tolerated the intrusion so long as they did not know what effect it was to have upon the substance of Hutchins's story, now finding that the objection only touched a very immaterial point in it, cried out to him to go on, and never mind about the goddess Diana. Indeed, one small fellow, who seemed to have studied to some purpose, supported Hutchins, by saying that "the goddess Diana *did* keep girls from getting married as much as she could."

"There, Remsen! Meadows knows," said another, a big and rather loutish fellow, whose hat, turned inside out, sat on the back of his head. "Hooray for Third Form! Hooray for the Great Middle Class!"

Then, as the young mythologist was about to follow up his success (as even grown-up human nature will sometimes do) with communications of learning at greater length, the new speaker set himself against any indulgence of this sort.

"That'll do, Meadows," he said: "you ain't reciting now;" and the young scholar, discomfited, resorted to the feeding of the fire.

Hutchins, however, came to the rescue of his learned supporter:

"Yes, Meadows has done very well. Towne, you may go on where Meadows left off."

And a laugh went up against Towne, who said,—

"Oh, I don't pretend to know any thing."

Hutchins, now re-enforced by Meadows's classical contribution, restored himself again to his own satisfaction, and to his leadership, by saying,—

"I knoo she did something o' the sort," but then seemed at a loss where to begin again.

One of the company—a pretty large little fellow—set him going once more.

"But that ain't *boys*. Because they have 'em for girls, that don't show that they have 'em for boys."

"Hooray for Villicks!" said Towne, at the expiration of this speech.

Now Hutchins recovered the full swing of his argument.

"Why *shouldn't* they have 'em for boys jest as well as for girls? Can't a woman watch, I should like to know? 'The Black Watch' I call her."

"The Black Watch was an English regiment," said Towne, who seemed to have read something, and to have information of some sort.

"Don't I know that?" retorted the chief speaker. "Haven't I got the book? But if she's black, and if she watches, ain't she a black watch?"

Having thus settled Towne, he took up his interrupted story about Brade.

"Well, after that he turned and looked after her ever so many times, and began to cry, too."

This story seemed to have gained and grown in its travels, not otherwise than as men's stories generally gain; for the same boy who had taken exception to the name "diana" now undertook to set Hutchins right in other points.

"Why, I was there, and he didn't keep turning round, and he didn't cry. He only looked queer-like. Perhaps it wa'n't at her at all, — bashful."

"There!" said Hutchins again, "I leave it to anybody if Remsen ain't backing up all I said. I said she was most likely watching him; and Remsen says he was frightened as soon as he saw her. Where's the difference? I shouldn't wonder but what she'd had the charge of him before he came here. I shouldn't think he'd had much schooling."

"That's a likely story!" said Remsen. "He must be a very smart fellow, indeed, if he hasn't had much schooling, to get on the way he's got on. An' I don't say he was frightened, — he was queer-like, jest for a little; but he laughed and talked and played like any person else after that."

Tom Hutchins had no thought of giving in. Feeding the bonfire with such sticks and bits of combustible material as were at hand, he answered, —

"He signed his name in the big book, there, with a kind of a tail to it, just like a *y*, jes 's if he was going to write 'Brady,' and then he made an *e* of it. Burgeon told me, — he comes next to him. So he couldn't write his own name very good, if that's the way. He's a pretty educated man that can't write his own name without blundering."

"Much *you* know!" said the same thin, light-colored, nervous fellow, who looked a little younger than the other. He was still standing opposite, as if waiting his chance. "He writes enough sight better'n you, Tom Hutchins, any day. He writes better'n any fellow in the school."

"Don't be personal!" said the loutish young fellow before-mentioned, and whom Hutchins had called "Towne."

Here several boys, — mostly pretty small, — as silent as Indians before, broke in, —

"That's a likely story!"

"A fresh chap like that!"

"Better than Lawrence?"

"Better than Lamson?"

"Better than Mason?"

All which supplementary helps were gathered by Tom Hutchins into one final and conclusive argument,—

"You tell that to your grand-aunt's granny, Nick Remsen."

It was evident from the number and eagerness of the interrupters that the point interested a good many.

"Well, I was going to say" — began the interrupted speaker, rather confused, as if his explanation was not quite ready.

"You want to make out that he's goin' to take the shine off Gaston," said Tom Hutchins, quietly, as an elder, to Remsen, not heeding his attempt to right himself with the company. "Now, I tell you it won't be one, nor two, nor three Brades that'll do that, if he does belong to Third Form, an' a big old Dutch family as long as your arm."

The incongruity of this descriptive phrase of Hutchins seemed not to strike any of the boys; for with the young race fancy adjusts itself more easily, and is less hampered by taste, than in grown-up people; and Remsen accordingly took no advantage of it.

"Who said he was a big Dutch family?" said he. "He ain't Dutch at all, but some sort of a nobleman, or something that nobody knows any thing about."

"That's the way with a good many o' those kind o' fellahs, — those noblemans and counts and kings, I guess," said Hutchins. "Nobody knows any thing about 'em; and the first thing you hear one of 'em's got cotched in the paper, an' they find out he wasn't any king and nobleman and such stuff, but a great, long-tailed Irishman."

Hutchins had resented the comparison of the new-comer Brade with Gaston. He was not the only one to rate Gaston's scholarship highly.

"I believe that fellow Gaston could pretty nearly enter college now," said a boy, who had a large mouth, easily worked, and which gave him a look of drollery in saying a very common thing.

"I guess he could enter that 'Ulterior College' you're always talking about, Blake," said Hutchins. "What do they ask there for admission?"

"When a fellow comes," said Blake, "they ask him whether he's made up his mind that he really wants a degree, so that they can be sure he'll take it when they give it to him. That's their examination. Then they make him give bonds that he'll pay 'em five dollars for his degree when he gets it."

The boys laughed at Blake's way of saying this.

"But what do they do all the four years waiting till it's time to take their degree?" asked Towne. "I guess that's the college for me."

"Well," said Blake, "they take it as comfortably as they can. Most o' their real work is writing petitions. If it's a fine day, they send up a petition to the President, — he's an old man, a hundred and fifty years old for all I know, — and they tell him they think they should enjoy a walk for their health; and the old gentleman says 'walking's very saluberous,' or some such word, — he's awful good-natured, — 'and he'll go with 'em;' and so they send him back word 'they're afraid they'll walk too fast for him,' and he lets 'em go without him."

"When 'tain't a fine day?" asked Hutchins; and added, "How do you spell that college?"

"Ulterior;" said Blake. "I don't know how they spell it. When 'tain't a fine day, they tell him the light hurts their eyes. — Then he takes off a few days at the beginning of a term, because they've just come, and a few days at the end of a term, because they're just going, and so" —

"Look here, old Ultimatum," said Hutchins, "do they use any books at that college?"

"They say they do," said Blake; "but they give 'em three or four days to look over a book before they go into it, and express their sentiments."

"That's my college!" said Towne. "They'll hear of *me* there some o' these days."

"It's the only place you ever will be heard of, I guess," said Blake.

If our readers, further on in life, on the upper side of that easy slope which leads from college or young ladies' school straight up to the heights of fame and fashion and fortune, and all that, object to the language of our very young friends, that it is not elegant enough or grammatical enough for the members of a great school of the first class, let us remind them that most boys disencumber themselves as readily of the hindrances of grammar and spelling-book, when they can, as of those of dress; and that even "lady teachers," sharp and sudden as they may be in rebuking mistakes, and thorough in exacting spelling and parsing and syntax and prosody in their classes, fall back easily from art to second nature when out of recitation. For boys, too, beside the attraction that other people find, common old words and queer words have a little interest and adventure, as well as homeliness, about them. These boys will come to good English by and by.

The conversation (like most conversations of boys round a bonfire, at any rate) was rather rambling; but, as nobody was in a hurry, so there were some who kept hold of the thread of the main subject. As soon as the laugh settled down, Remsen began treating all that had been said for some time back as altogether a mere side-talk, and going back, —

"I don't say but what there are impostors; but Brade

ain't one of 'em. Why, if you just barely look at him, you can see he's a gentleman. He ain't a common person. A common, vulgar man never has a handsome skin, — soft, that way, like Antony Brade's got; and he don't have handsome hair and handsome eyes, that way."

The late interrupters allowed all these points to go unchallenged; and even Hutchins seemed not disposed to argue them. He took another ground now: —

"All boys are gentlemen, ain't they?" he asked; but, as objections were beginning of a sudden to rise from every side, he changed the form of his expression, and limited its generalization: "All *our* fellahs, I mean, of course. What do you say, Wilkins?" he said, appealing to the largish small boy, who was ready and waiting to speak.

Here many hands poked the pieces of wood and brands together, and several mouths puffed up flames.

"To be sure, all Bartlemas fellows are gentlemen," said the boy who had been called upon, and whose features and complexion perhaps imperfectly satisfied Remsen's requirements; for he had a smooth skin and soft hair, if not the very expressive eyes which made part of Remsen's catalogue of gentlemanly qualities. "Every rich man's son's a gentleman, ain't he?" he asked, a little doubtfully; for, in truth, the question was a deep-going one, and these boys were groping among the elements of things.

"Not without you give him an education, an' *make* a gentleman of him," said Tom Hutchins; "and not always then."

Remsen was inclined to go further than this: —

"I know they used to say that anybody couldn't be a gentleman if his father and grandfather wasn't one too."

"And the boy himself, three (Arithmetic, ain't it?)" said Tom Hutchins. "But look here!" he added, as a still brighter play upon Remsen's words occurred to him: "you say the father and grandfather were one gentleman, — that makes each of 'em a half-gentleman, don't it? Remsen's an old Dutchman. You go back to Adam's flood, I guess, with your family, don't you? Rem, Shem, and Jacob, — the three patri-arks, the fellows that made the Ark, — Rem's son, you see: that's where Remsen came from."

Our smaller scholar of antiquity, who has been called Meadows, undertook to correct Hutchins's loose and latitudinarian quotation.

"It wasn't 'Rem, Shem, and Jacob,' you old Hutchins," he objected.

Hutchins laughed with the most absolute confidence, and answered the objector as if he had him safely in the palm of his hand, to be crushed or let go.

"Why wa'n't it?" he asked. "Ain't his name Remson to this day? And after he'd been so long in the flood, didn't his family settle in Holland, where it's always been half under water?"

While the conversation was beginning to lag in this way, several members of the company got upon their feet, as if to disperse, the chief subject having been quite forgotten, and this last poor witticism of Hutchins's serving, like the cracker in the bottom of the Roman candle, to scatter them.

"Let the little fellows go home," said Blake, "because their legs are short, and they want to start early. I propose to see this fire out."

The natural effect of this speech was to stop all the younger boys who had started to go.

"*My* fathers and grandfathers," said Wilkins, glad of so large an audience, "were all gentlemen." This he said with much satisfaction, and with that kindliness, and that condescension, and that easiness to be propitiated, which mild people show who are secure in the enjoyment of a privilege which cannot be shared by others.

"Your father used to make real good clo'es, I know," said Hutchins; "but" —

"But he didn't make 'em himself: his men made 'em," said the scion of a noble stock. "He had ever so many men."

Wilkins's gentility was allowed to stand where he put it. Hutchins's attention was drawn to something else.

"There's Brade, now, ain't it? Don't he walk like a lordship?" he said; and a boy drew near, with one of those gaits peculiar to childhood, — a sort of canter, — in which that age, feeling (no thanks to Mr. Darwin) its born sympathy with lower living beings, expresses it often by imitation.

Instead of coming up to the ring round the fire, the subject of Hutchins's remark turned off down the playground toward the West Road.

The boys, remembering suddenly, began to ask, —

"Where's the woman in black clothes?"

While they are waiting and watching, we leave them, to take the reader to the house of a person who is growing interested in the mystery of our hero.

CHAPTER IV.

MRS. WADHAM IS INTERESTED.

In Eastham, at that time, was living a Mrs. Malvina Wadham, who had two sons at St. Bart's, and who heard, in due course, the defective and conjectural story of Antony Brade. For her, indeed, all ears were wells into which ran countless underground rills of information, and out of which she drew, as she pleased.

To Mrs. Wadham few things were impossible. Her style of self-assertion was of this sort: "When I say a thing's got to be done, it must be a very strange case, — that don't often occur, — or it's got to be done, just as I say. When I put down my foot" (and she was in the habit of putting down one of her solid instruments of locomotion), "something" (very emphatically, and with a pause) "has *got* to start." She had sent her husband out to some far land of promise to make his fortune, while she administered, at home, what was generally thought to be a pretty snug fortune, already made. That she should take comfort out of it, if she did ("though Dear knows," she said, "the worry of managing so much — the brain-work and the mind-work — is worth more than any satisfaction there is in it)," — but if she did take comfort in it, she "had a good right to," she said, "for it was by her advice, and by her lookin' to things, and seein' to every thing and advisin', that it was what it was. She hoped his children would realize that. Her advice had always been jest right, — jest the thing that was wanted."

The name was said to have come, by some law of "development," through "Wad-DELL" from — shall we say it? We do not like to confess, but yet, after all, do find a certain pleasure in it. The "origin" of this "species" was "Waddle."

This lady lived in Eastham, in a house which illustrated her assertion of herself. She had bought a small bit of ground, and run up upon it a slight, thin, spreading structure of boards, with gables and bows, and bays, and pinnacles, and pendicles, and dormer-windows, and (for any thing that we know) a clere-story, and something atop that was not a clear story, but half-roof; and so had covered her ground up. Then she had hired a barn, of a farm-house close by, for "her carriages and horses," and she was complete. "It's only a summer veranda — I call it. That's just what it is, — only a summer veranda. It'll do for me in my widowhood," she said pleasantly, "and when I go away, I shall sell it; and that's the last of it, as far as I'm concerned. — That's all there is about it."

Climbers and creepers everywhere, and flowers in pots on the piazzas and window-sills, had supplied the place of trees and shrubs in summer; and now what were left of them made a fresh and cheery house inside. A good solid wood fire was blazing one November morning, on handsome French andirons, toward which Mrs. Wadham was stretched nearly at full length in her chair.

This lady, as we have said, had heard of Antony Brade and what there was of his story, and still more what there was not of it, and she reasoned about it in this way: "Who says you can't find out a boy's history, and his antecedents?" (this word with much distinctness). "I should like to see a boy that I couldn't find out, if I tried to" (and it is to be borne in mind that her face was very square, and very set, — when it was set, — and rather hard).

Her daughter Minette (whom, for some reason of their own, the young men of her acquaintance called "Toby") was much like her mother, perhaps, in substance, but smoothed off considerably by some years of costly education. To her, too, it seemed that the secret of the boy might be found out. They both agreed, — the mother that any thing of that sort ought to be known; and the daughter, that any thing of that sort might as well be known. "There was no occasion for any concealment," the mother said: "if a thing was honest and honorable, there was no necessity for it; and if there was any thing wrong about it, it hadn't any right to be concealed, and the sooner it was known the better for all parties."

The mysterious character of the Ryan family was by no means unknown or unconsidered by the Wadhams.

"I'm sure, Ma," said the daughter, "there's nothing about them: they're just like any other family that has risen up. The mother 's not educated much, — a foreigner. The girl's a bright girl, — I know from having her in my Sunday class, — and she's lady-like enough, considering she can't have had advantages of society, and all that; and then," continued Miss Minette, making a concession that not every young lady will make, even in case of a person whom she does not consider quite on her own level, "she's pretty."

"Yes, baby-pooty," said the elder: "big blue eyes, and a smooth skin and a dab of red; but then, as you say, where does all their money come from? *I* say they're employed, most likely, to have an eye to this young heir to — whatever he's heir to; for I take it" (dropping her voice, and giving a tone of inquiry to it, and looking scrutinizingly at her single listener) "he's heir to something, if it's only a common fortune, and no title nor nothing."

But the daughter had either heard much less, or attached much less importance to what she had heard, for she said, —

"I can't see exactly what ground there is for supposing any connection between that boy and this family. Why couldn't he be as great as you please, and yet go to school, like anybody else, without a family set to watch over him secretly?"

The mother was equal to meeting this suggestion.

"Why! that's their way of doing things, that's all. Yes, that's their way. Why! he bears it on his front, I'm sure, unmistakable; and he has the finest of every thing, — no matter how I know it, but I *know* it, — the finest of cloth for his coat, and his vest, and his pants, and the best of shirts, French fashion, and handkerchiefs, plenty of 'em all, and all of the best (I've seen 'em); and all marked and numbered just as pooty" —

"But all that," said the daughter, who seemed to have powers of reasoning at least equal to those of her mother, "don't show what the Ryans have to do with him. It may all be, — and I don't say it is not; only I don't see what reason there is for thinking so. I don't see any objection to any one's following up this clue (in a proper manner, of course); and if it leads to the Ryans, or through the Ryans, why, then he'll find out two secrets, instead of one."

The good-natured tone in which she spoke disarmed the otherwise formidable and murderous-sounding words "to the Ryans or through them" of any terrors.

"Then you agree," said the mother, as if right and wrong, in any case about which they formed judgments, were settled by the agreement of the court, — "you agree that it would be well to find this thing out, — to probe it to the bottom. Now *my* way would be this: *I* should go straight to head-quarters. I should" —

"But, Mother," said the daughter, "you can't make it your business" —

"That isn't the way I should do it, at all," interrupted the mother, in her turn. "You don't understand. I shouldn't make it my business. I should go — where's Eldridge?" she asked, interrupting herself in the middle of a sentence; and then, looking round and not seeing him, she proceeded: "I should go to Saint Bartholomew's School, and I should say, 'I want to see your alcoves' (any parent, or anybody, has a right to go and *demand* to see every alcove at any time, to see what the accommodations are, and how they're kep' up). Mr. Parmenter maintains that principle. He likes to have 'em goin' and then comin' and tellin' him, so's to show that he looks after things up there. Anybody is; an' I've got two sons there."

"But, Mother," interposed Miss Minette, "you wouldn't want to go and *demand*" —

"That isn't the way I should do it," said the mother, who seemed equal to any emergency. "You don't understand. I say anybody's got the *right.* I wa'n't a-goin' to use it. I should go there to see the alcoves. I should find out from Albert — no, from Edmund (our Edmund) — which Brade's was, and one or two more. I should have a friend with me. I should say, 'Look here! this alcove is very pooty, or neat, or snug,' whichever it might be; and I should see all there was there. Then I should send for the boys, 'with Mrs. Wadham's compliments,' and apologize to 'em for having made free with their alcoves; and I should send for Brade last, and I should compliment him, and put him in good humor; and then I should mention, incidentally, souveneers from home, and make alloosions; and then, if I saw that he was close, I should say, 'Never mind, dear, — another time: it'll do jest as well.'"

As Mrs. Wadham said this, in a very small and tender voice, she patted, with fat and many-ringed fingers, the air, which, perhaps, to her quick mind, represented the head of the mysterious boy. Having finished this scene, she presented another.

"And if I should find his heart tender, and his eyes swimmin', I should jest draw him up to me" (here she suited the action to the word, and drew up to her the shapeless air), "and tell him to put his head on my bosom, and think I was his mother, and what a tender name that was! — there wasn't any thing like a mother; and not to be afraid to confide in me, for I was used to such things. So I should sort o' pave the way, you see."

Here she made a gesture with both hands, not quite like any form of paving, but something like brushing slight trifles out of the way, which, perhaps, was as much in her thoughts.

"Well, — but, Mother, what would Mrs. Warren think?" asked the daughter.

"Fiddles!" said Mrs. Wadham, loftily, "for what *any*body thinks, when you're in the right." Then, being carried off her feet (metaphorically) on the tide of her own words: "Civility is a very good thing; and courtesy is a very good thing; and ceremony, and politeness, and all that, — all very good things; but not to interfere with dooty. Ceremony's one thing, dooty's another."

"But, Mother," interposed the daughter once more, "Mrs. Warren might be hurt, if you" —

"I shall make it all right with Mrs. Warren," said Mrs. Wadham with dignity, feeling that she was older than her daughter. "I shall make a point of sending for Mrs. Warren, and tell her, in a lady-like way, 'I hope I haven't interfered with any of her arrangements in exercising my privilege of visitation; and I'm happy to find (if it should be so) that she doesn't need any sudgestions,' — not *reproof*, nor instructions, — I shouldn't use that word, — 'doesn't need any sudgestions.' That will make *that* all right."

The daughter, who bade fair to be one day as big as her mother, and perhaps to carry as much moral weight, was not yet quite able to withstand the solid bulk of her mother's advance, and perhaps, indeed, was inclined, by curiosity, to let her go on.

At the moment, catching sight of some one coming toward the open parlor-door, she got up from her chair and walked toward him; but her mother, who kept herself in the practice of putting things together, having observed her look, or hearing a footstep, called out promptly,—

"Eldridge! Oh, it ain't Eldridge," she said, as no answer came.

"Mr. Greenwood," said the daughter, and a small, soft-voiced, sharp-faced, and rather melancholy-looking gentleman, wishing the ladies "good day," came in and was made welcome.

"Fine growing weather!" he said, as he sat down, after squeezing his soft hat into a pocket, and rubbed his hands together.

"I do'no' what you'd grow in it," said Mrs. Wadham, "unless you mean grow cold. It's cold enough, I'm sure, for this time o' the year," and so she poked the fire, and, with a vigorous thrust or two, brought forth obedient flames.

"Oh!" said Mr. Greenwood, stretching out one leg, and rubbing the side of the knee, "didn't they use to call these growing pains?" and the face looked suddenly and unaccountably droll.

Miss Minette smiled an appreciative smile. The mother set her face with a special grimness, and then formally relaxed the special grimness, and said,—

"Oh, a joke!" then paused. "What do you think of our *mystery* now?" she added, after giving time for things to settle from her guest's humorous effort, which chilling pause he seemed to enjoy under his sadness, as did Miss Minette, who laughed a short laugh.

"Oh," said Mr. Greenwood, "isn't that all settled yet? I hear but one opinion; but then you know I live a very retired and studious life."

"Settled! How?" exclaimed the solid lady of the house, turning round upon her chair and facing him, with the poker in her hand, and a fixed and steadfast gaze in her face, her chin being a little dropped, and her mouth hanging a little way open.

Mr. Greenwood certainly could be as sad-looking at times, by nature or habit, as if the whole of life and the world, and whatsoever is and whatsoever appears, were a standing painful mystery to him. He was, when one looked into his eyes, especially sad-looking. Miss Minette seemed already amused, or ready to be amused.

"I thought it was all settled that he was a young foreigner," said the visitor, giving little encouragement to any expectation of fun, but speaking very seriously and gravely.

"Oh!" said the lady, with a toss of her poker, "that's an old story, — that isn't up to the times. He's a foreigner, we know. Now the question is, what sort of a foreigner? If we've got a young dooke, or a prince, or a premier among us, I think we ought to know it, — I do! I think it's no more than our dooty to society." And again she fixed her gaze upon him squarely.

"Well," said Mr. Greenwood, "society's a good thing: let's discharge our obligations to her. You say he's a Russian?"

"No, I didn't say he was a Russian; but it wouldn't be strange if he was a Russian. But he may be a Russian, or he may be a Cir-cassian. What's the great difference, when you get to foreigners, provided, mind you, that they belong to the upper classes? Only, if there's any deception, we ought to know it. Deception's tryin' to outwit us, — that's what deception is; and we mustn't let 'em."

"I'm sure," said Mr. Greenwood, solemnly and earnestly, "I'm willing to give my little help to the detection of a plot against society."

"'Taint consistent with our republican institootions," she said, taking a fresh start.

To this Mr. Greenwood answered deliberately that "he was not sure that it was." "And then," said he, "if your sons are likely to be associating with a duke in disguise, or a Czar of Bohemia, you've a right to know what company they're keeping."

Mrs. Wadham's face relaxed; but she could not accept the political geography. "I guess you won't find any Czar of Bohemia. Bohemia's a part of the empire of Austria. I've been through it. Come to Russia, and you're more like it. But the next thing is," she continued, "what you're going to do about it?"

"That's it," said her visitor, "what *are* you going to do about it? If a little knowledge of foreign languages — but I hear the boy don't know any thing but English."

Mrs. Wadham did not overwhelm this suggestion about English with irony or with scornful eloquence; but she met it with much shrewdness:

"He don't know! What's he going to know except just what's put into his mouth? But ain't he goin' to have memories of his native land? Squeeze a leaf, and ain't there an aroma?" She illustrated this with a geranium leaf, successfully.

Mr. Greenwood, in a low voice, said that, "if it was a memory of the native land brought that out, he wondered what sort of country one particular kind of cabbage remembered so strongly, that Mr. Parmenter was raising, on his low grounds?"

She continued, without check: "Yes! can't you appeal to 'em? Haven't we known of foreigners that were as hard as you please; but give 'em a little toone upon your dulcinets and your castanets" (here Mrs. Wadham illustrated, with her fingers, first the twanging of melodious chords, as of a stringed instrument, and, next, the airy touch which draws the responsive soul from ivory keys), "and then you've got 'em." (Mr. Greenwood applied his handkerchief to his eyes, but only passingly, and said "that was human nature.")

Miss Minette was a musical person, and sat a little impatient under this figurative representation. "I don't know about those musical instruments," she said, "but, Ma, that's the way it is in story-books."

"No, it isn't story-books! That great, fat Gretkins Warter wasn't a story-book, that fell down flat, like a shot, and kicked out her two great feet, as stiff as that poker! Now," said she, "that's just what I should try, — that's just what I should try."

Now Mrs. Wadham had said enough to warrant her sitting still, and looking him broadly and steadily in the face again, as having presented him with a very complete "case."

"I think that's just what I should like to *see* tried," said Mr. Greenwood. "It's like a chemical process, I suppose," he continued, in a pleasant voice. "You" —

"That's just it, exactly," she said, accepting the simile as soon as she knew that a simile was coming, and before she heard it. So Mr. Greenwood did not follow out the figure.

"Or like a mechanical appliance."

"Yes, yes, — 'a mechanical appliance.' It's like a good many things. Now what we want," she said, getting the lead again, as became her, "is a little — what shall we say? — Russian? Yes! a little Russian."

"I thought," said Mr. Greenwood, diffidently, "that we'd *got* a little Russian, and wanted to get *into* our little Russian."

Miss Minette smiled. Mrs. Wadham did not recognize this harmless attempt as a joke, but took it seriously, and wasted no time over it.

"Well, we want the Russian language," she said.

"If you say so," he said, accommodatingly, "let's have the Russian language. What's the evidence that he's Russian? That's settled, is it? Certainly, his hair curls, — that's like Peter the Great; and he's thin-skinned. The air in those northern countries is so sharp it takes off all the outside, — 'the cuticle,' as the doctors call it."

"Let's see the book! Where's Peter the Great!" cried the mother; and as Miss Minette turned to a bookcase, Mr. Greenwood added one little particular, to prevent a possible disappointment: —

"Unless they've got him there in his wig, which was straight."

Miss Minette smiled. Presently, having found the book, and opened it, she proclaimed the result: "You're right: his hair is curly."

"What else *is* the child?" Mrs. Wadham asked, with a conclusive air, and repeated, "What else is he? He ain't an American, — that we know; nor he ain't an Englishman, nor a Frenchman. Then what is he? Why, here's a story that says 'he's Russian.' Now where does that come from? Where there's a grain of fire, I say, there's a spark. I mean where there's a spark, there's fire."

"Both propositions are true and logical," he answered. "I suppose we may say that where rumor asserts a thing persistently, when there's no reason for it, there must be something in it."

Mrs. Wadham was too close and clear a reasoner, as we have seen, to accept any poor work, for her argument. "How do you mean 'there's no reason for it'?" she asked, looking at him with a most searching and unflinching stare.

"Why, in this case," answered the acquiescing visitor, "there's no interest to be served by representing him as Russian. Nobody's going to gain any thing by it."

"Now, I see, you talk reason," she said. "What we want is to try the boy with something that'll remind him of his far-off home, you know; and my opinion is if we try him with a pretty little scene from his native land, and a little song, or a few words of his mother-tongue, we shall do it. Who is there that can talk Russian? There must be Russian ships coming into Boston and Noo York every day."

"Not so often as that," said Mr. Greenwood, — "not so often as that."

"Well, they must have Russian Bibles; and if I had a Russian Bible, and a dictionary, I'd get enough, in half an hour, to find him out, I'll be bound. He's only a boy."

"You wouldn't undertake to make a 'Ranz des Vaches' out of a Russian Bible and a dictionary, in half an hour, Mother!" said Miss Minette, laughing.

"I should like to see her have a fair chance," said Mr. Greenwood, gravely. "She wants to prove to this little chap at St. Bart's, and the rest of us, that he's a Russian, of noble birth; and if she could take him unawares, and sing him a little simple, artless song, in what she calls his mother-tongue, who knows what the effect would be?"

But this was going beyond Mrs. Wadham's limit, and she applied a check.

"I haven't said any thing about singing a song, ran-des-*vaches* or ren-dez-*vous*. No, I beg you not to mistake me. I know very well what I'm saying. I say, if *somebody*,— *not* I, — *not* I, — if *somebody* would only sing a few words to him, — a song of infancy, — a song of home, — he'd touch the hidden springs, and there'd be a gush" (there was a little confusion in the imagery, here, but she evidently knew what she was saying) "and a rush, and there it would be, — you'd have him."

Mr. Greenwood, before the weight and force of these words, sat very meekly, and at the end he said, "Of course *you* wouldn't sing it. Miss Minette would have to do that for us" — ("I beg you'll excuse me from singing Russian," said Miss Minette) "of your mother's composing," continued he, turning to her, with much earnestness and a wave of the hand, all which precipitated the young lady into a fit of laughter, in which he left her and turned, gravely and silently, to listen to the mother.

"It needn't be poetry," she said. "If I had to get it out of the Bible, I should, most likely, choose an appropriate text: 'We confess we're strangers and pilgrims; we want a better country, for this isn't our home.' *That* would do! *that* would do! something like that."

"Why not?" asked Mr. Greenwood, "if you could only get the Russian Bible and the dictionary?"

"They'd have 'em at the Depository, to give to the sailors as they come in."

"Well," said Mr. Greenwood, modestly, "if we could be sure, now, that every man in New York or Boston, with a Bible under one arm and a dictionary under the other, was a Russian sailor — don't the Swedes, and the Danes, and the Portuguese, go the same way?"

Mrs. Wadham was not to be led off by any senseless suggestions of this sort.

"What are we going to go round the streets after sailors for? What I say is, 'Go to the Depository;' there you'll get your Russian Bibles, as many's you want."

"The trouble is," said Mr. Greenwood, "Russian ships don't come to this country, and so they wouldn't keep any Bibles for 'em, — that is, I don't think they would."

But Mrs. Wadham knew something about trade: —

"Why don't they come to this country? Who brings all the Russia duck and" —

"Why, I suppose," said Mr. Greenwood modestly, like a man ready to learn, "Russia ducks, like other ducks, are migratory" —

"Well, well!" said the lady, "this doesn't bring us any nigher to our point. If you can't try one thing, try another, *I* say," and she looked straight forward into the boundless realms of thought, abstractedly, to see what that other thing should be.

"You want to touch his feelings," said Mr. Greenwood, now proving himself more serviceable and purpose-like. "How would it do to show him some affecting scene from his native land, — the murder of Peter the Great, or something like that?"

"Was Peter the Great murdered?" asked the lady,

turning from her meditation, and speaking like one who was not in the habit of taking things upon trust.

"A great many Peters were, at any rate. Peter something was; and, I suppose, you'd be safe in saying any Peter, for you know what the Russian way is. They take the rightful heir, and put a crown on his head (a splendid crown, — heavy gold, and all covered over with jewels), and then he sits on a great throne, — you've seen representations of them. Well, then any man in the Empire has one shot at the crown, — I don't remember what the distance is, — and, if he knocks it off, then the emperor abdicates, and the man has the first jewel he can pick up. 'Succession by Shot,' I believe it's called."

"Suppose the emperor gets hit?" asked the lady, not committing herself by look to a favorable or unfavorable estimate of this information.

"If he dies, then that's called 'Succession by natural Order' (or 'by the Order of Nature,' I forget which); if he doesn't die, they try it over again."

Miss Minette was not as gravely affected by the tragical character of the tenure of the Russian throne as this story was calculated to make her. Indeed, she laughed at it, and said it was a pretty state of things in the Empire of all the Russias if that was the way with them.

"This may be a little Czar sent here to escape that ordeal," said Mr. Greenwood, diffidently.

"Well, well," said the mother, "that's neither here nor there. You *might* have something out of history that everybody would know. There was that burning of Moscow, — they used to have a panorama of it going round. *That* would do, — *that* would do. We could easily get that up."

"How was it got up? I haven't been in the world as long as that?" said her visitor.

"Why," said Mrs. Wadham, "here were great flames darting out, and smoke rollin' off, and a drumming and a thundering, and the Kremlin Tower comin' down" —

"The *Crum'lin'* Tower you mean, perhaps, if it was coming down in that style?"

"No, I don't: I mean the Kremlin Tower. I know very well what I mean; and then the great bell come down, — ding-dong! ding-dong! — and then the curtain fell."

"And speaking of bells reminds me of the fair," said Mr. Greenwood, with a great bow to Miss Minette. "We can have the Fair of Nijni-Novgorod, on the Ice; and we're pretty sure of killing one bird with two stones, — if there's no member of the 'Prevention of Cruelty' about."

"'Two birds with one stone' it is, I believe," said Mrs. Wadham, gravely; for it was evident that he had got the proverb wrong.

"You're right, it is so," he answered, accepting the correction handsomely; "but why can't we have some tableaux, whether we catch this little chap or not? It would be fun for the Bartlemas boys, if you can get them, and fun for everybody."

"Why shouldn't we?" asked Miss Minette, eagerly. "It would be just splendid, wouldn't it?"

"*Now* you're on the track of something," said the elder lady, who had set them upon this track. "Now there's some prospect. Well, Mr. Greenwood, say the word. When shall it be? You shall be stage-manager and costumer."

"Are we going to have 'The Russian Succession,'

too? or only 'The Burning of Moscow'?" he asked. "We can have the one, or the two, or the three. The Succession would be very effective, especially as we should have to put Brade through it."

"Oh, let's have it by all means!" said Miss Minette, to whom the prospect seemed very suggestive of fun.

"We must have your mother close by to catch him, if we knock him over, and to take his head in her bosom," said Mr. Greenwood, whose plastic eye set up for him already the future mimic scene.

"No, you don't, I thank you," answered that sensible lady. "I ain't a-goin' to stand up and be shot at, — not for nine hundred and ninety-nine dollars a second. He'll have to have somebody else for his mother, if that's what she's got to do,— I can't mother him."

"We can take out the balls, for any but the good shots," said Mr. Greenwood.

"No, you won't catch me, good shots or bad shots, if it's only pop-guns."

"Well, somehow, we must get his head into your hands, and have that little song of home."

"That you won't get from me, I guess," said the matron, again smiling, but with decision.

"And where are you going to get your Russian words?" asked Miss Minette, conclusively.

"I suppose we could get those on a pinch," said the future stage-manager.

"Then you begin to think there *are* ships coming in," said the matron.

"No, no; but men who know Russian. I didn't mean to mention it though."

"*You* don't know Russian?" asked Miss Minette, apparently in doubt whether he was in jest or earnest.

"You say so;" said Mr. Greenwood, with a tone of regret: "I wish I could say as much. I had a painful experience in that way." (Both ladies looked at him with great interest and curiosity.) "I shouldn't like it mentioned, for the aspirations of an ambitious young man were crushed. I was appointed Secretary of Legation to Pekin, — St. Petersburgh, I mean; but Mr. Everett died, and the embassy didn't go. Nobody knows that here, and you won't tell it, will you? Now, I am just working very hard, in a respectable and remunerative way; but that was a sad damper. N'importe!" he added, with a manly spirit. "Good morning," and bowed himself out of the room, — followed hospitably through the entry by the younger lady, — and left the house.

CHAPTER V.

THE BLACK WATCH.

Our young friends at the bonfire were questioning where the lady in black clothes, who had gone up the West Road, now was; and began to answer themselves.

"It's getting dark, down there: soon you couldn't tell her."

But in every boys' gathering, as in every gathering of men, there are always some who, finding themselves gifted with extraordinary faculties, are not disposed to keep the discovery to themselves.

"Oh, *I* could!" said one of these lucky young persons; and his reputation was at once extended by Towne, who caught up his words and proclaimed them.

"Will Hirsett says he can see in the dark!" which gave Tom Hutchins a chance to try his hand at one out of the stock of figures of speech to which each generation comes fresh: —

"Oh, yes! he's an owl."

Meadows took a higher flight for himself: —

"*I* could see in pitch dark, — I always could."

Another, a doughy-looking boy, having witnessed the strength and dexterity with which Hutchins had wielded a grown-up man's metaphor, in calling Hirsett an owl, immediately handled one which he thought as good, or better:—

"Meadows is a fowl. Look here, fellows! Meadows is a fowl."

If Meadows was quick at his lessons, he was also quick in his temper, too; and so he took this latter right up:—

"And Fatty Dover is something else which begins with *f* and ends with *l*."

Here Hutchins, who had all along been the chief speaker, hastened to use another opportunity:—

"Take care, Meadows! If you ain't a fowl, don't get afoul of him."

But before the audience could fairly see this joke, Remsen, Brade's champion, exclaimed in a low voice:—

"There she is, now! She's coming back!"

"The Black Watch!" said Hutchins; and the time being propitious for the taking up and fastening of a name, several voices adopted it.

"Well! Meadows and Hirsett are bright fellows to see so fast, ain't they?" said Hutchins. "Now for magic and mystery! Where's old Peters, with his 'shrivelry,' or whatever it is, he's always bragging about? I should like to see him stick his nose into any thing that's got any '*adventure*' in it, as he calls it!"

The boys started from the fire, and hurried over to that side on which the mysterious woman (dressed just like a mysterious woman) and their own school-fellow, with whom they supposed her darkly connected, were approaching each other. They were away before Peters had found utterance for the assertion that "they'd find he wasn't a coward, when the time came." Squads of twos or threes got behind any thing (trees, or whatever else) which offered a pretence of a screen. Some — as Will Hirsett, Fatty Dover, and others — kept themselves aloof from all entanglements, on the open ground.

"He ain't a bit afraid," said a low voice.

"That's what you'd be, Fatty, if you were down there," said another, louder, which might be recognized as Towne's.

"He don't care any thing about her, I bet," said Will Hirsett, still, however, keeping his face toward the centre of all interest. By degrees all came forth of their hiding-places, but it was to draw down nearer to the West Road. It was strange how they had wrought themselves up.

"Look here, fellows!" cried Tom Hutchins, "I don't think this is very gentlemanly. I'm going off," and accordingly he and others left the ground.

Remsen had not, like the rest, gone into covert, but had followed Brade, at a slower pace, down toward the road.

The silent figure in the black dress went steadily onward; and Brade and she, without ever showing any consciousness of each other's neighborhood, or ever turning toward each other, were drawing nearer to the same spot.

"Hold on!" said the boys on the lookout, and Will Hirsett as eagerly as any of the others. They even advanced a few steps toward the two, over whom, to the eyes of these fresh wearers of manhood, a mist of glamour was thrown (how easily these things happen to childhood!).

"I bet ye he's got to go," said Will Hirsett, getting a little behind two or three boys.

"Hold on! hold on, fellows!" said others. "Le's go down!" said one or two, who were soon checked.

At length, while they looked, Brade stood still, just as the dark figure went by ("Now! now!" said excited voices). Remsen hastened to join him, when suddenly, with a shout or cry, Brade started up the hill, eluding all Remsen's efforts to stop him, and then Remsen, too, followed him at full speed. The dark figure, as some boys said, turned once; but the general impression was that it moved on with the forward steadiness of Fate.

But there was a commotion among the watching boys; and Will Hirsett ran round the corner of the laundry, from behind which he peeped out.

As the two boys came on, Brade slackened his pace, and then stopped. Remsen, in his furious speed, was carried on beyond him.

"What did she say? What did she do?" asked the boys of Remsen; Will Hirsett's curiosity overcoming his fear, and bringing him forward from his hiding-place doubtless, with his eyes staring and mouth yawning.

"Nothing," answered Remsen, panting and out of breath.

"No, no! but what *did* she say? what *did* she do?" the boys persisted in asking.

"Why, I told you the exact truth," answered the besieged boy. "Now you want the exact falsehood, do you?"

"Yes, yes! do tell us what she said," they besought him.

"RUN FOR YOUR LIVES!" said Remsen, in so peremptory and threatening a voice that Will Hirsett and

Dover instinctively started to run, although, to be sure, they soon checked themselves, under the laughs of their companions, and put the best (metaphorical) face upon it that they could. Will Hirsett said that he "was in fun," and Dover claimed that he "only just thought he'd go away."

The appetite of these boys was not satisfied with what they had already got. Some of the smaller fellows began again the inquiry: —

"Did she really say that, Remsen?" which, though a rhythmical utterance (indeed, not a bad 'trochaic dimeter acatalectic' for young scholars, if we take accent in English for quantity in Greek), had no effect upon the obdurate ears to which it was addressed; for Remsen was already running off; and now, calling Brade, he, with his friend, left the company to themselves.

Towne was moving about, as if particularly important and full of meaning: —

"I know something," said he, mysteriously; and notwithstanding Arthur Meadows's joke (which Arthur, at least, enjoyed exceedingly), that "he was glad to hear that; for he had always supposed that Towne didn't know any thing," Towne lost no time by attending to him, but began bestirring himself, and calling out, —

"Wilkins! Wilkins! Say! look here, Willicks!" and, having brought that worthy to himself, said loudly enough for others to hear, "I've got a way to find out!" and then, in a low voice, drawing Wilkins apart, at the same time began detailing to him some plan, over which he himself chuckled a good deal as he told it.

Then, aloud again, he asked his confidant "if that wouldn't be splendid," and received his assurance that it was "first-rate."

If nothing has yet been cleared up, possibly this plan (still more possibly something else) is yet to give us all more light.

Here, as we wish to keep the good opinion and good will of all our readers, we advise those who have no mind for thought, to skip over this next half page or so, which is written for such as will read it, — if there are any such.

As mysteries in human life are things which have their whole being in human consciousness, and that is an element more changeful and shifting, more full of tides and currents, and waves and eddies, than is the ever-flowing sea itself, so a mystery may, like a thing afloat upon the water, be wafted into a sheltered cove, where it falls and rises with the ebb and flow of tide, and is left behind when the water has run out; or it may be flung aloft into sight on the cresting top of a breaker, and drawn back in the blind disorder of its recoil, and carried off; or it may be cast up and abandoned on a beach, a thing of no account, or a clean and harmless thing, or a thing foul, offensive, and pestilential; or it may, ere it be borne fairly within grasp of hand or ken of eye, sink into the depths, and never more come up to light of day.

This mystery of young Brade may be perhaps but a harmless, pretty thing, — perhaps no mystery at all; perhaps, if we may keep up our figure, not more a mystery than a summer boat, riding in still water a little way off shore and not adrift, but fastened, although the moorings chance to be on the further side from us unseen.

Perhaps, too, there is more in it than this.

CHAPTER VI.

THE BOY'S OWN ACCOUNT OF IT.

Meantime, it must be supposed that the boy himself, though generally seeming indifferent, as boys do in such cases, was sometimes annoyed at being the object in this way of constant conjecture and occasional watching.

That afternoon, when they had got a little way from the rest, he stopped, hot and panting, from his run with Remsen, and said, after some delay and with some difficulty, though at the same time without whimpering or breaking down: —

"Remmy, I wish the fellows would stop, now! They might plague me, or just us boys in the school, but they've got no business with other people."

Remsen, for his part, was willing to take a friend's share: —

"I'm sure they're welcome to plague me, too, Anty, if they want to; I don't care," he said.

"But," said Antony, seriously, "they've no business to bring Mrs. Ryan into it."

"Oh!" said Remsen, "that's only their nonsense, and it won't do any harm. They've got a notion she's put here to watch over you."

To Remsen, at his time of life, a romance of that sort would, perhaps, seem as natural as any other happening.

"But I never made-believe I was any lord, or any thing; so I don't care about that," said Brade. "I don't suppose any person believes it, and I don't mind" —

His young companion was not quite so ready to let a romance go out of life · —

"But I *do* believe you are something, Bradey; I'm pretty sure of it; every thing looks like it," answered Remsen, laying on piece after piece of probability, until he had a pretty good pile. "And they do send away their sons in disguise: don't we read about 'em in books?"

"But I told you I wasn't, Nick, — I said I wasn't. I never told anybody such nonsense. I'm just a man's son, like any of the boys."

"But you never saw your father, Anty," argued Nicholas; "nor your mother."

"No, I never saw them," said Antony; "but, then, I know about them."

"But what was he?" asked his friend. "Do you really know?" and it might have seemed as if he were at the very brink of the mystery.

Brade was a little fellow to have the keeping of a secret big enough for a man; but for a moment he was as thoughtful as a man, and then said: —

"I know a good deal about him, — to be sure I do;" and now again it might have seemed as if the mystery were already almost open to the eye.

As they were drawing near to the buildings, they turned off toward the play-ground again.

"Well, won't they let you tell?" asked his companion, eagerly.

Again Brade was silent, as they walked, and then answered: —

"All I know isn't much of a secret. I should like to tell you, I'm sure, Rem. I will, some time;" and he locked his arm with Remsen's. "I can tell you my mother was very beautiful, and very good," — and he hesitated and was bashful, as most boys would be, — and he put up his free hand and clasped it with that which held Remsen's arm.

"Oh, I know she was! I'm sure of it! She must have been!" said Remsen, who evidently felt almost, if not quite, as strongly as his friend, and whose voice hesitated just about as much. He drew Antony's arm in closer to himself as he spoke. "And what was your father, Anty?" he asked.

The fading of the daylight and the chilling of the air very likely intensified the feeling of both, although they probably had no thought that coldness and darkness were symbols of separation and mystery. Here there was a silence again, as they walked, and then what seemed like an agitated movement of the young sharer in (more or less of) a great social or family secret. Remsen hastened with his sympathy: —

"Oh, no matter, Bradey!" he said: "if you can't tell, I won't ask."

"It isn't any thing very strange, only I can't, now," said Brade. "You tell people there isn't any thing at all, won't you, Remmy? There really isn't, — I'm sure there isn't. If anybody asks you, you won't tell them there is any thing, will you?"

Remsen promised, as strongly as if he knew the whole already; and they turned again toward the buildings.

After another silence as before, Brade went a little further in his confidence: —

"I know my father was an honorable man."

Remsen was quick to take this up. "There, that's it! I knew it!" he said.

"Oh, I don't mean that!" said Antony. "I don't mean so; but she always said 'he was a man I might be proud of.'"

"Why, I thought she died before you knew any thing," said his friend. "I didn't know you ever saw her."

Here was another bit of mystery.

"Oh! my mother died before my father did," said Brade, not clearing it up much.

"I'm just the same way," said Remsen, glad to be able to share his orphanhood, "only I've got a father. But who was it told you?"

This question seemed to throw Antony all back. "I don't know; let's let it all alone," he answered. "Mr. Warren knows. Only I know there isn't any thing very wonderful; and there isn't any harm in it, I know that."

To this last assertion Remsen answered: "Oh! nobody ever thought of that! What bad would there be, if you had a great title?"

Young people are pretty much like older people in the matter of curiosity, only more frank and straightforward with it. So Remsen tried once more at another point, leaving these that his friend might be expected to feel too strongly about.

"Has Mrs. Ryan got any thing to do with you?" he asked, in this way bringing them back to the point from which they had wandered.

Poor Antony seemed to be struggling with the difficulties of his position, — unwilling to be so reserved with his friend, and yet unable to speak freely to him.

"Remsen!" he said, pulling the arm which was between his two hands, "I don't want to talk any more about my things. You see, if I know any thing, I can't tell, because I haven't got any right to; but it isn't much." And, when his companion had promised, Antony made a little further advance:—

"Now mind, Nick, you won't say there is any thing, if anybody asks you or not." Remsen promised again, and Brade continued: "Then I'll tell you as much as I can. She doesn't meddle with me at all, but I know she's good. She's one of the best persons that ever lived in the world,—everybody'd like her,—and the boys mustn't insult her!"

Nothing that he had said had shown more feeling than this; and Remsen, too, was very much moved. They were near the buildings again, and lingered. Remsen answered for the boys: "Oh! they won't, Bradey! they didn't mean any harm,—they won't!" Remsen's question had been fairly answered; and yet, if the boy thought it all over, he would see that little change had been made in the mystery. Who Mrs. Ryan was, and what she used to have to do with Brade, was rather deeper in the dark than ever, because now it was plain that there was something between them; and yet they had nothing to do with each other. Moreover, it had been told him that Brade's father was a "man to be proud of," and an "honorable man;" but who, or what, or where the father had been, was still as unknown as before. And then, too, there were some people that were keeping Antony Brade from telling all he knew, which might be little or much, but which was, of course, not so much as those other people knew.

Some writers of novels describe what passes in the minds of their several characters, as positively and minutely as what these say and do. We cannot treat the personages of our little drama in this way: they seem to us too real. And so, of Remsen, we can only say that boys of just about his cleverness, and bearing such a relation as he bore to Brade, are capable of good argument (wanting only experience of life), and are more under the influence of feeling than men. The track of reasoning which we have pointed out, Remsen, we think, would be likely to take; and we think that Brade's positive statements, as to what his father was and was not, being both few and slight, would be likely, as time went on, and as he thought the whole thing over, now and then, to grow less and less, in proportion; while that which was unknown and behind the bars of secrecy, being capable of shaping into grandeur and wonder, which Brade would well befit both in body and spirit, and also, being capable of unstinted stretch and growth, would be likely to fill more and more place in his thought and memory.

The lamps were lighted when the two young friends went in, and streams of boys, up stairs and down, and this way and that, in the entries, were moving, as they usually move in idle times. One boy, occupied with a book, and another, idle, were standing under a lamp, in a corner.

Boys never escape banter, from some one or other of their fellows, when there is any occasion for it; and traces of the strong feeling which Remsen and Brade had so lately gone through were still to be seen, when they showed themselves in the hall, to the knots and pairs of standers and walkers there.

"Hillo! what's the matter, Emperor?" called out one of the loiterers, as the light fell upon Brade, who was hurrying quietly past toward the school-room.

Brade neither stopped, nor made answer of any sort; but Remsen took his place, and, going up to the boy who had spoken, said quietly, —

"Look here, Charley Leavitt! he's just been telling me about his father and mother, and he feels bad: don't trouble him!"

"Why, can't a fellow talk about his father and mother, without feeling bad about it?" Leavitt asked, but lowering his tone, considerately. "His father and mother may be very big; but I suppose every fellow's father's the same to him."

"Well, but his father and mother are dead," answered Remsen, "and he don't know very much about 'em, because they died before he was born" —

Just then an unexpected diversion was made, which drew the conversation away from Brade, as well as could have been wished.

"Look here!" said Towne, who was just coming from the school-room, as Remsen had reached this point, "how's a fello' goin' to be born when his father and mother's dead?"

Blake, who was standing, reflectively, under the lamp, now showed that he had his ears open.

"You needn't try that *now*, Towne," he said very gravely. "It's how you can get along, now you *are* here."

Brade and his orphanhood, and all that was unknown about him, were forgotten by this time; so Remsen followed his friend into the school-room, and found him there, surrounded by half a dozen others, who were making out their Latin, asking him questions which he answered without book.

Brade himself seemed entirely happy now; and, when their hanging light needed turning up, mounted to the top of a desk with great alacrity, before any one else, to set it right.

As he stood there, for a moment, he was certainly a bright-looking fellow, and, to those who can be influenced by looks, decidedly interesting. He happened, to be sure, to be a well-dressed boy, — and, for that matter, altogether well-dressed: from his collar and neck-ribbon down to his well-cut shoe, with silken braid for tie, all having the air of a refinement inborn in him, and showing itself in every bend and joint of his body; and it was his good shape and features that made his dress particularly becoming. Two or three words more, as he is the hero of this story, we will add, with our reader's leave, to his portrait. He had dark hair, cut short, after the manner of school-boys of the day, but wavy even in its shortness. A few freckles, on his cheeks and across his nose, did not disfigure him, but only showed the fairness and delicacy of his skin. In fact he was, outwardly, a very good specimen of school-boys.

An odd-looking, indeed a fantastical-looking boy had been hovering not far away from this group during the time that Brade had been among them, and with his eyes very often turned to Brade, — eyes which showed a good deal of white between the iris and the lower lid, and gave their owner a dreamy expression. Sometimes he drew near, and was apparently just ready to speak, and sometimes moved off again, but never to any considerable distance. As Brade jumped down to the floor, the boy, starting suddenly forward, took him by the arm, drawing him toward the side of the room, and saying, at the same time, —

"Look here, Bradey! I want to tell you something."

"Never mind Peters, Brade! he can wait. What does '*obvenerat*' mean?" called out one of the studious company engaged at the desk. "Oh! here's Meadows! Come along, Meadows: we want to pump you." But the new-comer, winding between desks and across seats, found his way to his own books, and sat down by himself.

Brade, who had moved a little way off with Peters, now stood still and asked, like one going against his will, whether it was "any thing very particular."

"Yes, yes!" said Peters, "something very particular, indeed. It won't take a minute;" and he tried to draw Brade aside still further.

"He wants to tell you about St. George and the Dragon, or Sir William Wallace, or something he's been reading!" Nick Remsen called out.

"No, I don't, — really and truly. Really I don't," pleaded Peters. Brade yielded again, and went a little way further apart.

"May I trap with you?" Peters asked. "You know I'm pretty lucky."

"Oh! that's all!" said Brade. "You must ask Remsen: I don't mind, if he doesn't. Was that all?"

"No, it wasn't all," said the other boy, hesitatingly, as if he had some reluctance about saying all that he had to say. "Look here!" he began, with a queer sort of abruptness, "you didn't want any succor out there, to-night, did you?"

The most important word in this sentence not being a boy's word, he slurred over, in his pronunciation, as if a little afraid of it.

"Why no! I didn't want any supper out there," said Brade, laughing. "I don't know what you're talking about;" and he looked over toward the others, as if to see if they were watching.

No one seemed to be attending to them (Remsen being engaged in lively conversation with one or more of the Latin-readers, the chief speaker of whom he called Wadham); and Peters, having apparently satisfied himself of the same fact, said with great earnestness, as if he had something on his mind or conscience till he could get rid of it,—

"They used to call it 'succor' when they went round helping everybody, in the old times," — he did not say days of chivalry, — "but I mean when that black lady was there. You wasn't afraid of her, were you?" The poor fellow was thinking more of what he wanted to say than of his grammar.

"Afraid of her?" asked Brade, impatiently. "No! what should I be afraid of?"

"You don't believe she's any thing but a common woman; *do* you?" Peters asked.

Brade fired at this. "What do you mean by 'a common woman'?" he asked.

"Why, a woman with great power," answered the other, innocently, "one that can do more than a common person. They were laughing at me about chivalry; but I'd have dared to go, if it had been necessary. I would, indeed!" Peters pleaded as if his character or happiness depended upon Brade's believing him.

Antony's expression of indignation was changed, at

once, for an expression of contempt, which Peters seemed to feel deeply.

"She can't do you any harm, can she?" Peters asked.

To Brade, at this distance of time from the late scene on the play-ground, and the talks with Remsen, no painful recollections needed to have been called up by such a reminder as this from Alonzo Peters; but he seemed now inclined to be angry at any reference to what had passed; and having turned his eyes again toward the other boys in the school-room, as if to see if any of them were hearing, he answered: —

"No! what harm do you suppose she's going to do me? You needn't come meddling between me and anybody."

"I don't want to meddle," said poor Peters, who was pitched upon such a key that he could not make himself understood.

"I should think gentlemen's sons would know better than to insult a woman," said Brade. "If they want to plague me, they may."

"Did they insult her?" asked Peters. "That's just what the knights were for, — to prevent people's being insulted. But the fellows thought she was a sort of a watch, or a sort of a woman with great power" —

Brade interrupted him: —

"But what fools they must be! They're not babies, to believe any such nonsense."

"Well," said Peters, "*I* didn't mean to insult her (you know I've only got a mother), — only, if you wanted anybody to stand by you, I wouldn't be afraid." (It was strange what a valorous young person this slight, large-eyed, flaxen stripling professed to be.)

"I don't want anybody to stand by me about that," said Brade; "and I only wish not to hear any more about it, please."

At this moment they heard the Tutor's signal, and became aware that every one was hurrying to his own seat for roll-call; and so their conference suddenly ended, with a hurried request from Peters, taking Brade by a button, —

"I *can* trap with you, can't I?" so eager, that Brade laughed, as he answered that "he didn't care."

"What did that old Peters want?" asked Remsen, as they went to supper; and when he heard the proposition about trapping, which was all that Brade reported, objected strongly to "taking that moony fellow in." He yielded, however, to his friend's good-natured mediation, and was persuaded at last that they could get along with Peters easily,— a conclusion which he filled out by adding, "We needn't have him with us much, anyhow."

CHAPTER VII.

TOWNE'S PLAN.

BOYS' secret plans may not be very deep; but there is in laying them and carrying them out often immense excitement and profuse concealment, which last, indeed, sometimes defeats itself, and is the cause of discovery. There are some boys who think themselves more cunning than all the race of tutors, who may be abashed perhaps, and depressed momentarily, by a discovery, and then rally their self-confidence again, and brag as before. So, too, there are others who accept these heroes' estimate of their own capacity, and follow them; and others again, who, whether they believe in their leaders or not, are ready for a frolic or a plot, and tumble into it as they would tumble into a boat which another was pushing off shore. No adventure is without attraction for boys. Towne, as we may remember, had professed to know a trick for discovering the hidden relation between the woman in black dress and Antony Brade, and from the moment of its conception worked pretty sedulously at it.

Wilkins was one of the first of his confidants, and enjoyed the enterprise extremely. A good deal of this confederate's activity was bestowed in giving intimations, aside, to boys — particularly boys larger than himself — that something good was going on. Others, not saying much themselves, laughed meaningly, when spoken to about the secret, and gave it to be understood that they knew all about it. In this way was created a pretty general expectancy in the school. Towne himself was going about making requests or holding conferences, apart, with different boys, generally laughing and gesticulating much while he talked, and having the appearance of being very busy.

He was not indiscriminate in these conferences, for at the approach of certain boys — as Remsen and others — he was at once silent, or drew away his listener. Tom Hutchins he often addressed, and was listened to a little loftily, as by one in advance of him. Most of his confederates were of his own Form or lower. One thing very inopportunely interfered with the devotion of these cunning fellows to business, and very much cut up the spare time which they could bestow on their preparation for carrying out the plan, whatever it was.

This inconvenient and ill-timed obstacle was the keeping-in of many or most of the knowing ones — Towne pre-eminently, always — for disorder somewhere or other, in school or dormitory or wash-room, or elsewhere; for not knowing lessons, or for chalking backs, or kicking other fellows' feet, or tickling ears in the recitation-room, or setting crooked pins, like Bruce's caltrops at Bannockburn, with the point up, on the seat of an unfortunate fellow reciting, who is using all the wits he can find in his head upon Cæsar's *accusatives* and *infinitives* and *se* and *sibi*, or the Greek aorist participle, which he takes for a second person singular. Day after day, as the sun slowly went down the western side of the sky, he described his wide segment of a circle over the head of Towne and his companions in misfortune, scattered in the school-room with dreary faces, sometimes bent over a book, and sometimes turned reproachfully at the unsympathizing school-room clock. The time had been when Towne had tried the persistent practice of not learning, and persistent assertion of his inability to learn the "lines" imposed, quoting his father and possibly his grandfather in support of the assertion; but as this, instead of bringing him an easy remission, had heaped up the unlearned lines unremittingly, he had of necessity conformed somewhat to inexorable conditions, and taken to doing some reluctant and indignant work at his task. He made amends (as far as it would go) by complaining aloud, out-doors, when at length, with all kept-in boys, he was set free for the afternoon at half-past four o'clock.

What time he had to himself, however, he used pretty industriously. In a corner of the gymnasium, seated on one of the mattresses, until the noise of foot-ball or hockey grew too loud to be endured passively by a boy who certainly had a constitutional love of play, if he had not a constitutional inability to learn "lines," he was busy at "some black thing" (so it was said), and had a door-keeper to watch against sudden intrusion. As may be supposed, few of the boys cared for Sam Towne's secret operations; and Blake, of "Ulterior-College"-notoriety, said, in his absurd way, that "old Towne was one of those fellows that would climb up a tree to get a good tumble." Almost everybody would be content to wait the development of time to know his great secret. The post of door-keeper, therefore, even though it combined the duties of general watch, grew tiresome and stupid, for there was nothing to do in it. While things were in this state, on the second or third afternoon, the shortening days and chilly evenings giving warning of winter coming, and making the blood in healthy boys run fast to keep warm, Towne was singing "Dixie" in his corner, when Nick Remsen walked quietly in, to look for a hockey-stick, which, as he said, he had left there, and (as it happened) under the very mattress on which Towne was sitting.

That industrious fellow, almost before Remsen had taken the place of his shadow inside the door, had managed to thrust under himself, and to spread himself over, the greater part of a quantity of black stuff on which he had been working with needle and thread while he sang.

The song he continued, looking aloft at the beams of the ceiling, and trying to seem very much taken up with it. As soon, however, as he allowed himself to espy the intruder, which he could not help doing soon, and had asked him the apparently purposeless question, "Where he came from?" Towne rolled himself over, carrying the mattress over him, and leaving the floor bare for Remsen to satisfy himself. Now, of course, Remsen, seeing so good a chance, instantly rolled the mattress as far over as it would go, — suppressing Towne entirely under it, — and then put himself on top, to keep him down; and of course Towne, like Enceladus under Ætna, made mighty struggles, which Remsen set himself to resist. There is a wondrous leverage in the joints of legs and arms, which, the moment Towne could bring them to bear, carried mattress and boy together right over, — for Remsen's weight added to that of the mattress was not much; but, as the mattress fell to the floor, there fell, at the same moment, Towne's secret. This looked like a black gown, but whether feminine or academic there was scarce time to see; for Towne gathered it hurriedly up, and, keeping it on the further side of himself, made it into a parcel, while the other boy, swinging his hockey-stick, departed, being met outside by Antony Brade.

At this juncture the door-keeper made his appearance, and was sharply reproved; "for what business had he to go away just when a fellow was going to poke his nose in where he wasn't wanted?" Poor Wilkins (for he it was who was officiating in the undesirable post of watchman) excused himself on the ground that "he hadn't been away more than a minute," and also that "he had been there all the time," and ended with the unanswerable appeal, "who could tell that a fellow would be coming just then?" — which excuses, as there was no help for it, and Towne was not an absolutely irresponsible despot, with bowstring or beheading-block at his service, were necessarily accepted.

Then Towne, taking the state of things as it was, told Wilkins that "they must hurry up and get through with the job, or their secret would be all found out; that he himself was not quite ready, but was ready enough, he guessed; and now was the time!" Wilkins began at once to be impatient, and danced, and looked out at the door for other untimely visitors. Then, by the leader of the great secret, three extraordinarily significant whistles were given, outside of the gymnasium, and then (having failed of effect the first time) were repeated, and again repeated, and again and again repeated, until at length, as Towne kept marching about like a bagpiper, while he uttered his signals, one boy after another, as if just waking up to the meaning of things, came running to him, to the number of four or five, — for the most part pretty small lads.

One of these was sent straight off, with much authority, to summon Wadham First, who was within sight, and the others were kept waiting till the leader was ready for them.

Towne advanced, like a man full of a good deal, to meet Wadham, and sent the messenger back to the rest.

"Look here, Wadham," said Towne, "I've got the best thing! I want you to get a black dress from your house, — I'll take good care of it. I'm going to dress up like that Mrs. Ryan, — only in fun, you know, — just to see what Brade 'll do. I was making one, but they found me out, and I don't want 'em to know it."

Wadham, if not as enthusiastic as the contriver of this scheme, entered into it with some spirit, possibly because he may have known the state of things at home. Accordingly, he undertook to supply what was wanted; and Towne, having pledged him to secrecy, left him, to join his own followers.

These, with a lofty summons of "Come, fellows!" he drew off, not into, but behind the gymnasium, and there held a secret conference with them, laying out plans and assigning duties.

Wilkins (of gentle blood, late door-keeper) claimed and obtained the general office of what he called "peekin'," asserting also that "a fellow'd got to know what he was about to do 'peekin'' well."

"Now, Wilkins," said Towne, "you'll have to be sharper'n you ever was in your life." ("Why, I'm always sharp," said Wilkins.) "And," continued Towne, not heeding this suggestion, "you'll have to give a signal, — you'll have to say something if a tutor comes. But Fatty Dover's most importance. Now, Fatty, you've got to rig right up, as soon's the lamp goes out, and come to Royalty's alcove, and walk right in, — you ain't to show your face, remember, — and, quick as you come in (I shall be there, you know), quick as you come in, I'll show the dark lantern right on you, and say, 'Why, Mrs. Ryan,' or something, you know," he said, with a little bashfulness, when he came to authorship in the English language, however bold and self-confident about the other effort of his mind, which he was detailing. "I'll say something. Then you see what he'll do." So said the author of this cunning plan, confidently. Whether one plot would or would not have differed much from another, to their apprehension, certainly this seemed to meet their approval. Allowing a moment for his allies to take in the character of his contrivance at this culminating point, and taking as cheers and as what grammarians call "rhetorical question" their inquiries, What he thought Brade would do? would he fight her? or would he be frightened? he then went on to show how he had provided for all emergencies and contingencies; how he first, and "Fatty" next, were to get out of Brade's window, at the first alarm, and, as the contriver expressed it, "put for bed, flat-footed, over the schoolroom roof."

"But they'll find that dress," said Fatty Dover, looking into the future, as so many plotters have done before.

"No, they won't find that dress," answered Towne.

"You strip it off, like a duck sheds water, and chuck it right over the roof, and get into bed, — that's all you've got to do; and after they've gone and all quiet, I'll go down and fetch it. Well, suppose they did find it," he continued, second thoughts coming up to him, "it'll be fun to have Wilson hold it up in the school-room. Only," — here third thoughts came in, showing that our young friend had not bad feelings, — "I wouldn't like any disrespect of a respectable woman; but I've got that all fixed complete."

From the smile which brightened the leader's face, as he contemplated his own skill and sure success in providing for the recovery of the dress, — a smile, indeed, which might be said to pervade his whole body, for it not only drew out the corners of his eyes, and mouth, and nose, but drew his elbows out also, and bent his back and knees, — it might be thought that, on the whole, this last contemplated piece of cleverness was the crowning contrivance of the whole plan.

The allies were eager to share in this part of the secret, and in the leader's satisfaction; but he put them all off, with the assurance that "they'd know, bymby." Wilkins claimed special confidence, on the ground that "he was goin' to peek out for everybody." But he teased in vain, Towne telling him that if he used that word so much they'd call him "Peak o' Gibraltar" next (asking if he wasn't right in supposing there was a Peak of Gibraltar). There were some things that, like a leader, he knew how to keep to himself; and, in short, Towne kept his secret, and, having cautioned Fatty Dover and the rest not to say a word or give a look to anybody about the business, he dismissed them.

Now, having Wilkins alone, he satisfied that worthy

confederate's curiosity; for by this time, very likely, he was itching to communicate.

"Look here, Willicks," said he, "if this ain't the best thing yet. You know that old empty cask the masons put there, by the school-room corner? Well" (and here he chuckled), "a fellow that's only half good at gymnastics can let himself down off the roof there, as easy's not. But that ain't all: it's big, you know; and I wouldn't be afraid but what I could hide in there against anybody, — if he wa'n't too near. There ain't any moon, now; and you know my gymnastic dress is all gray. Well, you can't see that, in the night."

"Loose, too," said Wilkins, "so you would not look so solid, would you?"

This support from the science of Optics, Towne neither accepted nor rejected, in words, but continued on his own line: —

"You know the rebel cruisers were painted gray, in the war, and our vessels couldn't see 'em. They'd run right before their noses, an' they couldn't see 'em. As quick's he'd gone by, I'd go up on the roof in a jiffy, and into bed, before he'd get along upstairs."

To most of us the American navy is synonymous with whatever is daring and successful; and no doubt these two American boys had the true feeling of American boys toward the pet and pride of the nation. But Wilkins had yet a standard of comparison which held its own, even in face of the American navy. "Would you run in those clo'es, right before a Tootor's nose?" he asked.

If we had heard this sentence spoken, we should very likely have laughed at the ludicrous figure presented of Towne, in his athletic suit, capering invisibly before the unsuspecting eyes of an official, or we should have seized upon the rhyme, and rung the changes on it, perhaps. But Towne heard it in the same sense, probably, in which the author conceived it, and to him one word drew off the force of all the rest. "Yes, sir," said he, "I don't believe but what I could."

"I don't believe you could before Mr. Bruce," said the propounder of the question, — "you, nor nobody else."

The conversation had been turned aside by this new element brought in; and, as if the private conference were over, the two boys walked away. As they passed the gymnasium door, a new turn was given to their thoughts; for Remsen and Brade were chasing each other on the ladders, up one, across another, down the third, by the hands, as busily and as noisily as if their lives depended on it.

"There's Remsen and Royalty!" said Towne. "I wonder we didn't hear 'em. I hope they didn't hear us, — there's a window open."

Wilkins found comfort in the fact, to which he called his friend's attention, that the two boys were a great way off from the window. But this did not satisfy Towne, who said that "boys could move."

"Let's go in and chase 'em all over those timbers, in the gymnasium," he proposed; and added, in a whisper, "if they've been listening, and heard what we're going to do, you take Royalty (he's the smallest), and I'll take Remsen, and if I catch him, won't I — ?" And he slapped his thigh with strong emphasis.

The notion of the wise contriver, Towne, seemed to be that a little advantage gained over the two boys would keep up the ascendency of the great plot. Let

4

us, therefore, look upon the athletic contest which is coming as a little skirmishing before the lines of the great battle; boyish, indeed, but into which, for the time, is turned the whole current of young life.

Wilkins excused himself from his share, as not being "much of a gymnast," and being obliged to save "himself for bymby, when he'd have to be pretty sharp."

"Come on, old Gray-breeches," cried Brade, who, though a good way off, seemed to have overheard the conversation. "Wilkins is pretty sharp, and he won't try me. You're the man, and I'll give you plenty of chance. I'm so 'small,' you know."

That epithet "Gray-breeches" might or might not refer to the "gymnasium suit" which was to play an important part in the approaching adventure. Brade's face did not show whether it had or had not any special application, for he was full of excitement for the play.

Towne, too, as soon as Brade, sliding down a rope, began to "dare" him, set off, at the utmost speed of longer legs than Brade's, in pursuit.

Then, if their mothers could have seen them, there would have been many a shriek, and possibly some hysterics. Up and down ladders, up ropes and down ropes, and down and up the same rope, along crossbeams, springing and catching by the hands, swinging up and catching by the legs, heels over head and head over heels, — what a race that was, with Remsen and Wilkins cheering! Remsen, it must be confessed, twice to Wilkins's once.

Where length and strength would have an advantage, Towne gained; where litheness and nimbleness, used as fearlessly as on flat ground, could play their full part, there Brade got the better, for he turned faster.

Towne tried familiar sleights, to lure his antagonist within his reach. He sat up, with folded arms and closed eyes, at a beam's end. He sat, with back turned, in the middle of a beam, and counted aloud. He asked such thoughtful and abstracted questions as whether his hearer, whoever he might be, "supposed there really ever was such a man as Duncigetorix," or "What's the cube-root of a quotient?" He busied himself with carefully untying and tying a shoe. By all these devices he got nothing but to be told that there was such a place as Dunci-Towne, and he had better not try scholarship.

Great struggles have their breathing-times; and when, flushed and panting, the two antagonists sat astride of different beams, watching each other, then, too, Towne offered, like greater generals, when worsted or unsuccessful, — like Artaxerxes to the Ten Thousand Hellenes, or Pyrrhus, the Epirote, to the Romans, — that "Royalty" should give in. In return he received a shout of scorn, and a challenge to reverse the order of things: he might run, and Brade would follow. This he accepted, and again the flight and chase began, hotter than ever.

Brade got, every now and then, near the shod ends of Towne's long legs and close to his hands. But once, as he came, in the eagerness of pursuit, to the top of a rope which Towne had just slid down and clutched it, he swung over, and falling came down in a heap on one of the mattresses, as still as a stone. Remsen rushed up with a cry of alarm, and Wilkins, too, rushed up; and although Towne held off, and called it a "make-believe," yet when he saw the two sympathizers in earnest, and the lithe and handsome boy lying silent and helpless, he also hurried forward to help.

Remsen had not succeeded in getting the cap off the face over which it had been thrust in the fall, and Wilkins had not yet thought of any thing to be done. Towne had probably seen or heard of such things before.

"Stretch him out! stretch him out!" said he, bending over, and laying hold of one of the half-doubled hands: "that's the way they do."

In an instant he was dragged down, and had taken Brade's place, receiving, as he went to it, two or three sharp applications of the two friends' hands, such as he had himself intended to apply. Then Wilkins, his supporter, was tumbled down on top of him, with as many or more like applications; and then Brade made his escape by the door, followed by Remsen.

"I knoo he was only makin' b'lieve," said Wilkins.

"Let 'em go!" said Towne, not questioning his ally's sagacity, but wiping his own wet forehead with a great colored handkerchief. "He can't try that dodge again. Come along, and I'll show you something. Look out for those two fellows."

The coast was clear outside; and Towne, with Wilkins in company, went warily but quickly over to the hogshead.

"Look here!" said he, peering in and lifting up a piece of board, "I'd squat down low under this, and then, if anybody should feel in, he'd think it was the bottom, in the night, or he'd think there was something under it, and he wouldn't want to feel down. Hullo! there's some water! it's good I saw it. Villicks, you pour it out, while I look out for those two fellows."

Wilkins proceeded with alacrity to his task, but made no more impression upon the strongly grounded hogshead than he might have made upon the crater of Vesuvius, by pulling at one side of it. Then Towne gave his length of arm and weight of body to the work; and then the two together soon brought the further chines of the huge vessel over, and, as they got it to a balance, Towne cautioned his far-descended friend "not to let it come down too hard, or they would have Mr. Stout after them, for he was in the barn."

Slowly and wisely they were lowering it, — Towne, with successive mechanical appliances, was at the same time working and teaching. They were standing now at that angle at which Atlas is represented in his most authentic portrait, where his great hands grasp his knees and prop his body, on which the world is resting. The boys' hands were at the level of their knees, on which the lower lip of the hogshead was resting, while the experienced Towne was showing his subordinate how "they were going to lower it to its side so softly it wouldn't break a robin's egg," when, without the slightest warning, while the boys were thus stooping, — one talking and one listening, as they worked, — the storm-house door, close by, burst open, a rush was made, "Oppidum!" cried Brade's voice, and down upon the most prominent and exposed part of each laboring workman fell a flat blow, loud and far-resounding. The effect was instantaneous.

"Outch!" cried Wilkins, at his share of the infliction. "Hold on!" said Towne, in spite of his. But at the word the hogshead went heavily to the earth, rolled swashing and lumbering down the little slope, gained strength with going, broke short off at the ground one weakly clothes-post, and laid it low with a crash, then, sidling round, was making across the green for another, with a hollow rumbling, that sounded as if it enjoyed mischief. Towne and Wilkins, with one glance, seeing most likely from the beginning what was likely to be the end, followed the two aggressors, overtook Brade, whom they treated as he had served them, and could not overtake Remsen, who in running easily kept out of reach. As Mr. Stout came from the barn, with a quiet but quick and business-like step, to the late scene of action, Towne and his follower began to come back, having evidently no intention of running away.

Mr. Stout was a thin, middle-aged man, with a strong New England face. He walked with a hitch in his step, as if from rheumatism.

Now he, having cast a look after the riotous hogshead, and also called to it to "stop when it got ready to," proceeded to the broken and overthrown post, lifted its lower end, and gave a short glance at the break, and ended by a nod of the head. The vagrant hogshead had by this time missed the other clothes-posts and brought up, lengthwise, against a bank of earth. Mr. Stout called to Towne and Wilkins.

"I want you boys should bring that cask back, as fast as it went away, and set it up just where it came from." And this he said like a man that was accustomed to do what he ought to do himself, and have other people do what they ought to do.

"I'll do it, Mr. Stout," answered Towne, with great alacrity.

"And when you've got it there, I want you should leave it there," continued that definite man.

"Mr. Stout!" said Towne, "we didn't roll it down at all, sir: all we did was, we tipped it down just as carefully as we could, or as anybody could, — I don't care who he is, — we did, really."

"Yes, that's plain to be seen," said Mr. Stout, grimly, as he set up the late involuntary agent of mischief firmly on its broad base again. "You found him here so dreadful uneasy and mischievous, and thrashing all round, you thought you'd just lay him down where he'd be quiet. I see all that plain enough. But now, boys, I want you should let it stand where I put it, and I guess it'll take about as good care of itself as you'll take care of it."

"We will," said Towne, leading off. "Yes, we will," added Wilkins. Then, turning back, the leader asked, "Do you want us to put that water in again, that was spilt?"

"No, — I thank you," said Mr. Stout, with a pause before the thanks.

Towne led off again, saying aside to Wilkins, "All we wanted was to get the water out. Let's go and have a turn at shinney." And they ran off.

As they disappeared, the other two came up hastily, after stopping to confer a little on the way, and caught Mr. Stout half way back to the barn again. Brade planted himself in front of the busy-looking man, and with a strongly persuasive look in his face, and holding by the front of Mr. Stout's waistcoat, and being drawn along, he said, —

"Mr. Stout! Mr. Stout! Won't you put that water in again, with your hose? and won't you let us see you? Do, Mr. Stout! won't you?"

"Boys are very good at asking for what they want, don't you think they be?" said Mr. Stout, walking on, as straight as he could.

"The engine's pumping now," urged the boy.

"And we'll see how long it takes to fill it half full with the hose," said Remsen, adding an inducement to Mr. Stout's curiosity.

"*May* we?" asked Brade, shaking the front of the waistcoat which he held.

"We never saw it go; and I've got a watch," said Remsen, continuing the line of his appeal. "Oh! do now, Mr. Stout!"

"S'pose I should, what's the great hurry?" asked the man, used to boys.

"We want to do it before the other fellows come," said Remsen.

Mr. Stout during all this urgency did not change a muscle of his face, and now, with the same unchanged look, he brought the colloquy to a happy end, by saying, —

"Well, there's no getting away from boys;" and he turned and walked back with them, amid their profuse thanks.

Brade was stationed near the corner of the laundry, to watch and give warning; and Remsen took upon him to handle the hose.

CHAPTER VIII.

ON THE EDGE OF IT.

TIME was going on: the dark evening was drawing near, and with it that chill was closing in, which seems to wait a little way off for twilight. The shouts and cries of boys engaged, not far away, "at shinney" or "hockey," came round the corner of the house, while Brade stood anxiously on watch, and Remsen impatiently coaxed the utmost out of the hose. Just as the quarter-bell before tea began to ring, Remsen gave a shout of success, to which Brade answered.

Towne had not stopped to look on at hockey, but had with all his might, and with his friend behind him, gone in for a share in that eager play. With no fear of consequences, he rushed into the thick of the game, while Wilkins, acting like a fellow who had knowledge enough of anatomy to know where his own shins were, and had sense enough to take care of them, kept well outside.

On his way to the wash-room, and afterward, on his way to tea, Towne was a little noisy and exultant over some "high old time" that he was going to have. He and Wilkins each got a few "lines" for disorder at the table; and in the school-room, after tea, "lines" fell upon them and others of their allies from time to time, for idleness and whispering, and passing notes; and when, at last, the signal for First Bedtime was given, Towne and Wilkins and Fatty Dover were all called back and received a few more lines for disorder in hurrying out of the school-room.

"Never mind, fellows," said Towne, partly in a loud whisper, and partly in a low voice, as he saw the coast clear of the departing tutor, "now for it! You, Fatty, must get your dress on as soon as the light's out in the dormitory, and tutor all gone. I'll give the signal this way: 'Ahem! ahem!' You'll have to be listening, for it won't be loud, but just the way you heard, —'ahem! ahem!' Nobody'll ever suspect that;" and, to do him justice, the signal had a very innocent sound. But Fatty Dover was in a condition to need stiffening. He did not seem to himself at all calculated to carry out the chief part.

"'Tain't the chief part," said Towne; and as Dover objected that Towne had told him it was, he was assured by the leader that "it was the principal part, but it hadn't got any talking, and it wa'n't dangerous, for he, the leader, was to be in there, and he was the only one that had got any thing to say."

The irresolute subordinate objected that "it was close by Mr. Cornell's door."

"Do you s'pose I haven't looked out for that?" asked Towne, scornfully. "What sort of a fellow should I be to manage things, if I didn't know enough to look out for that? Mr. Cornell's going out, and he's going to be out the whole evening. I heard him say so to Mr. Bruce."

"So did I," said Wilkins. Others confirmed this statement.

"You've only got to be spunky!" said Wilkins, whose

blood of generations was in a glow. "Why, I've got to be peekin' out all the time, and that's more dangerous than any thing else, ain't it, Towne?"

Without heeding this question, in the press of his duties, Towne gave or repeated his hurried directions. "There's the five-minute bell!" said he. "Now remember! You, Fatty, get ready, as soon as the lamp goes out, and start out when I give the signal, and come right to Brade's alcove; and, Wilkins, you come out by Mr. Cornell's door, and watch; and, if you hear any stirring, ask if you may go and get a drink; and, Fatty, that's the signal; quick's you hear that, follow me right out the window, and then shut the window down, and along the roof, just the way we've been doing; and, Leavitt, you and Ransom have got to make sure and light a light in the wash-room, as quick as the tutor's gone, and be washing away there like every thing, — all over your heads. There! there!" said he, summarily bringing his instructions to an end, as the tutor called out, "Towne! Dover! Wilkins! Ransom! Leavitt! Tarleton! late!"

Towne tried the persuasiveness of words, and began pleading that "he had had something very particular to say to those boys, and they didn't know how time went." But this well-devised though not strictly original phrase fell flat, and answered no good purpose: the leader and his followers were hurried away to their alcoves, and left to find comfort in the coming success of their scheme. In due course the lamp was put out, and the tutor departed.

CHAPTER IX.

THE DOING.

WHOEVER has lifted the curtains of boys' alcoves, soon after their inmates have gone to bed, and has looked lovingly in, has seen a pretty sight. Generally, the faces are lying most restfully, with hand under cheek, and in many cases look strangely younger than when awake, and often very infantile, as if some trick of older expression, which they had been taught to wear by day, had been dropped the moment the young ambitious will had lost control. The lids lie shut over bright, busy eyes; the air is gently and evenly fanned by coming and going breaths; there is a little crooked mound in the bed; along the bed's foot, or on a chair beside it, are the day-clothes, sometimes neatly folded, sometimes huddled off, in a hurry; bulging with balls, or, in the lesser fellows, marbles; stained with the earth of many fields where woodchucks have been trapped, or perhaps torn with the roughnesses of trees on which squirrels' holes have been sought; perhaps wet and mired with the smooth black or gray mud from marshes or the oozy banks of streams, where musk-rats have been tracked. Under the bed's foot, after a hard share in all the play and toil of the day, lie the shoes, — one on its side, — with the gray and white socks, now creased and soiled, thrown across them; a cross is at the head, some illuminated text at the side; and there, in their little cells, squared in the great mass of night, heedless how the earth whirls away with them or how the world goes, who is thinking of them or what is doing at home, the busiest people in the world are resting for the morrow.

All was still, that night, after the Tutor's going. Then, as the great constellations, made up of tremendous worlds, and the huge separate glowing stars, were all going through their vast turning in the boundless emptiness of space, so the lesser plan of Towne began its working in the Lower Dormitory at St. Bart's.

Scarcely had all grown still, when two sounds, by no means noisy, from the throat of the leader, announced to the associates in enterprise and peril that the work was to begin. A flash of light might have been seen in the dormitory, and possibly something like a chuckle from some young voice was followed by another chuckle from another young voice. As the light lasted, many curtains were shaken, and many faces appeared looking out from them as suddenly as flashes of northern lights show themselves all over the side of the sky. All in the same moment came a cry of alarm from the upper end of the dormitory, something like, "Get out, you!" and in that part might be seen, by a dim light prevailing there, a female figure in black dress and hat, retreating precipitately from a counterpart female figure in ghastly white dress and hat, precisely like, in shape and making, to the other, though on a somewhat larger scale.

In another moment the black female had scrambled away from before the white, and disappeared behind the curtain of an alcove, from which came forth repeated cries of, "Keep it off! keep it off!"

All this could not be gone through with without excitement, as indeed what street is there, in what town, where a scene like this could be enacted, with faces on all sides looking out upon it from windows, without a good deal of excitement? Curtains were suddenly drawn aside, and now a gathering of young figures in long white dresses began to take place in the middle of the room, the white counterpart of the woman in black having disappeared as effectually as the black figure. There was still a faint light at the upper end where the two apparitions had been.

The elder boys were asking and answering questions, with here and there a little fellow standing near; but, of the small boys, most stood in the doorways of their alcoves, holding the curtains aside and looking forth with curiosity or apprehension.

Even the younger boys at school learn a good deal of self-control; and therefore none of these committed himself, hastily, by words. Two or three seemed to understand the whole thing, and were laughing heartily, and trying to keep down the sound.

One voice was heard, but half-restrained, exclaiming, "What a fool that fellow is, to be frightened! He thought it was a ghost, most likely; and ghosts have been dead these thousand years, — there ain't any now!" And so, venting his indignation, the owner of this voice was walking up towards the light which still burned at the upper end, when all at once there was a general flutter and dispersion of the small boys; the light went out, a tone of authority was heard, close by the side of this malcontent, saying, "Towne, go to Mr. Cornell's door, and wait there!" and a whining sort of appeal from a third voice, "Mr. Bruce, sir! please, sir, may I go and get a drink?" at which there was a many-throated laugh of derision from curtained alcoves at the untimeliness of this request. Towne, also, laughed a short laugh, as he walked. Moreover, while these things were going on, all at once the larger boys in the middle of the floor at the same moment were saying, "We didn't have any thing to do with it, sir; we only came out to see what was going on," and were told mildly to go to their alcoves, and thereupon dispersed.

Mr. Bruce had lighted a candle which he carried, and went straight to the alcove in which the black figure had disappeared, and from which the cries of terror had come, but which was now as silent as all the others.

"Dover!" said he, drawing aside the curtain; and Dover, in his usual voice, answered. All around was altogether still.

"What were you making all that noise about?" asked the Tutor.

"I didn't know I was making a noise," said Dover.

"I judge it was you by the voice," Mr. Bruce said, "calling, 'Get out!' or something like it."

"I was frightened, sir," answered Dover, treading along the dizzying brink of discovery, if not with strong and dauntless stride, yet with unexpectedly firm step, if one might judge by his voice.

The Tutor bade Dover come to him after breakfast, and in the mean time to keep his bed and go to sleep; and then went across the dormitory to the opposite alcove. Here Remsen was in bed, and, like a sensible fellow, was not making-believe to be asleep; and near the curtain, as the candle showed, was standing our young friend Antony, looking somewhat sheepish, but quite as much amused at the recognition.

Mr. Bruce did not smooth the front of authority: —

"I'm sorry to have to speak to you" (Brade, though he said nothing and looked down, had certainly not a very guilty expression). "You know it's a very serious offence, Brade," he said, "to be found in another's alcove."

Young Brade looked up, ready to speak, but did not interrupt. The Tutor paused.

"I *didn't* come to anybody's alcove, sir," he answered.

"Of course you know what you're saying," said Mr. Bruce. "You were in Remsen's alcove a minute ago: do you mean to say you were *brought* there?"

The boy stood in his long white night-gown, with his bare feet on the bare floor, half full of fun, half full of fear.

"Oh, no, sir, not that," said Antony. "But I mean I didn't come up the dormitory to go to anybody's alcove: I only ran in there to hide away."

Mr. Bruce's voice changed, decidedly for the softer, and doubtless his face showed as great a change.

"Come to me immediately after breakfast," he said, as he had said to Dover. "Now go to bed instantly, Brade, and go to sleep as soon as possible."

Before the words were well spoken, Brade, in his white night-gown, was scampering down to the other end, and across the dormitory.

Mr. Bruce looked into each alcove as he went down, and then up the other side. Towne, meanwhile, danced and took different attitudes, as if to keep himself warm and occupied, at his tiresome post. At length the Tutor came back and found time to attend to him, making this little address:—

"Now, Towne, it's very unpleasant to find you at the bottom of all the mischief that's going on."

"I don't see how that is, sir," said Towne. "You only found me walking along the dormitory as peaceable as could be."

"Where do you *belong*, sir?" asked the Tutor, sharply.

"In Brunswick, sir. No, I wasn't thinking, sir: my alcove's"—

"Twenty lines for impertinence! (Not a word, sir!) Go straight to your alcove, and don't be found out here again," said the Tutor.

"I won't, if I can help it, sir," answered poor Towne. "I didn't mean"—

"Not a word, sir!" said Mr. Bruce; and Towne went away, with an inarticulate murmur, to his place. The Tutor, having seen all safe, went his way.

When the flap of the spring-door, at the further wash-room, showed that he was out of hearing, Towne exulted as loudly as he dared, that, by that cunning trick of impertinence, he had made Mr. Bruce forget to tell him to come after breakfast.

Mr. Cornell's door was ajar, as it had been all the evening, with a light shining through; but no change had taken place there implying that the occupant had come in. Mr. Bruce had left every thing, outwardly, as it ought to be. The dormitory had taken on again the stillness of night, broken very slightly by what seemed to be calls from one side to the other at the upper end. The adventures of the night were not over, however, for that unrestful place of rest. Towne's alcove and Dover's adjoined each other; Towne's being the uppermost, on the right hand, on that floor. Between those two went a loud whispering, growing often to a deeper voice.

"I want to go to sleep," said Dover, at last, a little more loudly; "and Mr. Bruce told me to. I chucked 'em over on to the ground," he added peevishly; but the other's success in pulling the wool over one tutor's eyes made him anxious for further adventures.

"Good boy!" said Towne, patronizingly. "If you're afraid, I ain't: so here goes!"

A voice from the opposite side came across the six-foot alley-way, sounding like Ulterior Blake's: —

"I say, Oppidum, you daresn't go out! Mr. Cornell 'll snap you up. He'll be just coming home, humming a toone, just now, and he'll snap you up just as a toad does a fly. I'll bet you two cents you don't dares't to go out!"

No answer came from Towne, though the speech was intelligible, if not good English. In the stillness which followed, a window might have been heard slowly opening. Immediately a boy came from the opposite alcoves, and, in a whispered shout, called out: —

"Fellows! fellows! Look out on the roof! Towne's gone out, in invisible clo'es, to dodge Mr. Cornell! Won't there be fun!"

"It's dark as Erebus!" said a very assured voice, louder than the rest, as many windows were hastily thrown up. "*Οὐδὲν οὔτ' ἀκοῦσαι οὔτ' ἰδεῖν ἔστι.* Remsen, how do you expect us to see?"

"Hear that fellow!" said another. "I say, Gaston, do keep your" —

"Fellows! fellows!" said another voice, which was certainly our friend Brade's, almost bursting with fun and excitement, as he ran by several alcoves, "Towne has gone out there to run before Mr. Cornell in his gymnasium suit, so that he shouldn't see him;" making pretty clear, in spite of the confusion of personal pronouns, that Towne had gone out on the roof to execute some daring and hazardous feat of activity, with which Mr. Cornell, the Tutor, was in some way associated. There was a stir and flurry on all sides. Objections and hasty discussions took place in several alcoves on the school-room side, as between boys wanting to go through and boys not willing to let them.

"Fellows! you'll catch your death o' cold! What's the use?" said some elder, gravely, probably the deliberate Blake.

Then a more authoritative voice: —

"Thompson! Mason! Lawrence! don't let those little fellows out on the roof! Do make 'em go back to bed!" And, in compliance with this exhortation, Brade, Ransom, Leavitt, and others, were called by name, as if already on the roof, and bidden (without apparent effect) to go to bed.

"We've got blankets round us," answered several voices. "Russell better come out himself."

Meanwhile, from the slight murmur to be heard outside the windows, and the low cries of "Look out!" "Isn't it dark?" "Don't walk off!" it might be known that many boys had got through all difficulties to be near Towne's feat. Cold had not stopped them; darkness had not stopped them; and there they were.

"Sh! — sh!" —was cried, to enforce silence; Remsen, as before, explaining that there was going to be great fun.

"Have you got it?" whispered a voice, somewhere in the darkness below the common level.

"Yes!" answered another, somewhere in the same direction, speaking in his ordinary tone, and therefore easily recognized as Towne, and going on like a hero, as he evidently felt himself.

"Now don't I wish Mr. Cornell was about three rods off! — but it's cold, I tell you!"

The words reminded some of the others that their clothes were thin, and they began to move; but the boys' proverb about the nearness of a person talked of was strikingly illustrated on this occasion, as on so many others. A good, manly tenor voice, a little way off, was heard singing "Days of Absence."

"Mr. Cornell! Mr. Cornell!" was the cry. "Down!" and some were heard fleeing; and some were heard going down on the tin roof, with a sudden thud; and some were heard struggling with laughter.

"Sh! — sh!"— said that fearless and eager lad, Remsen, again, going about. "Hold on! Towne hasn't got through yet," and the audience was still enough to catch the faintest sound.

Feet without shoe-soles scurried over the ground below.

"Sh!" said the same eager lad. "Now look out! sh!"

There was a sort of scramble down there below, where Towne seemed to be, and then a splash! with a suppressed shuddering "Oh-h-h!" and Towne had evidently met with a sudden surprise.

A roar of laughter started from many of the boys on the roof, suppressed as soon as possible, and as much as possible, but beginning, as hearty and genuine laughter will, to spread.

"Get under the cover, Towne! get under the cover!"

said Brade, his voice scarcely recognizable, for trembling so with laughter.

"You better hold your clack, Royalty, or I'll crack your crown!" retorted the poor fellow, splashing.

"How do you suppose that water got back?" asked a quavering voice. "'Tain't rained, has it?"

This sounded like Wilkins.

"Wilkins, why didn't you let that water out?" said Remsen.

Down below, the state of things had changed within a few seconds essentially. Towne, whose leap to the back of his great adventure (to use a figure), had been so vigorous and masterful, now— soused in chilly water — was not the same boy. His stout and tutor-defying voice was changed.

"I ain't a-goin' to stay here and freeze! I don't care if he *does* catch me!" he muttered. "I'll give it to somebody for this!" and then a floundering, and the brattle of the water in the cask, — cold-sounding enough to make the very listeners shudder, — implied that the unexpectedly immersed hero was retreating from his position.

"It is written," said Gaston's voice, "that the Greek philosopher lodged in his cask; but, as Towne ain't a Greek philosopher, I don't see what he wants to take up his habitation in a hogshead for."

Strangely enough there was no interference of the much-talked of Mr. Cornell.

"Are you visible, Towne?" Brade asked.

"I'll visible you!" said the interrupted adventurer.

"He can't see you in that gray suit," said Remsen "Look out, fellows, if you don't want to get spattered, if he comes up. Mr. Cornell wa'n't there at all," he continued, confidentially turning to those near him. "That was Lawrence: we got him to sing like Mr. Cornell."

But now a new element came in.

"Towne!" cried Mr. Bruce's voice, which had been heard so often that evening, and which now came, not from the ground, but from one of the dormitory windows, showing that he had stolen a march upon the absent inmates. The boys on the roof scuttled or fluttered, — whichever may be the better expression for a noisy motion, which partook of those of tortoises or seals, or the like, at the water's edge, and birds startled from a brake.

"Come to that storm-house door, and I'll let you in," continued Mr. Bruce.

"Whoever put that water," — said Towne, going away shivering, "wish I had him — head in it."

The boys — silently retiring at the presence of the Tutor — began to giggle, as poor Towne vented his threats.

Mr. Bruce, having lighted the dormitory lamp, went down, being doubtless listened to closely as he went, step by step, and heard to turn the key of the back door.

"Wait a moment, Towne," said the Tutor, who seemed to find it necessary to repress the boy's eagerness to reach his alcove. "Follow me, if you please;" and then might be heard, coming along the hall and up the crooked stairs, two sets of steps, — one brisk and trig, the other heavy, flat, and wet, even to the ear.

In the "Cross Dormitory" the boys were sitting up in their beds, as the Tutor, with great gravity, and poor Towne, looking pretty sulky and savage, went by.

From the sounds which came forth, it would seem that neither admiration nor sympathy was the overpowering emotion with the witnesses of the adventurous Towne's present condition. Mr. Bruce stopped, just inside of the large dormitory and near the lamp; and near him, of course, stopped Towne. The Tutor did not look strictly along the alcoves, or he would have seen that many faces, with very slight effort at concealment, were peering out at the sides of the curtains.

The victim of misfortune was certainly a most ridiculous figure; for, whether the hogshead had been nearly full, or whether he had gone into it "squatting," he was soaked and streaming from his neck to his feet.

"Move about, Towne, until I've done with you," said the Tutor, "or you'll spoil all the ceiling of the schoolroom below. Distribute your streams a little." And poor Towne began traversing, like a machine, a large circle, laying the dust (if there was any) effectually.

"Mayn't I go to bed, sir?" asked Towne, in a voice intended, perhaps, to be severe and distant, but which came near setting the whole dormitory off in a fit of laughter. Tittering and repressed sobs did make themselves heard. Towne, nevertheless, kept up his best dignity, and uttered one more sound: —

"I'm" —

"Oh!" said Mr. Bruce, "you've been going through a preparation for going to bed, have you, sir? Where have you been since I saw you last? I told you not to let me see you here again."

"No more I wouldn't, sir," said Towne, "if you'd let me have my way; but you wouldn't."

Even the gravity of Mr. Bruce gave way a little before the boy's pitiable figure. "You didn't remember the rules about bathing, I think?" he asked, smiling.

"I'm sure, sir," said Towne, stopping his round, and dripping where he was, "this is pretty good keeping the rules; for if I went 'a-bathin' out of doors' it can't be said but what I had a tootor to see to me."

This time the furtive laughter may have been with Towne instead of at him. His pluck appealed to the boys' sympathy, and possibly conciliated also the kindliness of the Tutor; for he certainly immediately released the unsuccessful adventurer from his enforced round.

"Come, Towne! have you got a rough bathing-towel?" said he; and, having secured one from some volunteer in an alcove, he took him into a bath-room, where, after making him strip himself of his slight clothing, which clung closely to him, and throwing the soaked garments into the bath-tub, he gave him so thorough a rubbing-down that poor Towne more than once cried out, and came out of the operation glowing all over.

Then Mr. Bruce sent him to bed in a night-gown, borrowed, like the towel, and bade him "good-night!"

"Isn't that hogshead a good place, Towne?" "Did the water fit you, Townie?" were questions addressed to the retiring adventurer, interrupted suddenly by the arrival of Mr. Cornell in his room.

The dormitory, after this, was still.

CHAPTER X.

THE NEXT MORNING.

THE sun came up, next day, as he usually comes up at St. Bart's, at that time of the year. First comes a scattering of golden largess far forward on the sky; then a crowing of all the cocks, as if they had not begun and kept it up for three or four hours already, to be sure to hit the time when it did come; a general standing-round of all trees, damp and frosty from the night; next the comfortable salutation of farmers, smock-frocked and respectable, across the way; then the blowing of the horrid steam-whistles; next the cheery ringing of St. Bart's bell; then the slow, sober sun himself.

The first use that Fatty Dover made of his morning strength and intelligence, that next day, was to rush out of the storm-house door, and by the hogshead, and over the triumphant part of Towne's track of the night before, searching all sides with his eyes, as he ran. He went the length of the school-room, and along the western end; and then from where he stood he surveyed anxiously the neighborhood, and then, disappointed, turned back.

The wash-rooms were noisy that morning, with anecdote and laughter, all drawn from the fruitful experience of the night before. The jokes were poor, as most men's, and almost all boys' jokes are; but boys' jokes, if not those of men, also, answer as good a purpose in the world as a great many devout and unselfish writers profess to expect or to hope from their books, which, as their authors say, will have answered their purpose if one pious soul shall have received comfort or edification from them. The amount of gratification given to at least one person by each witticism here would have pleased those friends of mankind.

Gaston, who ventured more into the province of classic history and invention than his neighbors, had given Towne the nickname of "*Ἀναδυόμενος*" (anadyomenos), which, as it was not generally understood, he explained at large. "As Venus," he said, "had risen from the sea, so Towne had risen" —

"From the *sea*-a-s-k," said Thompson Walters, trying a pun of his own.

This proceeding necessarily took from the freshness of Gaston's joke; but the boys, in the end, got as much satisfaction out of it, for they called the hero of the last evening "Venus;" and young Meadows, who, like Gaston, in lesser degree, had pushed into mythology, started a demand of him for apples.

The hero himself tried to show that "that water was one of the best things for him that could be; for, if anybody had tried to find him in it, ten to one he'd have put his hand on the water, instead of him."

Remsen was spoken of as having been the woman in the white dress, or the ghost, and commended; but Dover was quizzed by pretty nearly everybody who knew how to quiz after any fashion. It seemed a tender point with him, this morning, that he had not been able to find the black dress, which Towne in his adventures had dropped and left behind; and he was asked "how he would feel if he should see Mr. Wilson in that gown, making a fool of him before the whole school."

Russell, a Fifth Form boy, had caught, and brought away, a "poetical" outpouring of Antony Brade. This Russell read, with great enthusiasm, and it was received with much appreciation by the public in the wash-room: —

"'A Towne leaned over a hogshead's brim,
To see its own face far down;
And tumbled in. If it could not swim,
What else could it do but drown?'"

"Pooh!" said Hutchins, almost as soon as the reading began, "you say Royalty wrote that? I'm sure he never wrote that! I know I've heard something like that, — something about a 'town' and a 'cask,' — a Senior in college couldn't do that."

"Blake's the fellow to tell what college fellows can do," said Gaston.

"Where's Blake?" asked several voices; and when Blake appeared, with his face and hair all dripping from a wash-basin, and blowing water from his nostrils, Hutchins appealed to him, —

"Look here, old Ultimatum! wouldn't it take a 'Senior' to write that?"

"He hasn't heard it," said the chorus.

Blake, however, was above any such necessity: —

"That don't make any difference," he said. "At my college, out there, the fellows get through with all their literary work before they get to be Seniors. Seniors, at Ulterior, do as they like. It's all practical work, then,

—'scientific' they call it,—they keep tally at base-ball, and keep 'time' for fellows rowin'."

"Let's have the rest o' the poem," said Thompson Walters; and Russell went on reading:—

> "'A Tutor's summons came o'er the spot:
> That Towne began to rise:
> A very wet Towne,—by no means hot,—
> But all right otherwise.'"

So well received was this second stanza that when Hutchins began to object that he "knew a poem by some great poet,—De Kalb, or De Forest, or something,"—he was called upon by many voices, in language more vigorous than elegant, to "shut up."

"That isn't all of it?" said Thompson Walters.

"Oh, 'lame and impotent conclusion'!" said Gaston, quoting, no doubt, from some of his great books.

Russell was not inclined to forsake the rhyme, or hear it disparaged:—

"You'd better try it yourself, Gaston," he said.

"And do it in Latin," said Walters.

"I can," said Gaston, "if I try," and began to think:—

> "De Oppido audivisti,
> Et ejus sorte tristi"—

He had gone pretty glibly over two lines,—as far as most rhymesters go well,—and the flow of verse was obstructed.

"And there you grow rather misty," said Walters.

"Now give it me, please, Russell," said the author of the English verse, who stood at the wash-room door, blushing; and, receiving it, blushing he disappeared.

In the younger wash-room a crowd of lesser fellows

surrounded him and teased him for a sight, for the fame of it had already reached them; but he tore it into a hundred pieces, and flinging them into Leavitt's face escaped again.

At this point the veritable Towne himself appeared, and a sudden whim seized several boys, all at once, to shoulder him, and give him a triumph. There was little time, but that only made them go about it the more quickly; and for the first thing had him up with his head pretty hardly thrust against the ceiling. Gaston called out from a distance, —

"'Sublimo vertice sidera feriam.' Fellows! Fellows! you've made him *see stars!*" which could hardly give Towne any comfort.

The rest, full of their work, said that "Towne had taken cold, in saving himself from drowning;" and were just going to toss him in a blanket to cure him, when suddenly the two-minute bell (which they might have expected) struck. Down tumbled Towne, as many a hero before has tumbled from a triumph, and was left sprawling, to gather himself up, and go back, as he was, to every-day life. The others scampered up stairs or down, according as they were, or were not, nearly enough dressed.

Many were the delinquencies, besides Towne's, at roll-call that morning, and many the losses of breakfast; but among those who were in their places at that meal were Dover and Wilkins, both of whom had been summoned to Mr. Bruce's room after breakfast. Dover had begun to eat and drink with his usual appetite, which was one of the best; but a certain piece of intelligence which gave, as it passed about, a pleasurable excitement to his neighbors, disturbed Dover to such an extent that he accomplished far less than he was in the habit of doing; and when the tables were dismissed, he rushed hatless and breathless out of doors, and then — with a question at random, "Where is it?" — forward, toward a most conspicuous object which had already attracted the attention of passers-by on the road.

This object was a black dress, hung up and spread out, to full length and width, on one of the pear-trees, and surmounted by a woman's black hat. At first a sort of astonishment seemed to open his eyes and to slow his steps. He may have wondered, perhaps, how it got there; he may have been questioning how it could be got down; but, with his eyes wide open and his lips apart, he made steadily for it, as if nothing else existed.

Already boys began to pelt this tempting object with whatever they could find; and then (alas for Dover!) a large boy (Phil Lamson) set himself, as large boys sometimes will, directly in the way, and faced him off from whatever way of escape he tried. The shower of missiles, for some reason, slackened and then suddenly ceased; and then Dover tried as hard as he could, and entreated his stopper to let him go. It was all in vain.

Dover saw Brade under that tree; and with him Remsen, longer-armed than he.

He begged and besought to be let alone ("There's Brade and Remsen now!" said he), but could not get away.

The cause of the stoppage in the flight of stones and sticks was soon evident. "Dover!" said a voice behind him, as exactly measured as the fling of a lasso, "I thought I told you to come to me after breakfast;"

and Mr. Bruce appeared, with Mr. Cornell, walking leisurely.

"So you did, sir; and I'm coming, sir; but" — answered the boy, looking round toward the tree.

"If you don't want to make a butt of yourself, Fatty," said Phil Lamson, aside, "clear out and thank me."

On the South Road, close by the school-grounds, a carriage had stopped in the way, within near sight of the tree with the black dress.

"Eldridge!" said a lady's voice, of that courageous sort that is not afraid to go across any open space, and encounter any ears (as in this case, Mr. Bruce's and Mr. Cornell's), "how much time have we got? I don't want to miss that train. There! that's an effigy! It's something those boys have been getting up. It's Science or Learning, or something. (I wonder Mr. Bruce don't see us.)"

The proper name she pronounced with great distinctness.

"Ma!" said Miss Minette Wadham, who was with her, "don't you see what that is?"

"To be sure I do!" said the mother. "I understand it. Boys" —

Eldridge ventured an assertion that "it looked to him amazin' like one o' Miss Wadham's dresses."

"What? No!" exclaimed the lady, in excess of amazement. "What? That ain't the dress I lent" —

While the occupants of the carriage gazed at this extraordinary exhibition, Antony and his taller companion were very busy at the tree, but without climbing into it.

"Brade!" said Mr. Bruce, calling from a little distance.

Just as he spoke, — almost at the very word, — a sudden flame began to creep, and then to climb, and then to leap up and over the dress, which was of some flimsy cotton fabric; and in a few moments the tree showed nothing on its leafless limbs but rags of glowing red, and then of black tinder. There was no wind, and the boys had had to run away from the falling shreds of flame which for an instant came down thickly. The two Tutors continued their leisurely walk to the scene.

While this was going on, Mrs. Wadham worked about in her seat, and seemed on the point of speaking, and of course looked very red. It could not be but that she should feel her dignity involved, at this public destruction of a garment formally borrowed of her; and her daughter, we may suppose, could not help sympathizing, as daughters do. Miss Minette, however, had a smile on her face; and, turning herself away from the scene of the catastrophe, looked steadfastly in the opposite direction.

"It was loaned," said Mrs. Wadham, beginning the process of recovering her self-assurance, "for the purposes of investigation, — of an investigation. Well," she continued, a little flurried, but showing her native strength, "all are to perish in the using. It ain't showing much ceremony; but we'll sacrifice ceremony on the altar of investigation! — Yes, on the altar of investigation! — Drive on, Eldridge! Do your pootiest!"

"There's the Caput!" was cried; and there, sure enough, — not on the ground, but at his study window, looking out, — he stood.

Most of the boys were already hurrying away, to

make the utmost of their short time between breakfast and prayers. Foot-ball was already in active play, and foot-ball was the only thing in the world, now, to every boy but Dover, Brade, and Remsen, and such others as might have to do with the authorities, for the activities of last night.

"I set it on fire, sir," said Brade to Mr. Bruce.

"And I gave him the match, — I did, indeed, sir," said Remsen, seeing the Tutor smile.

The scene at the tree over, the Tutors sought the Rector.

They felt clear that the thing had been a masquerade, to look like Mrs. Ryan ("the lady that came to church with her daughter," as Mr. Bruce explained), "because the boys thought she was a watch over Brade."

"And Brade has set it on fire, I suppose," said the Rector, "and no wonder."

Mr. Bruce added another piece of information, — that "he believed the dress was one of Mrs. Wadham's."

"Well, certainly, if she lent it, that's her look-out," said the Rector. "We must punish playing with fire; but I'll take off a good deal for the provocation. I'm sorry to have Brade's score lose by another boy's fault. Towne may learn wisdom some of these days."

Though the few minutes before Prayers, and the Recess in the forenoon together, were not enough for the examination of the young fellows engaged in the fun of last night, it was all done with before dinner, in time to go on the school-room slate that afternoon. The result was that Towne came out, poor fellow, with a special infliction of lines and bounds, as the chief offender; and the rest of the boys in that dormitory were treated pretty evenly with lines proportioned to their technical age or standing in the School, in order of Forms.

The fire was not forgotten, but handled lightly this time, with the reason given.

With this all were pretty well satisfied, except poor Towne, who muttered that "when a fellow got wet through and shivering, the way he'd been, they ought to have compassion on him, and not punish him hard, like that."

CHAPTER XI.

MR. PARMENTER DRAWN TO THE FLAME.

THE blaze of that dress of Mrs. Wadham's, if it had not flashed into a great many eyes of Eastham people, had yet been heard of in the post-office and the store, and in many a private house and homestead of the town, within a few hours after that dress had become tinder. Public opinion had not satisfied itself "how Mrs. Wadham's dress came to be on that tree," or "how it came to be set on fire." That "she had lent it to be a *sacrifice* or something," was part of the general information, and was wrought-in through the public discussions of the subject, but did not help to make things plainer.

This contribution to the fund of general knowledge was, most likely, made by Eldridge, who, in coming back from the cars, made visits of some length to both store and post-office.

One man there was in Eastham to whom the affairs of Town and School were alike near; and to him was many a question proposed, to find out "what those boys had been up to, there, at Saint Bartholomew's School."

Mr. Parmenter, a leading man and a leading trustee of St. Bart's, had the reputation of keeping himself pretty closely informed of whatever took place there.

The School, as it had happened, though still in its early infancy, had had the benefit of more than half as many heads as it had seen years; and this variety and abundance was said to be owing to the vigilant supervision and unremitting interest of that active trustee.

Sometimes he was coming out of the stable; sometimes he was looking into the kitchen; sometimes he was talking or asking about arrangements in the cellar. He was occasionally bringing information to the Rector of the School, and occasionally asking information from him; he was corresponding with parents, and he kept up continual intercourse with the under-masters and the boys.

This assiduous devotion was said not to have been approved by any of the different heads, so far; and one after another, like swiftly circling stars, had rolled off into space.

Mr. Parmenter's way of discharging the duties of his office of trustee, if not properly appreciated by the several rectors, was very efficient in its kind. He never left the other members of the Board in ignorance of weak points in the administration of the School; and he never failed to administer comfort to the existing Rector, and to excite him to noble effort, by showing him how inferior his predecessor had been, and making him familiar with the chief short-comings of the former administrations.

With this active spirit in him, we may be sure that it was not long before Mr. Parmenter put himself in the way of possessing all the information that was to be had.

The Reverend Mr. Warren, Rector of St. Bart's School, was walking up and down upon the piazza, and apparently in that state of settled thoughtfulness in which one rests himself now and then, or draws himself off from his care by looking for a while at this thing, or listening for a while to that person.

As he paced to and fro, he stopped at one time, and fixed his eyes steadily, though not very actively, on the figures of a horse and rider coming along the South Road, and leaving behind them a little cloud of dust, such as can be raised, even just before winter, in certain conditions of our soil. The horse, as could be seen, even from a distance, was a good one; and his gait, an easy gallop, showed good training. Having looked in that direction for a moment or two, Mr. Warren turned and walked again.

The rhythmic sound of iron-shod hoofs drew nearer, was deadened for a moment, and then clattered up the short road-way to the School buildings. The walker had turned, at the end of his beat, and was coming back, just as the rider was close at hand.

About the latter there was something of what is called "air," as he sat his horse, with his heels decisively down, the rein held lightly, and the whip under his arm. He was a little stiff, perhaps, but looked as if he knew that he was right, and as if there was no other way of doing what he was doing than that. His salute was something very definite also.

"Good morning, sir!" he said, from the little distance near the side-gate. "You've been having quite a piece of fireworks, I hear."

"Why, no; nothing of any consequence, that I remember," answered Mr. Warren, and invited Mr. Parmenter, his visitor, to come in.

The horseman excused himself for want of time.

"One of our ladies has lost a portion of her wardrobe, I'm told," he continued, smiling. "No disorderly conduct among the boys, I hope? — It occurred to me that it might be necessary to make some atonement. Of course, we couldn't offer compensation exactly."

"I don't think any thing is to be done on our side. If the lady lends a dress to her son or another boy, she must look to the boy," said Mr. Warren. "I don't propose to do any thing about it."

— "If it don't bring the School into any trouble," said Mr. Parmenter, like one who felt that there were a good many things to be thought of by men in responsible positions. "People have a way of talking. You find Brade, I suppose, a high-spirited fellow?" he continued, changing the subject a little, after having given his hint.

"A very fine boy, and a very promising boy, every way," answered the Rector of the School; "with the stuff in him to make a good Christian man, and a satisfaction to his friends."

This thorough commendation apparently gave much satisfaction. Mr. Parmenter called to Mr. Stout, and very courteously desired him to take his horse ("he would be only a minute or two"). Then he formally, and with precision, dismounted, and, coming upon the piazza, seated himself on one of the settees, and busied his hands with setting right some of the twisting of the rattan, of which it was made, while he talked.

"I believe," he said, "young Brade's birthday comes to-morrow." Then, after a pause to give effect to his minuteness of information, he said, "Am I right, sir? Perhaps it has occurred to you already, without any suggestion. Of course" (with a bow, and interrupting himself) "I haven't any fear of your neglecting any thing that concerns the *intellectual* part of the boys' education. There were some things it was impossible to make your prede — "

Mr. Warren's face, it must be confessed, showed less interest than annoyance. Mr. Parmenter proceeded: —

"It's the custom, I believe, in foreign countries, — and a very graceful one, as it strikes me" (the word "graceful" he made emphatic), — "to have a good deal of ceremony on birthdays. We can't make a difference between one boy and another, but Brade is a little homesick, and we might" —

"Brade isn't homesick," said Mr. Warren. "There isn't a happier fellow in the school."

"Perhaps our information differs," said Mr. Parmenter, with sufficient gravity. "I commonly have independent sources. I thought you might make a little more of him. Perhaps a little special attention" —

Mr. Warren had changed color, for some reason or other, during this speech. He answered: —

"Thank you: he won't be neglected."

Mr. Parmenter changed the subject again.

"I saw a very beautiful drawing, — by one of your family, I think, sir. Would it be too much trouble to let me see it? It was lying on the table in the front room. That's it, I think," he added, having left his seat and looked through the window.

Mr. Warren obligingly brought it, — a crayon drawing.

"By your sister, sir, I think I understood?" continued Mr. Parmenter. "There's a great deal of *depth*" (emphatic) "in that. Is it after an old master?"

The drawing was of a western sky and sunset, as was indicated by the attitudes of such animated figures as appeared in it. It was really so good that the splendors flung upon the clouds, and showing through a row of leafless larches and other trees, on a rising ground, seemed scarcely to want the gorgeous hues of gold and scarlet or crimson.

It even seemed to change, under the eye, to deepening or lightening of red, and burnishing or dimming of yellow, as the colors change aloft while the sun is going down, and promising a fine to-morrow.

"That impresses me very much, sir," said Mr. Parmenter. "I wish you'd allow me to have it framed. It's a jewel worthy of being set in an appropriate case."

Mr. Warren excused himself, very absolutely, with thanks.

Mr. Parmenter drew a parcel from his pocket.

"Perhaps you'd do me the favor, sir, to give that to Brade, with my wishes for 'many happy returns'?"

"Certainly," said Mr. Warren, "unless you'd like to give it yourself."

On this point Mr. Parmenter, a man of business and experience, had notions of propriety, and said: —

"I think it better to have every thing, as far as possible, pass through the Rector's hands. You haven't observed any communication between Mrs. Ryan and — you know, I suppose, they say she's a watch over him."

"Oh, no!" said Mr. Warren, impatiently. "There would be no harm if there were."

"I don't feel so sure of that," said Mr. Parmenter, deliberately, like one who felt his own responsibilities, if not those of others also. "I'm not clear that it would be safe to shut our eyes to any possible harm which might befall one committed to our care. Have we? I think not."

With this expression of opinion Mr. Parmenter took his leave; mounted his horse in true style, grasping the reins and a lock of the mane in his left hand; setting his foot deliberately in the stirrup, while Mr. Stout held the head; springing and swinging himself over the saddle. When he found himself handsomely in his seat, he promised to do as much for Mr. Stout when Mr. Stout should need his services in the same way, and, putting his horse to an easy gallop, rode off.

CHAPTER XII.

A DISTINGUISHED FOREIGNER, WHO, PERHAPS, HAS SOMETHING TO DO WITH IT.

THE main building of St. Bart's was large; but the chief merit in its appearance lay in the variety of its outline, occasioned by the additions of different shapes and sizes, according to the need of the time.

Its front doorway was good and substantial, a fair oval of plate-glass showing, when the door was shut, a large hall, with a handsome, winding staircase, on the first landing of which stood one of those long clocks, which hold so fast a place in the mind of one who knew them in childhood. Over the doorway, and in front of a lengthwise window, was a carving, which, to an intelligent eye, was evidently heraldic: a "wreath," or "torse," of red and white, bore an upright something, which one, who knew the name of the School, and the conventional symbol of its saint, might recognize as a dagger or knife. The blade and handle of this were of the same colors respectively, or, as they would be called in heraldry, *gules* and *argent*. Beneath, in golden church text, was the legend, "SURSUM," (*upwards*).

It was a harmless joke of successive Forms, as they advanced in Latinity, to say that this motto was an invitation to the Rector's study, in the second story.

The implement which, as described, decorated the

entrance to St. Bart's, had puzzled a good many visitors. It was popularly called among the boys "St. Bart's whittle;" and new-comers to the School were mystified, where they were capable of it, by hearing it called his "whistle." The Rev. Mr. Merritt, one of the Trustees, when fresh in office, had innocently taken it for illustration one day as a church steeple, exhorting the assembled boys to "remember the badge of their school, — that sky-pointing spire, — and direct their flight with unflagging wing still upwards;" and when some one whispered an explanation, as he sat down, astonished at the laughter which greeted what was intended to be, and doubtless was, the point of his speech, said that "the fault was the carver's, and not his."

At this door, surveying this heraldic device, and whatever else ornamented and distinguished the place of entrance, was standing, on an afternoon in early autumn, a foreign-looking gentleman, of large size and distinguished air. He had tried the knocker with little effect. Apparently those who ought to have heard and come to this inanimate call were away, or were napping; and the only result of his experiment with the knocker was the stopping of a little girl in the road, at a short distance, who curiously watched his movements. He proceeded next to ring the door-bell. While he was still waiting, a small, slight, neatly-dressed man came up (whose most noticeable feature, perhaps, was a set of squarely trimmed whiskers and moustache), and said politely: —

"Perhaps I can help you, sir. I'm at home here. I'm a trustee of the institution. Did you want to see the Rector, sir? the Rev. Mister Warren?"

The foreign-looking gentleman turned at this address, and, like a very courteous and distinguished foreigner, saluted the Trustee, who had thus come to his help, and thanking that gentleman for his kind offices, — approving, perhaps, in his foreign heart, *στηθέσσι ἑοῖσι* (stethessi heoisi), as the boys of the Fifth Form might say, after Dan Homer, this American habit of keeping Trustees about the premises to wait upon strangers, — inquired whether the building was a hotel.

The Trustee, smiling as one whom a consciousness of wit made good-humored, informed him that, "though they had a good many boarders" (this, as conveying a joke, and that in a language foreign to the hearer, he pronounced quite distinctly), "this was not a hotel."

Answering this assurance with a simple interrogative "So?" and then asking pardon, the distinguished foreign gentleman, declining to go in, accepted a seat outside, and listened attentively to an account of the character of the institution, of which his informant was a trustee. Having heard this account through to the end (or at least to a convenient place for the end), the foreigner, drawing out his watch, said in outlandish but very intelligible English that "he wished the manufactories of Weston to see. Might the gentleman only be so good and tell him when he could next take the cars?"

Having been informed by the Trustee that he had "some two hours to wait," and having met this second disappointment with the same interrogative monosyllable as before, "So?" he returned his watch (a rich-looking and very foreign-looking watch) to his pocket, and addressed the courteous and communicative Trustee: —

"This is a school for boys?"

The Trustee accepted this interrogative affirmation

with a readiness which implied satisfaction at having made himself so well understood; and the stranger continued: —

"If it pleases, how is called that little boy, with curly head, who plays?"

"That is Brade," answered the ready Trustee.

"'Bread'?" asked the foreign gentleman, giving a foreign turn to the name. "That is the best thing: the first one of whom I ask is 'Bread'!" And he smiled, repeating the name, "'Bread'! that is good; that is the first wish. Might I with the young gentleman speak?" And to the Trustee's assurance that he might certainly speak with any boy, if he wished it, he asked pleasantly, "You think?"

"He is a foreign child, of very high family, it is supposed, — some think a Russian," said the Trustee, emphasizing the word, as if this intelligence would give the stranger an interest in the school or in the scholar.

To this information the distinguished-looking gentleman listened attentively, but showed no surprise, and answered only by the expressive monosyllable which he had several times before employed to so good effect. The Trustee hastened to call the boy; and Brade, with cheeks glowing and eyes bright from play, came forward, turning to bid the "fellows" go on.

The stranger rose at his approach, went forward to meet him, and at once engaged him in a conversation of question and answer; the Trustee having first discharged what he evidently considered a duty, to be gravely and seriously performed, by informing the boy that "the gentleman wished to speak with him." This duty done, the Trustee stood not far away from the interview, occupying himself, rather faintly, with several boys, who, under the pretence of "tag," or some other pretence, had contrived to bring themselves within hearing.

"You have a good name," said the stranger. "You are not of this country?"

"My name is Brade, sir," answered Antony, looking down a little and blushing, "and I came from Philadelphia." At the same time he showed the letters carved, in the fashion of other boys, upon a hockey-stick which he had in his hand.

"Ah! so!" said the stranger, looking to the Trustee, who drew a little nearer, as if invited by the stranger's look. The name the foreign gentleman, smiling, spelled out carefully, letter by letter, "B-R-A-D-E, Brade;" and then, giving back the stick to its owner, repeated, "B-r-a-d-e, Brade."

"You love to study very much?" the foreign gentleman continued; and having received the usual answer, "Pretty well, sir," asked again, "You like not to play at all?" and being answered that Antony "liked play very much," he laughed and said, —

"Your father liked to play when he was boy: this gentleman, also, I think," looking with a pleasant smile to the official of the institution for confirmation. "*Omnes, pueri, ludendi avidi fuimus:* know you what means that?"

This sentence, Brade, with the gentleman's good-natured help in repeating the words, and asking, "What is *subjectum* of 'fuimus'?" translated pretty well: "We all, as boys, have been eager for play."

This translation was accepted with a kindly smile, and the gentleman asked: —

"You learn Greekish? Not?"

Brade looked round, a little bashfully, to where the other boys were, and then answered modestly that he "had begun Greek."

At the mention of this new language the Trustee, who had not been unintelligent or unmindful, at once drew nearer.

"We teach Greek here, sir, of course," he said, "and I'm aware that it is the language of the Russians,—that is, of the Russian Church."

"You are learned in Greek, self?" asked the courteous foreigner.

The Trustee took care not to be drawn into a conversation in that tongue, if the lively foreigner had any intention of substituting it for honest English.

"You must excuse me, sir," said he. "I have two daughters that know botany, and talk about their 'monogramic' and 'cryptogramic;' but education was not so much attended to in my day. I can do one thing in Greek that not everybody can do, perhaps: I know how to make *Greek Fire*," he added, smiling with the consciousness of wit, and emphasizing the two important words.

The foreign gentleman recognized the witticism, and acknowledged it by a good-natured laugh. Some words in a *very* foreign tongue he uttered, at which the Trustee went through a shoulder-shrugging and grimacing and gesticulating action, which no doubt seemed to him most familiar and intelligible to a foreigner, and was then asked,—

"You were not soldier of the Greek-landish Freeings-war,—the Liberation-war, perhaps? Too young, I think."

The Trustee modestly disclaimed the martial character also, as well as the scholarly, "though he must confess that he loved freedom, of course," he said. "He had found out the Greek Fire when he was in the East Bartlett Chemical Works."

The polite stranger seemed to get no definite information from that hard proper name, although the Trustee repeated it very distinctly. The latter polite gentleman therefore changed the subject for one which he, doubtless, thought more hopeful.

"I believe, sir, if I'm not mistaken," he said, "Greek — the Greek language — is still the language of the Church?" Then, to make his meaning plainer, he added, "I think the service-books — the sacred books — are written in Greek?"

The stranger caught his meaning (as he testified by a courteous wave of both hands with a bow of the head), and answered, —

"'The Sacred Books,' yes; the evangelium, certainly."

"And of the *Greek Church*, I believe?" interposed the Trustee, with mild pertinacity. "*The Russian* is the same, sir, if I am not mistaken," looking as if he had "got" the stranger now.

The boys, who had contrived to come within hearing, at the beginning of this conference with Brade, now seeing what turn the conversation was likely to take, began quietly to withdraw. The stranger-gentleman, seeing this, hastened to take a formal leave of the little fellow with whom he had been talking, asking, however, very courteously, "permission" of the trustee. Having obtained this, the polite stranger turned to Brade: —

"I will give you," said he, "according to your name:

you are called Brade; I will give you some Greek by your name." And, taking a heavy gold pencil from his pocket, he wrote upon a plain card these words: "*Βραδὺς ἴσθι εἰς ὀργήν*" (*Brad*ys isthi, eis orgēn), and gave it to the boy; and, as he gave it, said mysteriously, "There is a great secret for you to find out. Some time you will find your name. I liked very much to talk with you. Adieu!"

So saying, with a very respectful gesture, he took leave of little Antony, who made his acknowledgments not uncourteously, though hastily, and who immediately, folding and putting away in a pocket the writing, ran after his fellows. These, of course, seeing him coming, loitered for him; and then, having apparently persuaded him to show them the paper, seemed to be for a few moments puzzling their boys' brains over it, as they walked with their heads all crowded together, the most pushing of them being Will Hirsett; and presently after were all at play once more, as at first.

While the stranger had been engaged in writing, the Trustee, seeing some one whom he addressed as "Mr. Stout" pass, begged "to be excused for a moment while the gentleman was engaged," and joined him, saying to any who might hear, that "he would be back immediately."

"A moment" is always longer than a speaker or caller or shopper (or any one except a person waiting) expects it to be. The strange gentleman, finding himself alone, walked quietly round the corner of the house, in the direction which the Trustee had lately taken, and looked. The broad barn-door stood invitingly open, and sounds, such as men make, were coming forth. He walked to it and entered.

6

Presently, from the opposite side, appeared the Trustee. He looked hurriedly this way and that; went round the corner of the school-room, as he had just come, and cast a hasty glance toward the boys' playground. Then he looked toward the different roads; then went to the other corner, and looked toward the barn, now sending forth no sound; then came hastily back to the front steps.

Here, having taken one last look all round, he opened, and shut behind him, the front door, and like one familiar with the ways of the place passed up the stairs.

CHAPTER XIII.

MR. DON FOLLOWS IT UP A LITTLE.

Hanging on the staircase was a very tolerable painting, on a large scale, of the Acropolis at Athens, and its ruins, by moonlight. Further up, on the same wall, was a smaller painting of the Field of Marathon.

Upon each of these, whether intending it or without any thought, the lively Trustee turned his eyes in passing. So, too, he looked in passing upon two engravings of the Coliseum and the Tomb of Adrian, which were hung upon the opposite wall of the upper entry. He smelt of one of the flowers, and plucked a leaf from one of the geraniums, which were standing in tiers in a sunny bay-window at the front of the entry; but he scarcely made the slightest pause until, with a familiar and assured tread, he reached a door, which he gently and slowly opened to himself, passing into the room beyond. Here he did stand still.

The character of this room which the Trustee had so confidently entered would have declared itself to any intelligent eye; for books, on their shelves, made its chief furniture and ornament. These were arranged, not straight along its sides, and from floor to ceiling, but in double cases, standing out as wings from the walls and reaching about two-thirds up, having books on the two sides and one end.

Busts and statuettes stood atop of the several cases, and behind and above these the room on the walls was given to handsome photographs and engravings. A long black cross occupied the middle of the chimney, with a strong-lined engraving of Rubens's Descent from the Cross on one side, and a like engraving of Raphael's Transfiguration on the other. Underneath the cross was an illuminated legend, "*Γίνου πιστός*."*

Perhaps a single intelligent glance would have taken in all this; and there was a moment or two that the Trustee lingered after coming inside the room, for the gentleman who was busy at the study-table took no notice of his entrance. Presently, without looking up, the student asked, "Who's there?"

"It's I, sir," said the Trustee, with a gentle voice and in unexceptionable grammar, such as became an official of a great institution of learning, "Mr. Don. I didn't wish to disturb you. How is Mrs. Warren, sir? She's well, I hope? and the children? I wanted to inquire, sir, if any one — a foreign gentleman — had been to see you this afternoon."

Mr. Warren laid down, open, a book on which he was engaged, and turned round to his visitor, deliberately, a large-eyed, thoughtful face, of thirty four or five years, needing a moment to bring his eyes to bear.

"Oh, Mr. Don, excuse me!" he said, smiling at the other's eagerness. "You came in so quietly that I thought it must be one of the family. No; no one has been here."

"You were not far wrong, sir, I believe," said the social Trustee. "I presume all who are connected with

* "Be faithful." — Rev. ii. 10.

Saint Bartholomew's School are, in one sense, of a family: are they not, sir? Have you a few moments to spare (I'll lay my things down here, if you please," proceeding to dispose of his hat and gloves, with much kindness and courtesy, on the study-table, and seating himself near them) — "for something," he then added, "which has an interest for us all, I think."

An announcement of this kind made a strong claim for attention; and Mr. Warren assented, very readily and definitely, and turned his open book, whose leaves had been a little fluttered by Mr. Don's movements, over upon its face, and sat all ready to hear.

"I was very happy, sir," continued Mr. Don, seriously, as if he were beginning an autobiography (and Mr. Warren listened with proportionate respect), — "I don't know what you may think of it, — in being on the spot as a representative of Saint Bartholomew's School, when something happened which, I think, may prove an entering-wedge, — a turning-point, perhaps, sir, in the history of young Brade." (At this name his hearer looked still more curious for what was to follow.) "Young Brade, you know, when he came to us was reported as fatherless and motherless, if I am not mistaken? I believe the conclusion now is, that he's a young nobleman from abroad, — ah! of course from abroad, if he's a young nobleman at all, for we don't have them here."

By this time his listener had changed his attitude, and his expression had become a mixed one of amusement and annoyance. As Mr. Don was about beginning again after this correction of himself, Mr. Warren said decidedly: —

"Oh, no; no, no! he's a particularly fine little fellow,

but I don't think there's any such mystery about Brade. I know some nonsense has been talked about him, in Eastham, — fun of Mr. Greenwood's, probably, — and the boys have got up wonderful fancies;" but, after this rather unsympathizing dash of cold upon Mr. Don's account of his marvellous incident, he stopped.

Mr. Don himself was for a moment quite taken aback; indeed, it might well be asked, Now, even if Mr. Warren's mind, being sedentary and studious, was not so active as those of others in inquiry, why should he feel inclined to set himself against so natural and reasonable an opinion? Mr. Don's face was clouded.

"Pardon me, sir:" he said, when he began to recover himself, and with a look of honest astonishment at the backwardness of the Head of the School in information about a boy under his charge which the community about him were well advanced in. "I thought it was taken for granted that there was a mystery about the boy, although we possessed a clue to it, or to a part of it."

"Oh!" said the Rector of the School, pleasantly, "I won't go so far as to say that there is nothing which might be called a sort of mystery in the case. I'm only saying that I'm sure there isn't a particle of that particular mystery about him."

"In your opinion, sir, if I may be allowed to suggest," said the Trustee, very gravely, proposing a correction; "but I must be pardoned if I can't quite agree with you, sir. I'm surprised that there should be so great a difference." Then he added very patiently, "Perhaps you will allow me to give an account of the adventure in which I was a party myself, and which is certainly not a little remarkable. It may affect your own opinion, sir. I hold in my hand an important testimony to the character of the stranger," and he produced what seemed a letter, or the envelope of a letter.

"Of course," said the Rector of the School, cheerfully, "I shall be glad to hear about the adventure, by all means;" and (having for whatever reason committed himself already to the other side) he looked both amused and curious.

"We may differ, sir, as to the bearing of the incident," said Mr. Don, who was at no loss for well-chosen words; "but I think we shall hardly differ as to its interest and importance. As I came up toward the School, about half an hour ago, I observed quite a foreign-looking gentleman — a man of distinction, I think I may say, sir — standing at the front door, looking at our emblem. I offered my services, and told him the character of our institution. At the time, a number of boys were playing on the upper ground: he singled out Brade, and asked if he might speak with him; said a great deal to him about his name, and said there was a mystery about it, which Brade would find out some day; said that Brade was like his father in being fond of play. Oh! I almost forgot, sir: he said it was his first wish to see Brade, and he gave the boy a Greek sentence, as he said, 'for his name.' The Greek was very striking, sir. If all I supposed was Greek *was* Greek, he talked it as I talk English. The remarkable thing about that is, that Greek, if I'm not misinformed (perhaps you can instruct me better, sir), is the language of the Greek Church, — I should say, of the Russian Church. That seems to me an important item, sir."

During the telling of this story, Mr. Warren's look

of amused curiosity had undergone some change, and he now looked a little puzzled besides.

"If it had been so, why should he say so much, and yet say no more? And did this remarkable foreigner say all this before *you?*" he asked.

"Not exactly before me, sir, — I was at some distance."

"He was at the house-door?" asked Mr. Warren, again.

"But he wouldn't come in, sir. I asked him, of course, and he made a pretence of inquiring whether this was a hotel."

"People do that, now and then: we're a big building, and look something like it, outside; and we were a famous hotel, you know, once."

"But you see, sir," said the Trustee, who looked deeper into things, "he would very naturally do that, if he was desirous of concealment."

Mr. Warren smiled; but it may have been that the Trustee was too much taken up with what he was telling, to see the smile.

"And where's the wonderful paper that he gave Brade for his name?" asked the Rector of St. Bart's School.

"Yes, sir," said the Trustee, with alacrity, "I took the precaution; but I would first take the liberty of suggesting, sir, might it not be well, in view of the peculiar character of the case, to send Mr. Stout after him? A little attention, perhaps, might not be altogether thrown away. Beside the immediate result to Brade, I see the possibility of an important connection for our school in the future." (Mr. Don was a business man.)

"But, if he declined to come in, I don't think we

can well force him in, can we? He's gone away?" said Mr. Warren. "If he had wished to come in, I should have been glad to see him."

"Yes, sir: he's gone away; but it'll be an hour or two before he can take the cars for Weston," said Mr. Don, taking out and consulting his watch.

"He's going to Weston, then, is he?"

"Yes, sir: 'to see the manufactories,' he said; though I suppose it would be easy to explain that consistently with the theory: he comes here first and sees Brade, and then says 'he has made a mistake, and is on his way to see the Weston factories.' I should say that might be easily reconciled: doesn't it strike you so, sir? It seems to me nothing is simpler," said the Trustee, with much animation over a living secret involving foreigners (perhaps, too, foreigners of the most exalted rank) which was now passing toward its discovery, in open air, through the channel of his own intelligence. "Perhaps, if it wouldn't be too much trouble for you, sir, to make a chance for a few words with him, you would easily" —

"No," said the Rector, with singular indifference to the opportunity, "I think I won't do any thing about him. You've got the paper that you were going to show me?"

"Yes, sir," said Mr. Don, with less animation, "I took the precaution (you think nothing is to be done, sir) to go round the house and head Brade. It was then he disappeared. I made this copy, however, hastily," — and here he presented an envelope. "If it will give you too much trouble, sir," he added, in a tone of disappointment, "Mr. Parmenter, I know, has Greek dictionaries."

"Oh! I'll give what help I can; but why not the paper itself, instead of a copy?"

"Why not, indeed, sir? You remind me; I didn't think of that. I'll get it, and return it to the boy;" and Mr. Don disappeared, after snatching up his hat and gloves, and bowing to the Rector of the School, who was sitting at the moment thinking, and smiling at his thought.

Mr. Warren, now, as his visitor was departing, recalled himself, and turned to his work again.

CHAPTER XIV.

MR. DON HAS HOLD OF A CLUE.

LOOKING neither at the Tomb of Adrian, nor at the Coliseum, nor at the Field of Marathon, nor at the Acropolis of Athens, on his way, Mr. Don, full of his business, went straight about his errand. The boys had moved; but he sought them out, secured Brade, and then, followed at a little distance by the rest, came back. It was a coincidence that, while with a single purpose he was walking toward the play-ground, the mysterious stranger came quietly along from the barn, and with Mr. Stout, acting apparently as guide, went toward the eastern road.

Mr. Don ascertained from the boy, as they walked, that he had no recollection of ever having seen the stranger before that day; and he also made sure, by judicious questions, that Antony had had no sympathetic or instinctive drawings toward the supposed agent. While Mr. Don, and Antony in his company, were thus making their way through the front door, and up the main staircase, the rest of the boys — Brade's playmates — went as straight to the back door and up by their own way, to the neighborhood of the Rector's study. From that room a sharp ear might have caught the confused sound of feet and murmur of young tongues after the door had opened and let in Antony Brade, together with the returning Trustee.

The mysterious boy (looking not at all mysterious) was affectionately saluted by the Head of the School, and was invited to a seat, but managed nevertheless to keep his feet; and then, with his cap in his hand, looked from side to side at the throng of books.

"They followed me, sir. I thought you'd allow them to come as far as the entry outside," said Mr. Don, as if in explanation of the sounds which had attended him. ("This is the paper, sir, that I spoke of. I brought Master Brade with me.) The others may possibly afford additional information."

Mr. Warren was looking at the card which had been put into his hand.

"Shall I find a lexicon, sir? (I think that's what we used to call them when I went to Master Bradish, at the Hollow, in our town"). And the intelligent gentleman, who with his eye-glasses was already scrutinizing, at random and afar, the backs of books in different directions, on the shelves, was eager to search.

At the word "lexicon," Antony first allowed his eyes to wander about the crowded bookcases, and then turned them timidly at the lofty embodiment of scholarship who presided over St. Bart's School, and to whom was referred now a question of interpretation in which the boy was himself concerned. Very possibly, if he knew of Pericles and Plato (and he at least knew of Xenophon), there may have been a question in his mind whether Greek was about as easy to the Rector as it had been to the men of old days. If so, he was probably comforted when he heard the Head of St. Bart's thank Mr. Don, and decline the help proposed; and he showed all interest when that learned man began to read from the paper: —

"'*Β ρ α δ ὺς ἴσθι εἰς ὀργήν.*' That seems plain enough, and a good motto too,—'Be slow to wrath.' The first four letters are emphasized"—

"Oh! that's it," said the Trustee. "I saw they were written wide" (which showed that the worthy man had good eyes). Then he added, with the scrupulous politeness which seemed habitual with him, "May I inquire what they are, sir, if you please?"

"They spell 'Brad,'" said the reader, who perhaps had some curiosity to know what all this inquiry of Mr. Don's was going to lead to.

"Would you be kind enough, sir, to read the original—the Greek—once more?" said the inquiring Trustee, sliding forward on his chair, to bring both ears nearer to the reader.

Antony listened in very good humor, if not so eagerly.

The interpreter of the cabalistic sentence complied at once, very obligingly, and read aloud the words, emphasizing distinctly the syllable which, as he said, was written as emphatic. "That first syllable 'Brad,'" said he, "must be, as the mysterious gentleman said, 'for our young friend's name.'"

"Yes, sir," said Antony, to this about his name; and then, when he found that he had spoken impulsively, without having been addressed, he blushed and looked abashed, like a modest young fellow, well brought up.

The Rector of the School smiled upon him, and said,—

"It's near enough, you see, Anty, for a play upon words. The truth is, a foreigner couldn't get our English *a* in your name very easily, and couldn't put it into Greek; but I think he must have been a pretty learned Theban. Did he talk a great deal of Greek?"

"I said I thought I could make Greek Fire," said Mr. Don, "and then he went off with what *I supposed* was Greek."

"A happy thought of yours, certainly," said Mr. Warren, laughing.

Antony modestly inquired whether the Thebans were very learned; Mr. Don listening, as to something which might or might not bear upon the main question.

"No," said the Head of the School, going very readily into the subject with the boy, "the Thebans were Bœotians. Pindar was a Theban, to be sure; but they were contrasted with the Athenians, though no part of their country was more than fifty miles, perhaps, from Attica. 'Boiotum crasso jurares aëre natum,' Horace says, as you'll find some day when you get to him. They were stupid."

By this time the Trustee was only politely waiting for a pause.

"Pardon me, sir," he said, as soon as he civilly might. "That first word or syllable, whichever it may be, I think you said was 'Brad,' without the *e*, if I understand rightly. Would you be so good as to read the next two syllables, or words, as the case may be?"

Mr. Warren at once complied, and read with patient distinctness: —

"'ὑς ἴσ'" — (us, is).

"Ah!" said the Trustee, whose ears must have been as good as his eyes, "there was another sound. What is the next syllable, if you please?"

Mr. Warren again complied obligingly, and read the syllable 'θι,' (thi).

"Thank you, sir; that's the sound that I missed. The two would make 'isthy.' Now, sir, pardon me for troubling you with another question (I think we may come to something). Are the syllables which, if I heard you rightly, you pronounced 'isthy,' emphatic, as you said 'Brad' was?"

Being assured that the two syllables were not emphatic, he continued, with animation enough to draw Antony's attention, and very likely to excite some curiosity in the Rector of St. Bart's School:—

"Then, sir, one more question: Could that be made 'inski' or 'iski'?" Then he added, as if repeating to himself, "Bradinski,—Bradiski."

"No: I wish it might, if it would do you any good; but Greek is as definite as any thing ever was. 'Ἴσθι' is ἴσθι" (*isthi* is *isthi*).

"Perhaps, sir," said the unwearied investigator, "you would do me the favor to write 'iski' and 'inski' in Greek?" and he supported his request by holding out his paper and pencil.

Mr. Warren wrote as he was desired, saying, while he wrote,—

"Now shall I dispose of your boys, outside there, and Master Brade, here? I suppose they would like to be off."

"Oh! certainly, sir; certainly," said the Trustee. "I thought you might wish to question them."

"Call them in, please, Anty," said the Rector; and in a moment three or four boys were ushered in, among whom was Remsen, and among whom, too, was Will Hirsett, conspicuous by the grinning of his broad mouth.

"Boys!" said the Rector, "we hear that there was a

wonderful learned gentleman here this afternoon. Mr. Don says he talked Greek; and I want to see if we can make out what it was he said."

Will Hirsett hitched himself up a little, as if preparing for his part of witness. The other boys looked a little blank.

"Mr. Don told him something about 'Greek Fire,' and then the gentleman said some Greek."

"We can't remember Greek, sir," said Remsen. "If it had been English, we might."

"If you was to say it over, sir," said Will Hirsett, less afraid of trying to fill a few gaps in authentic history than Remsen appeared to be.

The Rector laughed. "I must guess, you know," he said. "Was it '*τὸ πῦρ τὸ ἑλληνικόν*'?* or '*ἡ φλὸξ γραική*'?" †

"Yes, sir," said Will Hirsett, with gratifying promptness.

"Which, Will?" asked his Master, while the boys laughed.

"I think that was it, sir, — what you said," answered the well-inclined witness. Even Mr. Don seemed amused.

"'*Η φλὸξ γραική*?" † asked his examiner.

"Yes, sir," said Will. "I think that was it."

"Or *τὸ πῦρ τὸ ἑλληνικόν*?" *

"It's one or the other, sir," answered Will Hirsett, with unvarying satisfaction at being able to confer a favor of this sort upon the head of the school.

"Thank you, William," said the Rector, sending a glow of added pleasure over the boy's beaming face.

* Hellenic Fire. † Greek flame.

"Your testimony is worth fully as much as a good deal that people give, about a thing they don't know."

This commendation completed William's gratification; and he handled his hat as if expecting that they would all be dismissed now, because nothing could well be added to what he had done.

So it was.

"Now you may go and play. Don't forget that Greek, Will." And, promising not to forget, Hirsett modestly led the way from the Rector's study.

Mr. Warren took his book once more.

"How do you get on with 'inski' and 'iski'?" he asked of the thoughtful Trustee.

"If you say, sir, that 'isthi' couldn't be a hint for 'inski' or 'iski' — (certainly the sound might suggest ——). I won't take up your time," said Mr. Don, regretfully or almost reproachfully, as if, somehow, the Rector of the School was a little obstructive to science; and so he took his leave.

CHAPTER XV.

THE MAKING OF A LANGUAGE.

There are very pretty walks, in different directions, near St. Bart's School. One of the most beautiful of these, up hill and down, and with many windings among barberry-bushes and other shrubs and low trees, was, in spite of its beauty, very little used; for it was only a short lane off West Road, not leading through to any road, and was in one place — beyond the houses — wet, where it met a marsh. Just beyond that marsh it came to an end, near a disused brick-kiln.

It is not always bright weather, even in the wholesome country; and those rains had apparently now set in which are said to "fill the streams before winter." It was on a day which gave little encouragement to walking (for it had rained a good deal) that there were sitting on a smooth rock, under very thick evergreen branches, at the side of this lane, a girl and a boy. The grass which bordered the roadway was, by this time of the year, scanty and weak, and the leaves of most trees were much thinned out; but everywhere, unless under the covert where the children sat, was moist.

The boy we have seen so often before that we know him at once as Antony Brade: the girl, who was dressed in plain black, was pale, with an interesting and thoughtful face, but brightened now, as by the boy's company. She was rather older and taller than her companion, — possibly wiser also, for, at least just now, she talked less and listened more. Now and then she leaned forward, — sometimes leaving her seat and walking a step or two into the road, and looked each way. Then she took her old position and listened, smiling, and as if ready for her turn to speak. Young Brade was beating the damp ground with a stick, — his hat lying meanwhile beside him on the rock, — and all the time he was speaking in rather a low voice, but earnestly, and, as it would seem, upon the same subject which had occasioned so much speculation and discussion among people, young and old, of his acquaintance, — his origin or condition.

"Oh! I can do it!" he said. "But it'll be pretty hard, sometimes; but you'll see. Some things I don't like, — if I could only have your house for home: it's just as if I'd got no home and no family."

The girl very cheerfully answered, tossing her head with each merry exclamation of contempt: —

"Pooh! pooh! pooh! pooh! pooh! poo-ooh! Master Antony, never mind! it'll come right, by and by, please God;" (and she seated herself on her seat, adjusting her dress). "It won't be long, first, and then you can be as happy as you please, Master Antony Brade."

This she said with a tone of good cheer, that comes by natural gift to womanhood, young or old. The boy's spirits seemed more like the sky and the weather: still, as we have already seen, it was not another's strong spirit or cheery voice that was needed to give him strength. He turned to her, with a pretence of frowning, and raised his stick, threateningly: —

"Don't call me that! don't call me Master Antony!" he said drolly. "When we are all by ourselves, I am sure you might call me 'Anty' or 'Tony.'"

"No, no!" she said, shaking her head and smiling as she did so, and with a very lively and determined tone, indeed, "No!"

Then she added, with a very ceremonious voice and manner, "When would I do it at all, Master Antony, if not when we are all by ourselves? Come! we mustn't lose our time. Isn't it good we've got our bower?" (spreading her arms, but rather narrowly, as if to avoid shaking down the wet, and looking about upon their quarters), "and we are able to meet, so that any way we'll not forget each other." This, too, she said mirthfully, emphasizing rather excessively the last words. Here she turned her face round in front of his, putting up her chin pertly, and receiving in return a little slap upon the cheek. So their narrow retreat was pretty merry and comfortable.

"Well, we'll begin our language right off," said Antony, in his enthusiasm throwing up the stick with which he was beating the earth so high that he struck one of the heavy, low-hanging, evergreen boughs, and brought a whole shower of raindrops down upon them both. At this both burst into happy laughter, and he shook his curly head, and she wiped her dress with a handkerchief.

"Suppose," said he, as older philosophers have made their suppositions, sometimes stretching very far out into moving causes and into the strengths and fastnesses of nature, and sometimes, too, bringing great discoveries to men, — "suppose we should shake all the wet down, and then there wouldn't be any more to come."

Here was a philosophical principle involved which the girl seemed to regard with little respect. "Why, you foolish boy!" she said, laughing heartily again, "wouldn't you get all wet yourself, shaking it down? and wet all our bower, and our seats? What a boy you are!"

His foolish supposition coming back to him in this shape of absurdity, he could not help laughing again; so, under those trees, damp as things were all about, was as cheery a place as under many a well-shingled or well-slated shelter from the weather. The girl ran quickly forward to make her usual *reconnoissance*, and back again, and, having seated herself as before, smoothed out her lap, and said with great spirit: —

"Now let's begin! Who's got any paper?" and she felt, long and thoroughly, in the only pocket she had, without bringing out any thing more to the purpose than a crumpled bit, on which were what looked like sums in Arithmetic. This, they both said, would not do; and Antony kept on going through his pockets, which he had already gone through more than once; but his search resulted in his finding nothing more than a few small rolls and foldings and crumples of paper, — all of which, he said, were precious, as having parts of a WORK in Greek and Latin on them, — and a single brown scrap, in which were wrapped up three or four small stones, a few black seeds or berries, and a tangle of twine. He restored the first, carefully and ceremoniously, to his waistcoat, and folded and squeezed up the latter again, and put it back into his coat, and then they both agreed that perhaps they could find a place on the rejected sum-paper, and ended by saying that "there was plenty of room, and it would do splendidly."

Now they spread it all out, and, after hastily looking it all over, set themselves to their work; and with what spirit they went about it! One corner of Brade's pocket furnished a pencil, caught in inextricable meshes of pack-thread, and released after Alexander the Great's fashion.

Nothing (unless looks) was ever so touching, so moving, so overcoming, so full of life and kinship as words; and how hard it is for the fire of life to die out of them! Language — any worthy and noble language that we know — is so great and wonderful that men of long thought and study are arguing, in books, whether speech is a gift straight from God, or was felt out and followed on by men's own wit and need. But who has not, with some school-crony, knowing or not knowing what Cadmus did for Greece, boldly made up a language and sported it sometimes in the hearing of grown-up men; and initiated, with some show of form, a playmate or two into its secrets; dropped some of its words upon the pages of a letter sent home, and left them unexplained, — his heart beating pretty high, and his eye glistening at thought of what conjectures would be there indulged, about the very deep things that school boys get into! Let our readers who are curious in philepy, or speech-liking, look closely to the doings of these two intelligent children of different sexes. Here they will be likely to get as reasonable and fair an account of the way in which languages originate, as from the twins of Psammitichus, who *βέκος ἐφώνησαν* (made the sound of the goat) or made their first utterance in Scythian, or those of the Scottish king who pushed straight out into the world of speech with well-formed Hebrew.

Antony Brade and the young girl, his companion, were now set down to the making of a language. A difficulty presents itself before they begin.

"There are as many words in the English language," said Antony, "as one hundred thousand! we couldn't make as many as that;" and he laughed.

"Why, we don't want as many as that, to say all we've got to say," said the girl; and she belonged to the sex who make the most use of that and other languages, and might be expected to know. "We could say every thing with only a few."

"How many should we have to have, Kate?" asked Brade, — "two hundred? We couldn't get along with two hundred, could we, if people use a hundred thousand?"

"Let's begin," said Kate; "only you must remember and call me 'Miss Ryan.'"

"Pooh!" said Brade, at the last part of the sentence. She looked thoughtfully at her paper.

There they sat, and did not begin. The first start was made by Brade: —

"Let's call mud '*modo*,'" he proposed, working the end of his stick in the earth, "and we must change all the letters of the alphabet: how shall we do that?"

"We shan't have to do that," said Kate. "Different languages have the same letters, and yet that doesn't make the languages the same. If you changed all the words as much as 'modo,' you wouldn't have to change the letters."

"Oh, well," said Antony, brightening up as the task was narrowed down, "if you only want words, I know a way Russell made when he was in the Second Form;

but then he let everybody into it at last, so that a great many people could read it. We've got to have one that nobody can read but just us two."

"But we needn't do just the same that he did. How did his way go, Master Antony?" she asked, emphasizing the name, but looking up and smiling.

He was thinking; but, as soon as he understood what she had just been saying, he raised his stick, which he had still held, though no longer playing with it, and threatened her, drawing a frown upon his face over the smile which kept place at his roguish young mouth. Then he came back to business.

"Oh! let me see," said he, conning the composition which was to be the ground on which they were to work out their language.

"I must look out," said the watchful girl; and made her walk to the road, and turned her eyes up and down it quickly, and then came quickly back.

He had been studying the written words.

"Russell's way was to leave a letter out," said Brade. "But I don't believe he meant it to be hard; and, if a word was a long word, he'd leave out two. But anybody could find that out. Suppose we should leave out half a word?"

"Well, don't let's begin to write, until we've chosen what we'll have; because we haven't got much paper," said Kate. "Take a word."

Antony looked up into the air, as if words and ideas floated there, and before long had got a word.

"'Therefore''s a good word. Suppose I want to write to you, 'therefore I can't come.' I'd write 'fore,' but then," continued he, hesitating, — "you can't take half of 'I'" —

"Make it small," said Kate, — "make it little 'i,' with a dot: 'fore (little) i, not me.' There! they couldn't make that out."

"Now, suppose I want to say, 'I've got another ball,' or 'I've caught a muskrat,' — little '*i*'–'*e*' (how far have we got?) 'I've-got-a-muskrat,' — *I*, — no, *little i–e*, — how are you going to divide 'got'? — leave the *t* on? — No: I'll tell you. He had another way. It was: Take a letter from one place and put it in another place; take a hind-letter and put it in front. He left his book down for anybody to find out; but nobody but me ever found out, and I never told anybody. It's a real good way. Let's try that."

Now that things looked more definite, the paper came forth and was put to use. Antony had a pencil, and Kate Ryan wrote for both. Brade proposed the making of a regular letter, which was to run in this way: —

"'Dear Kate, I got your letter, and was very glad when I got it. I got it last evening. I am glad to hear that all are well. I went a trapping, and I'" —

"Not so fast!" said Kate, whose fingers went pretty well, considering the dampness. "There! now you've got enough for a beginning. There! you can take that" (tearing off what was already written). "Let's keep 'THE LANGUAGE' all on a separate piece. You read."

To this arrangement the boy assented with great readiness.

"You must only say 'Kate,' not 'dear Kate.'" ("Well!" said he, as if he did not care to argue that point any more). "'*Ekat*,'" — she continued, writing.

"Let's always put '*I*' on to another word," suggested Antony, following his paper.

"Well," she continued, "'*Ekati-tgo-*'" (following his dictation, which he said was like Cæsar's, — only he wanted a few more scribes) "'*ryou — rlette — dan — swa — yver — dgla — nwhe — itgo — ti.*'"

They did not get along quite so fast as we have gone, for they made and corrected a mistake or two; but this was the result which they came to, at the end of the first sentence; and there they stopped a little while, to compare notes and exult. They were satisfied with the look of it. They longed to put the acquired language to use in their correspondence; and, after the first flush of excitement over their success, went on to translate the whole of Antony's composition into their own private language. The preliminary '*Ekati*' they changed, on Kate's urgency; and at last the whole work stood complete before their eyes in this shape: —

"*Smis nryai tgo ryou rlette dan swa yver dgla nwhe itgo ti. imdgla ot rhea ttha lal ear lwel. itwen gatrappin dnai tcaugh eon tmuskrai. lwil eb ta rbowe sa lusua. B. A.*"

And then one thing struck one of the authors, — Kate Ryan: "Where a letter is doubled in a word, like two *p*'s in 'trapping,' why can't we leave out one? and so in 'letter'? I'm afraid somebody will guess 'trapping' and 'letter.'"

In the making of so important a thing as a language, the girl seemed to think the world interested, and likely to be curious. Young Brade accepted at once the proposition, and the dangerous '*t*' and '*p*' were taken out, leaving the words to which they belonged much less suspicious-looking and much less liable to detection, now that the letters had been taken away.

"Now," said Antony, "we must both have copies exactly alike, so that we can remember, and we can put a particular mark at those two words, so as to show that the letters were left out on purpose. Now can't we do any thing else to it?"

The makers examined the effect of several proposed improvements; but, because these did not make either The Language any better or the secrecy any greater, they were all abandoned; and it was resolved that, for the present, the language should be tried as it was. Brade, with many bows and much ceremony, and with some laughter, practised the "*Smis Nrya*" with which the letter opened, at first joining to these words others in the ordinary vernacular, but at length turning all into the Secret Language which had just come into being, as "*Smis Nrya, who od uyo od?*"

Now they did not believe that anybody in the whole world could make it out; and Brade would not fear to leave a piece lying on the ground so that anybody could see it.

"Wouldn't it be good," he asked, "if one of those great men that read inscriptions, or the Postmaster-General, should try a piece of it?"

These words apparently reminded Kate of her watchfulness, for she hurried to the road, looking longer than she had yet looked toward the highway.

"There's something stopping away over on the hill," she said, hurrying back. "Now we must be quick. Have you made a new one? If we could rub out one *t* and one *p* from this, it would do just as well as writing it over. Quick! quick! quick!" and she spread out the paper.

With all the hurry, Antony took occasion to show a little learning, acquired, as we may suppose, not long before in the class-room, and still fresh to him, that "the Ancients used to write with one end and rub out with the other, — *vertere sty*" —

Kate unceremoniously broke in, bursting into a laugh (children in good spirits are so ready to laugh) :—

"Never mind the Ancients!"

The Third-Form boy took good-naturedly this slight upon his Latin, and, turning his pencil, began to rub out the objectionable letters with its india-rubber; and, while he was busy with that work, Kate, finding the freest and cleanest part of her paper, made a copy for Antony, keeping for her own the first.

Then going into the road, and looking each way, as before, she called hastily to him: "There! go you right in back there, into the 'cuddle'" (this very likely was their private name for some inner retreat or fastness), and as she spoke she pushed him inwards from the road. "Mr. Parmenter's coming!"

"I don't mean to hide!" said the boy, positively.

"You must!" she answered, with equal positiveness; — "but I can't stay!" — and immediately set out in the direction of the main road, and of what had given her the alarm, walking steadily and quietly, without once looking back or turning her head.

She bowed quietly on meeting a vehicle in which were Mr. Parmenter and another person, to whom, as they drove slowly, Mr. Parmenter was pointing out with his whip, to the prospect on the grounds at the side. It was not likely that they would observe the young girl in black, who brushed the moist bushes in turning out for them. After passing them, in like manner she kept her way without turning, as wisely as any woman who wished not to show curiosity nor to attract attention.

CHAPTER XVI.

MR. PARMENTER STUMBLES UPON A SPECIMEN.

The carriage which Kate Ryan had just met went on at a walk, but was soon opposite the place where, in his nook of damp shelter, our young friend, the associate language-maker, had been left.

Mr. Parmenter's eyes, as he drove, were still fixed upon the fields, at the opposite side.

"We must turn before long," he said, "for there's a bad place in the road, just beyond here, that our town-authorities will have to look to; but I've shown you the whole ground."

His companion, whose tall neck showed a white cravat, implying that he was a clergyman, was perhaps less occupied with field and road than he, and at this moment exclaimed, —

"Well! there's a young chap has found a snug place for himself!" and Antony Brade appeared, sitting on his rock as before, — though not now with his head bare, — and beating the moist earth with his stick.

The boy looked a little conscious and confused, perhaps, but possibly not more than any boy of his age might appear, when found in a strange situation like this by two gentlemen, and having had their attention directed to him.

"Good afternoon, Brade," said Mr. Parmenter, in a

gracious tone, and lifting his hat from his head, ceremoniously, in return for the salutation of the boy. "I'm glad to hear you're such a good scholar, Brade. Don't you feel afraid of taking cold in there? I should think Mrs. Wales might have to prescribe for you, if you sit in such places."

Then turning to the clergyman he said: "Brade is the first scholar in his Form, I understand, Mr. Merritt."

"So this is Brade," said the other, looking well at him. "I'm glad to see you, sir, and hope you'll live to be the first scholar in the School." To Mr. Parmenter, he added, smiling, "Boys have boys' constitutions."

The boy, after the way of boys, made no answer to the compliments and complimentary wishes, but by this time had found an answer to some one of the several suggestions about dampness and danger, and was saying, "It's very dry after we've sat here a little while."

"Oh!" said Mr. Parmenter, graciously, "this is a place of resort for boys, is it? Rather a dangerous practice," he added, turning to his companion. "I think I shall have to speak to Rector Warren about it. Well, Brade, I shall be glad to see you at my house. Are you interested in works of art and taste? You know, Brade, where my house — Mr. Parmenter's house — is? I suppose all the boys of Saint Bartholomew's School know my house? Would you like to come?"

To this invitatory address, which was palpably at the same time dignified and elegant, and hospitable, the boy answered very much as modest boys generally do.

"Then I shall expect you, Brade: I shall request Rector Warren to give you leave," said Mr. Parmenter, even more graciously, and saluting him punctiliously. He then backed his horse and turned his buggy, neatly, on the narrow road.

"Did you observe any thing particular about that boy, sir?" he asked, in his formal way, of his companion. "You know he's the mysterious boy."

"Not very different from other boys in the same condition, I should say," answered the clergyman. "So that's the mysterious Brade?" and then he added, with a touch of that humor which is peculiar to a certain class of minds, "'Braid broad braids, brave maids.'"

"Yes," said Mr. Parmenter, accepting the quotation, with a courteous smile, "I suppose there may or may not be something under it? It might be quite an important thing for our School? You observed I mentioned 'works of art.' I don't go so far as some of our neighbors, in concluding right off that he used to live in a palace; but it *might* remind him of former associations and surroundings" (Mr. Parmenter showed a good choice of words). "I don't know whether you observed any effect? How do his manners strike you, sir?"

"I don't know how a *nobleman* ought to look" ("*I* don't," said Mr. Parmenter, without interrupting). "Doesn't somebody say he's a nobleman?" continued Mr. Merritt. "I should easily say he might be foreign."

"There's a strong feeling in Eastham, you know; and Mrs. Wadham and Mr. Don have got a theory, I believe," said Mr. Parmenter with an impartial dignity, like one who was ready to accept either side, according to the weight of evidence. "*They* think he's a Russian, and Brade stands for Bradinski or Bradisloff (I don't know Russian" —). ("Who does?" asked Mr. Merritt.) Mr. Parmenter smiled and went on: "or some other he mentioned, — a very distinguished family. Dr. Farwell's got a Scotch theory" ("I know he has," said Mr. Merritt), "a great family of Breadalbanes," continued Mr. Parmenter, dividing the stress of voice between the first and last syllables.

"Breadal'bane," said Mr. Merritt, showing superior knowledge by accenting the second syllable.

"If he should be a Russian," continued Mr. Parmenter, going on to weigh that side, "it might be an important thing for St. Bartholomew's School to be a connecting link between our Christian education and the highest classes in that country (they all belong, I think, to 'the Greek Church,' or to 'the Holy Eastern Catholic Church,' — you know about those things better than I do), and it might be a step toward intercommunion."

"Rather a short one, I fear," said the clergyman, again opening his vein of humor.

"I should think so," said Mr. Parmenter, smiling as before, impartially, as if this were just as much his opinion as the other.

"Don't you think it might be worth while to follow it up a little, in a quiet way? Haven't we a right, in justice to a pupil under our charge, and in justice to ourselves, to ascertain the facts about a boy that we're educating, if we can do it without exciting suspicion?"

Mr. Merritt smiled, as if catching his friend's thought.

"I suppose," said he, "we may gratify our curiosity,

if we can do it without exposing ourselves: is that it?"

"Mrs. Wadham puts it 'on strong moral grounds,'" said Mr Parmenter, by way of answer. He smiled as he spoke, but added: —

"I confess it admits of a question. *Is*n't it a moral duty to know all we can about one of our pupils? in case of wrong, for example, or danger. There may be something kept from him. Can't we, if we choose, put it upon the ground of moral obligation? — that is, if we think best. I should say it depended entirely upon that."

This last he said as if not committed to any course, but as being capable of seeing his way pretty clearly.

"Well, I don't know," said Mr. Merritt; "we might kick up a good deal of a mess. Somebody said (I believe it was Dr. Farwell) that Mr. Bates, the agent, or guardian, or whatever you may choose to call him, said Mr. Warren knew all about the boy."

Mr. Parmenter was hardly prepared for that supposition: —

"I think that can't be so," he said, coloring. "I presume that Mr. Warren would recognize my claim to be informed."

Here was a slight pause, and then he said, —

"The Rector is pretty clear-headed and sharp-sighted, I suppose, about learned questions, — the question whether Hector (wasn't it Hector?) killed Andromache; — but bring him down to daily life, and it doesn't follow that he'd use his eyes as well as those of us that have to keep our wits about us all the time. He doesn't think there's any thing foreign or remarkable about Brade (I should judge from what he told me). What should you say?"

"I should think there might be something a little foreign in his accent, — possibly Irish," said Mr. Merritt. "But I should be prepared to believe one thing as well as another."

"That's it," Mr. Parmenter said. "The ladies suggest that naturally, under the circumstances, — being *incog*, — he would be left a good deal to servants. I believe, however, Irish gentlemen have that — and Scotch, too — as well as the common people. In this country," he continued, drawing an appropriate reflection from his fact, "we should think it strange if any educated man was to have a peculiar accent. I believe I'm right, ain't I?"

Mr. Merritt assented, and then, sticking like a parson, as he was, to his text, said, —

"I think you told me once that you had never known of any foreign communication with him?"

"No: I ascertained that without raising any suspicion or any curiosity. I got our post-master, old Mr. Bancroft, to keep account of all the foreign letters that went through our office, so as to show the importance of the Eastham post-office. That took the old gentleman, and he kept account for two months. You see I looked out for that."

"What visitors has he had?" Mr. Merritt asked, at the end of the sentence.

"He hasn't had any, till the other day. I never told you about the stranger?"

Taking his answer from his friend's face, Mr. Parmenter went on: "Quite a distinguished-looking man. I tried to get him to ride up with me from the cars;

but he preferred walking. I went up afterwards to the School, and Mr. Don told me he had singled out Brade from quite a number of boys, and talked with him; asked what his name was, and when he said 'Brade,' he laughed, and asked him if he knew who his father was; and then 'if he knew any thing.' Brade said, 'Not much,' and then the man said, 'Good,' and 'he was just the boy he wanted to talk to.' I found, from the little conversation I had with him, that he was a foreigner; but I could not hear any thing about him, afterwards. Nobody, except just at the school, had seen him, or heard of him."

"That ought to be one of Robert Dale Owen's stories," said Mr. Merritt. "I don't see but what we're coming on in the world, at St. Bart's."

Mr. Parmenter had still his comments to make, and he made them, as follows: —

"What he said to Brade might mean a great deal, or nothing, just as you choose to take it. 'Does Brade know who his father is?' 'Does he know any thing about the mystery?' 'It's good he doesn't know much.' 'He's just the boy that was wanted.'"

"Well, but you don't suppose so much of a plot as all that?" said the other.

"I suppose," said Mr. Parmenter, confidently and sagaciously, smiling, "that a plot's a plot, ain't it? a spade's a spade. If there's a plot at all, why not a whole plot? It's just as cheap, while you're about it."

The sky had not ceased to threaten, and now looked more threatening than ever; and the clergyman, like a sensible man, held out his hand to the weather.

"Here it comes!" said Mr. Merritt; and, while he spoke, the two drew over and fastened the leathern top, and sheltered themselves, besides, with the boot. The rain came quietly and steadily down, in the surest way to soak the earth and all things on it. At the same time the horse took the road handsomely, laying himself down to his work, and the lumps of wet sand and gravel began to fly from his hoofs and from the wheels.

Mr. Parmenter had pretty well explained Mr. Don's views and his own upon the subject, when Mr. Merritt gave another turn to his thoughts.

"Our young friend 'll stand a pretty good chance of getting soaked, if he camps out there much longer. His high family won't keep the rain out. All the Braids-*in*-skies and *out-of*-skies won't help him."

"Suppose we turn back and take him in?" said Mr. Parmenter, reining up; and, Mr. Merritt assenting, he turned with some little manœuvring in the narrow roadway, and went back as fast as they had been coming.

"This was the place, surely," he said, stopping his horse at a particular spot, and looking out. "There's where we turned round before. Surely, that's where the boy was."

He drove on slowly, turned round in the former tracks, and came slowly back to the same spot.

This time, however, no opening in the shrubbery by the roadside appeared. They laughed.

"This is one of the old stories of enchantment that we used to read, — invisible gates and so on. You see what he's done, don't you? fastened those two boughs together," said Mr. Merritt.

"That's very well done, Brade," said Mr. Parmenter, in a very considerate tone; "but I wouldn't stay out here any longer, now it's raining. We've come to offer you a ride."

There was no stir or sign of animation behind the green door; nor to their repeated calling was there any answer, any more than if the boy had not understood English.

One part of the gentlemen's performance consisted of a repeated blowing by Mr. Merritt through his thumbs into his hands, so as to make a loud whistle. This he repeated many times, because, as he said, "he knew from his own experience that every boy understood that."

Mr. Parmenter was, it would seem, a man of resolution. "I should like to see," he said, aside, "what has become of him;" and, giving the reins ceremoniously to his companion, he jumped out and set himself to opening the way into the hiding-place. At the expense of a pretty thorough wetting from the drops shaken down and brushed through, he made an entrance, only to find the bare rock, and the place empty.

"That's the Russian way, I suppose," said Mr. Merritt, "though I should have called it rather '*French* leave.' But you're dripping, my dear sir," as from his secure retreat he saw his friend come back. "Where's he gone, do you suppose?" he asked, his curiosity again overcoming, for the moment, his sympathy and good manners.

"That I can't tell you, sir," said Mr. Parmenter, with several slight coughs.

"What's that paper?" Mr. Merritt asked. "Perhaps that's his father's patent of nobility."

Mr. Parmenter picked up the paper, — a damp and not over-clean bit, — and, glancing at it, said: "It's something I can't make out, — a strange language."

"A find! Suppose you bring it home," said his friend; "perhaps we can make some hand at it." And

Mr. Parmenter, having folded and put it into his pocket, took his place, wet and chilling; drew up the boot, and soon had his horse going faster than before.

Through that side-road, so pretty in bright weather, they splashed, and into the main road. Here was some moving life.

"That's a remarkably nice-looking girl ahead there," said Mr. Merritt: "we met her before. What new family have you got here? She'll get a precious soaking, though, won't she?"

"Yes, but there's Mr. Manson offering to hold his umbrella over her!" said Mr. Parmenter. "*He* doesn't care for weather either."

"But what's he got in his arms?" asked Mr. Merritt, — "a sheep?"

Mr. Manson (whom our readers may remember, the Rector and editor) had certainly something large on his arm, under his cloak.

"I see his feet hanging down," said Mr. Parmenter: "it's little Billy Carnes, the cripple. I saw him in Mrs. Rainor's window, as we came by."

"We'll say it's a lamb, then. If it wasn't so rainy, I should like to try Manson with your 'strange language,'" said Mr. Merritt.

"Yes!" Mr. Parmenter answered, keeping up his horse's pace. "That girl belongs to a very respectable family, lately moved in. Some people say the mother is most likely the person that had the charge of Brade, or else is appointed to look after him. I haven't made out yet, to my own satisfaction, whether there's any thing in it. There's no intercourse between Brade and them, that anybody knows of; but they're very well off."

"In a country place," said Mr. Merritt, "the neighbors would soon know it, if there was any intercourse, — to say nothing of scores of boys with two eyes and ears apiece."

"I should know it as soon as any one," said Mr. Parmenter, in a tone that implied a large reserve of power and means within him: "my position is such, you know, that not much is said or done that doesn't find its way to me. It's important that it should be so."

The rain came steadily down, in a way to check conversation; and the rate at which they were driving brought their faces and hats and clothes against it, and made it necessary to meet it manfully, or shelter themselves from it, as best they might. So, splashing through shallow puddles, and flinging the mud from wheels and hoofs, with now and then a snort from the horse and a cough from his driver, they made their way home.

CHAPTER XVII.

MR. DON AND ANOTHER JOIN FORCES.

THE reader will not expect that Mr. Don, who does not live in Eastham, should give up all his time to St. Bart's, or to his friends in our town. He is a snug man of business at home, and quietly thriving in the world; and this he would not be, if he did not look after his own business, which is that of calico-printing, on a good scale. It is because his business is in a safe way, and that he conscientiously follows up his duties in all other directions, that we find him so often treading the soil of Eastham, and making himself seen and felt at the School.

More than one thing here now took up his time.

We have seen that Miss Minette Wadham was not disinclined to let her mother go forward and work out her plan, if only she could be kept within certain bounds of propriety. We have seen the plan formed in their house to give harmless pleasure and to develop a most interesting and attractive mystery. It is while things are just in this state that our small but intelligent and courteous friend made his way in; and, in answer to the salutations of the ladies, said that "his wife assured him that he was looking very well; that he was not quite clear that she was right; but supposed that it was a proper compliment to her to think so."

Having thus smilingly introduced himself as put forward and sustained by his wife, and having next complimented the ladies on looking well, and remarked the beauty of their flowers, and the comfort of a wood-fire, he diverged a little. "You find your residence in Eastham still agreeable, I suppose, Mrs. Wadham?" he asked. "Our boys — the boys of Saint Bartholomew's School — don't disturb you?"

This he said like one who, though he felt responsible for the conduct of the boys, yet was pretty well assured that there was little misconduct to account for. The lady answered: —

"I've got two boys there myself, you know, Mr. Don; and my boys were always brought up to respect their mother, — to respect their father and their mother my boys were brought up; and, if boys respect their mothers, they can't be very bad."

This little sentence was uttered with so much decision as to make it clear that she considered Mr. Don's question met and answered. Mr. Don accepted it, apparently, in that understanding.

"True, ma'am," he said, "the parental principle — the principle of parental respect — in my opinion underlies (I think that's the phrase now), it's at the root of every thing. You commonly observe" —

Mrs. Wadham plunged into speech: —

"As for the *parental* principle, I say, teach 'em to know their mothers. I know it's said, 'it's a wise child that knows his father;' but I say let 'em know their mothers, and then you keep 'em in connection with all that's pure and holy."

"It may be as you say, ma'am," answered Mr. Don. Then gathering up again the thread of discourse, which had been brushed out of his hand, he followed it: —

"I've seen young men left orphans who have been brought up without that restraining influence. I have one in particular in my mind now" —

"Yes: speaking of that, what do you think of the mystery of St. Bartholomew's — I call it; there was a 'Massacre of St. Bartholomew's' once, you know."

Mr. Don moved in his seat, and looked intelligently at her; for, as our readers will believe, here was a subject that he was ready for. He answered cordially: —

"I think we're in a way to get nearer to it."

The answer was so ready that Mrs. Wadham seemed to doubt whether he could have understood her.

"About this young chap at the School, I mean, — nobleman's son, or whatever he is."

"That's the subject I had in my mind, ma'am," said Mr. Don.

"It's the subject a good many people have got in their minds, I guess," said the lady.

"But, excuse me, ma'am," said Mr. Don. "You spoke of a 'Massacre.' Am I to understand that you connect something of that sort with the history of the young person we referred to?"

"That I can't say," answered Mrs. Wadham, with much meaning and authority in her look and voice. "*Mystery* is what it is, now. I ask" (with a sort of official tone) "what you think of it?"

"Oh!" said Mr. Don, seriously, "I'm convinced there's something in it, ma'am. I think it altogether likely he's a nobleman's son, — my own opinion is, a Russian nobleman."

Mrs. Wadham looked as if she carried in her pocket a pass-key to the House of Things Unrevealed. "I suppose it can be known," she said, and sealed the sentence with a single nod, as significant, if not as conclusive, as that of Jove.

Mr. Don was not the man to shut the mouth of an oracular cave, or to put brakes upon the wheels of advancing discovery, nor was he the man to precipitate things. "You think it could be discovered, ma'am, do you?" he asked. "I remember a remark our Rector, Dr. Nattom, once made, that 'if we could encourage the hidden thing to come out of its shell, without rudely breaking it ourselves, we were following the order of nature.'"

"The 'order of nature' is all good," she answered; "but I take it we're meant to be lords of nature. I should say this secret will be discovered!" and, having nodded decisively, she looked steadily in his face. "There's Eldridge!" she said, suddenly, showing that she could attend to two men at once. Then, throwing up the window, she called out, "Eldridge! I want you to put Tommy directly into the light carriage, to drive me."

It is to be supposed that if Eldridge had received his proportion of that domestic wisdom which, as we have heard, had been applied to the sons of Wadham, he would go straight to the execution of an order, or a suggestion of Mrs. Wadham, with a readiness beyond that of submission to authority, with a feeling as if he were furthering the operation of one of the Elements of Nature. This time he answered, not strongly, "I haven't been to dinner yet, Miss Wadham."

"Oh, yes!" she said; "but I want the horse and

light carriage, right away. — I sha'n't be gone long," she added, considerately, for his comfort.

"Now," she said, "I'm goin' to St. Bartholomew's School: I've got an end in view, — I've got a purpose, — and a motive."

Mrs. Wadham's way of speaking a sentence like this was sententious: whether to choose the right words, or to give them a chance to take their full effect upon her hearers.

Mr. Don was a very good listener, — courteous and grave, but not demonstrative. To what had just been said, he answered, "Oh, yes, ma'am!"

Mrs. Wadham looked at him as if she were not sure whether he had altogether understood her.

"I say," said she, emphatically, "I've got a purpose and a motive!"

This phrase had evidently been chosen with deliberation.

"Perhaps you'd like to go with me?" she asked, and was assured that "he would certainly go, with pleasure, if it wouldn't put her to any inconvenience."

"No inconvenience about it!" she answered. "I ain't a living skeleton, and I always have plenty of room in my carriages. Now, Netta, *you* might go and set and talk with Mrs. Warren, while I'm about business. That'll be treating her with proper respect. — Yes."

To many persons, if they had heard the whole of Mrs. Wadham's plans, this proposition would seem like that among thieves, by which the one is to draw off a partner or a clerk, while the other robs the till. To people like the author of it, it seems to provide for all the demands of propriety and kindness, while it answers the first object, which is to enable the contriver of it to accomplish his own purpose.

"So we'll put on our things and get ready, if you'll go."

The daughter had more delicacy of perception, if not more kindliness of feeling than the mother, and she objected, while she nipped dead leaves from the plants: —

"But, mother, I don't see why you can't see Mrs. Warren and ask leave to visit the dormitory. I don't think there would be any difficulty" —

"That would just spoil my plan: I can do that afterwards," said the mother. "That is all very proper, no doubt, in general: I make no objection; but there are other considerations that outweigh propriety, this time. Well, Mr. Don, I'll go and get ready."

"And I'll beg off from going," said Miss Minette. "You'll have Mr. Don."

"Perhaps I can take your daughter's place with Mrs. Warren," said that mild gentleman. "I can't fill it, of course, — I wouldn't undertake to fill it; but just to make a call upon Mrs. Warren, and I could join you immediately, in the alcoves."

Mrs. Wadham was going, large and heavy, to make herself ready, and answered, turning to Mr. Don, as she went, "Yes."

"I can understand your feeling, — if you'll allow me to say so," said the gentleman to Miss Minette, who was still engaged in trimming her plants. "I should have some scruple myself, if I thought that any liberty was going to be taken; but, of course, that isn't the intention."

"Mrs. Warren may make no objection, and may not feel hurt," said Miss Minette ("No!" interposed Mr. Don); "but I don't like to ransack her house, without leave" —

"The house is, in one sense, Mrs. Warren's," he said; "but a school isn't altogether like a private house. It must be open to inspection to a certain extent, at any time. I can easily conceive that a lady at the head of it might prefer that some examinations should take place, informally, as it were."

Mr. Don spoke philosophically, and as one of the Trustees of a school; perhaps, too, as a man whose curiosity saw a prospect of gratification, if Mrs. Wadham could only have plenty of room and time. Miss Minette had more delicacy: —

"If mother was going on an official visit, — if she was a visitor, or on a committee, — why, even then" — but as the sentence would have had little effect, probably, if it had been finished, so it never reached any end, for it was cut across by Mrs. Wadham's entrance, and she filled a good deal of space, wherever she was.

"Couldn't you send a bouquet to Mrs. Warren?" she asked, as she came in. "You'll have enough to make a show, after you've cut off a good many."

"Of course," said the daughter, "we've got plenty of flowers; but I should prefer sending them another time, or taking them in my hand."

"Here! Here!" said the mother, "let me take 'em." And with very summary fingers she snipped and clipped, and crowded the flowers into one of her hands without any care for arrangement, and then putting the bunch into Mr. Don's charge, and receiving his very courteous acknowledgment, she said, —

"There! those shall be your share to take care of: I like always to have my hands free to take the reins, if any thing should happen."

During this time Eldridge had brought the carriage

to the side of the house, where, from the top of a natural rock which was as level and smooth as if made for the purpose, Mrs. Wadham and her guest stepped down through the doorway of the vehicle, and after she had given her daughter a parting direction to "keep Mr. Greenwood, if he should come, for she might have some use for him, — and tell him, 'Not a word!'" they were driven off. "Mr. Greenwood's been away," she explained, "and I want to have my party."

No prettier road has its flowers gathered in summer by children's fingers, and its stones piled by them into walls and causeways, and bridges and houses, and few smoother country roads have their dust raised by flashing wheels, than that over which they went. In the first place, there was a hill, and there were windings; and then the varied grouping and size and shape of trees gave change and beauty, even now, when their chief grace and glory was no longer hanging upon them, and made a shelter from the chilly winds; while, through the openings, the lake was seen, and the town, afar.

At St. Bart's, the cunningly devised programme was carried out, with one chief exception. Before leaving the carriage, Mr. Don had mildly expressed his purpose of going with Mrs. Wadham first, and reserving his visit to the Rector's family until afterwards. The flowers were left lying on the seat.

"Just as you please," said Mrs. Wadham, who would gain by the change a witness to her own cleverness, and an adviser, — and, moreover, a sharer in the questionable proceeding in which she was engaged. "Now I lead, and you follow. Eldridge, you'll walk the horse along the road, up there, and mind and be here in twenty minutes, — from fifteen to twenty minutes."

So saying, she led the way rapidly, and with her face set gravely and resolutely forward, not to the front door, but round to that storm-house with which the reader is sufficiently acquainted. Mr. Don followed, without trying exactly to overtake her. As she got her hand upon the latch of the door, it was suddenly pushed open with a force that, coming unexpectedly, and striking her not well planted on the ground, nearly threw her over backwards. Mr. Don supported her by one arm, and she successfully withstood the shock.

"A mite more," she said, gasping, "and my boys would have been motherless, and I shouldn't have been here to tell the tale!" She made the tragic character of the unhappened incident complete, by adding: "And it would have been their own school-house door that did it!"

The three boys who had made the unintentional assault stopped very politely to apologize, and Mrs. Wadham received the atonement graciously: —

"Only," she said, "I wouldn't come out of a door as if I was fired out, for you may hit somebody."

Mr. Don, for his part, addressed two of the boys as acquaintances, "Brade" and "Remsen;" and Mrs. Wadham promptly turned to one of them, whom the reader knows as Nicholas Remsen, and expressed great interest in him, as being in her son Edmund's Form. "Oh, yes! I know it's Albert is in your Form," she said, correcting herself, as the boy corrected her; and then, with great dignity, took leave of him, and said, —

"Now, Mr. Don!" and — the door having been opened more deliberately than the last time — passed through, into the house.

"You know Remsen, then?" Mr. Don asked.

"Remsen? No! I know Brade, — I spoke to him just now. I've looked at him, many's the time, in church. Now, this is our way!" and she went straight on upstairs, remarking, as she mounted stair after stair, that "if people could go up a slope, as they used to have it, up to the cupalo, in the State House" (Mrs. Wadham very seldom miscalls a word, but that crowning glory of the capitol is one that she names like most people), "it would be ever so much more comfortable."

"How d'y'do, Therese?" she said affably to a nice person, with a bunch of keys at her girdle and a pile of white clothing on her arm. "I'm come to look at your rooms, you see, to see if you've got 'em all right. — Mr. Don, you know," she added, partly withdrawing, so as to let a portion of the Trustee be seen. "I sha'n't need any help, Therese. I know my way. Who's next to my Edmund, now? Remsen? or Brade?"

Being informed that Thompson Walters was on one side, and Blake on the other, she said adroitly, —

"Brade's the one they call 'my lord.' I suppose his room is very splendid. This is it, I believe?" and she drew aside a curtain.

This time she had hit rightly, as "Therese," who kept close at hand, assured her, and disclosed a pretty little place, — not, at the moment, absolutely neat, for some shavings, with a piece or two of paper, lay upon the floor, and a roughish bit of wood, with a knife sticking in it, lay on the little table.

A good engraving, from one of Raphael's well-known paintings of the Mother and the Child, hung over the bed, and there were several pretty photographs upon the walls.

Mrs. Wadham seemed to see every thing at a glance, and she dropped the curtain.

"Very pooty!" she said, — "plain, but very pooty. Nothing very foreign-looking but the watch. Oh! perhaps you didn't see that watch?" and she drew the curtain again.

Mr. Don had entered into more general subjects of conversation with "Therese," whom he called "Mrs. Latham." He had started that of heating, and was on his way, doubtless, to that of ventilation and the rest, when this appeal was made to him. We may suppose that, whatever he was talking about, his eyes and ears were ready for discovery. The watch he set out for with all the alacrity that was in him.

"Indeed, ma'am," he said, as he surveyed it with his glasses, "it's a very curious specimen!" for under their eyes lay a large — as compared with watches of our day, we might say a huge — machine of silver, with a high and broadly-overarching dome of crystal; and from this body came a great stalwart ticking, as unlike the sound of modern time-pieces as was the accent of our fathers of two or three centuries ago unlike our own.

"Two angels," said Mr. Don. "Foreign!" Then, looking closely, he read: "Diependorper, Haarlaem."

"That ain't Russian, though!" said Mrs. Wadham, thoughtfully. Soon she added, in a cheery tone: "But *we*'ve got English watches and Swiss watches. — How do you suppose they ever carried such a thing as that?" asked the lady, having relieved her own anxiety. "Had a servant, I suppose, to lug it in his pocket, and take it out when his master wanted to know what the time was. Silver, you see: couldn't trust 'em with gold. That's the reason they did it," she continued, finding confirmations for her theory multiplying as she went on.

"Not very far out of the way," said Mr. Don, comparing the notes of time upon its face with those of a very good-looking gold watch which he took out of his pocket, and speaking a good deal as if the old horologe had brought down with it a current of time from centuries far off, and as if it were as marvellous that this should hit that of to-day as that the eastern and western shafts of the great tunnel should come so wonderfully together.

"Ah!" he exclaimed, putting his forefinger to the crystal. Mrs. Wadham's head went instantly down to see.

"That's some sort of lingo that's too much for me," she said, leaving Mr. Don at work, with pencil and paper, copying.

"Well, now for my boys!" said the lady, and she started off. "Have they got bedclothes enough?" she asked, feeling between the sheets. "Dear me! what's the child got here? A turtle, I do believe!" and she drew her hand hastily out again.

Mrs. Wadham was not a woman to take counsel with her fears, when any thing was to be done; so she assailed the work again, and flung the clothes down over the bed's foot; and there, uncovered, on the middle of the lower sheet, stood something more congenial to boys than "turtles," and perhaps less foreign to their beds, something between two plates of crockery, and looking like rich pastry. She lifted the upper plate, and showed a delicate, flaky pie.

"What things boys are!" said the mother. "Now, he's been home and got that, without letting anybody know. That's my china. Well, we won't leave it there," she added, taking it and looking round the little room. "'Twon't do to put it where it'll get him into trouble. (If a tootor should see it, he'd take possession of it.) What's in here, I wonder?" and she opened a small standing cupboard. "There! we'll put it in here," removing some of the rubbish of newspapers which nearly filled it. "Ah! what's this?" and she laid open another plate of pie, much like the former. "Well done!" she said, and then proceeded to explain: "That child has a very delicate stomach. He always liked to have something a little nice, between his meals, if he felt hungry: I was so before him. Entirely different from his brother. *He'll* hardly take any thing, if you'll give it to him, away from table."

A human sound, evidently coming from some hidden overhearers, not far off, showed that there were other occupants of the dormitory, beside those in sight.

She shut the door of the cupboard, and then called Mr. Don's attention to the furniture of the little room, among which a pair of boxing-gloves was conspicuous, with portraits of pointers and setters and some highly-colored lady on horseback.

"Every thing's very neat, Therese, — very proper," she said to the respectable person whom Mr. Don and she called by different names, and who, though she had in some way disposed of her pile of clothes, was still busy very near them. "Now we'll see the other," Mrs. Wadham said, and went across to the opposite side of the dormitory.

"This boy ain't like his brother: this boy's all for reading," in confirmation of which assertion copies of the "Youth's Magazine" and some closely-printed newspapers might be seen upon his table.

Mrs. Wadham was not, like many persons, satisfied

to have the character she had given her son rest upon her own statement only, but was entirely willing to put it to a test; either not observing or not regarding her companion's looking at his watch, as if he were becoming a little impatient, and felt the importance of time. The lady walked straight up to this son's little private lock-up, and, finding it fastened, went at once across, and borrowed the other's key. The inside of the cupboard, when opened, certainly showed a different set of contents from that of his brother with the delicate stomach; for here was an open box of "devilled" ham, and a large bottle of mixed pickles, in which was a fork of silver or plated ware. "*He* seems to be doing pretty well, too," said the mother, after a short pause. "But this isn't business, you may say" (turning to Mr. Don). "I ain't forgetting. Therese, I'm going to take home this fork," and shutting the cupboard-door, without any further remark upon the different characters of her two boys, she returned the key to its own lock, and, holding the fork, said, "Now we'll go! I saw a scrap of paper on the floor in a room we were examining: I don't believe but what I could wrap this fork in it, without hurting anybody;" and, going to Brade's sleeping-room, she picked up a piece of paper, calling Therese's attention to it, as she did so, and promising to return it, "if it was of any consequence."

"Let's see before we start," she said. "We can tell pooty well if it amounts to any thing," and she looked with some significance to Mr. Don, who was, or seemed, entirely calm and unintelligent. "It's a boy's writing," she said, having spread it open. "'itwen gatrapin' she read aloud, with growing animation, which seemed to infect Mr. Don also, for he certainly listened, without pretending to be unconcerned. "Well," she said, folding her fork in the paper, "I can't make any thing out of it, any how. Remember, Therese, I'm answerable. — If you're ready," she said, addressing her companion. Then, in a low voice, "This 'll come in very good at our tableau."

Mr. Don turned and bade "good afternoon" to "Mrs. Latham," and then followed the large lady out, and down the stairs. As they went, sounds of steps and quick voices (among these some quieter tones of a woman) could be heard in the dormitory which they had just left.

She took her way this time through the front hall. As they went, she said: "I've been put back a little with my party. I depend upon Mr. Greenwood; and he went off, just as I was giving out my invitations, to his sister. It's a complimentary party to Brade, — dejooney, in the afternoon, because Mr. Warren won't let 'em come in the evening. I had to write to the Russian Ambassador myself, and I did, — autograph. I told him about his young countryman, of exalted family. I said his interest in him would bring him; but I wouldn't ask him to take that step. I'd bear all expenses, both ways, here and back, gladly, gladly. I wrote a second time, because I hadn't got any answer, and set the day, and said my offer would hold good, if he come without any warning. I hope you'll meet him."

Mr. Don expressed his pleasure at the prospect of meeting so distinguished a personage, and they found themselves near the door.

People are apt if their thoughts are sufficiently collected in the moment of victory, to tax themselves with any excesses or short-comings which they can see in their own conduct, in the pursuit of that glittering prize. Mrs. Wadham said, as she went downstairs: "There! I don't know as I've hurt *any*body."

"You haven't disturbed the arrangements of the house, I think," said Mr. Don.

"I think not!" she said. "Now," — as she looked about her, outside of the front door, which she had chosen this time. "Oh! here! won't you take some flowers for me, with a message, to Mrs. Warren?" she asked of an abstracted-looking boy, so far off that he was obliged to come near, and she to repeat the message, before he could accept or decline it.

"A message," she repeated, "and a bouquet to Mrs. Warren, with my compliments, — Mrs. Wadham's compliments, — and say that I didn't see any of the family about. Eldridge! those flowers!" and having committed them to her messenger, who, without her recognizing him, was no other than our friend Alonzo Peters, and having taken in Mr. Don, and having settled herself thoroughly in her seat, she was driven away, at a very good rate, by the undined (if he was still the undined) Eldridge.

CHAPTER XVIII.

TRAPPING, AND SOME AFTER-TROUBLE.

BRADE had made his way thoroughly into the manifold life of the School. Remsen and Antony (with Peters added) trapped together; and it may be supposed that neither of them was so entirely taken up with lessons as not to have a considerable piece of his heart left to bestow upon the making and setting and visiting of traps. Cæsar, with his Belgæ and Ædui, and Allobroges, and Aduatuci, and Helvetii, and his indirect discourse, and whatever else there is about him, was construed and parsed and understood. Some way was made in Greek, too; and glimpses of flashing shields and spears and helmets were beginning to gleam athwart the lively boyish fancy. Already Antony, though hardly out of the alphabet, even professed a strong drawing toward this foremost of earthly tongues. On the other hand, Remsen, who was a bright fellow, though he did not get through his work always with the same steadiness, very honestly acknowledged that "he did not like either of 'em, but Latin wasn't as bad as Greek."

Trapping they both went into with equal heartiness. Remsen had, possibly, a little more skill in getting up traps; and Brade was as often good at choosing ground. They were both equally untiring in following up their business; and as they had got leave to "set" in Mr. Freeman's land, by being early in asking, they were thought to have as good ground as any boys in the School. In it was the pine wood, where, occasionally, a hare, called by the boys from his winter dress a "white rabbit," used to be caught.

Their self-chosen partner, Peters, was endured, and really showed himself to have some skill and a great deal of willingness.

One thing will be observed, that, as Brade's fortune has already brought him a good deal into contact with Towne, though they are not in any way intimates, so it happens that, somehow or other, they are still brought together in the life of the School. In this trapping, while on one side of them (for the whole neighborhood was parcelled out and appropriated) Will Hirsett had got leave, with Meadows;, on the other, were Towne and Wilkins and Tarleton. This last boy grumbled much that his party had not got the other ground.

Babble-brook (or Brabble-brook) ran through the whole; and one particular piece of marshy ground along that stream was in that lot. There was the most promising spot in the whole neighborhood (if not *πάσης τῆς οἰκουμένης*, as Brade exultingly said, when Remsen and he were making their first survey of their domain on a breezy, warm afternoon in early October) for finding muskrats. Tom Spencer, late of St. Bart's, had, as the tradition ran, been in the habit of catching them there "hand over hand." It was said that he had bought with the proceeds the best pair of skates in the School.

So now for the boys' trapping; and let the young fellows skip straight over to Remsen and Brade, except such of them as are wise enough to go along with a few of us old-time school-boys in two or three beautiful reflections here.

Are there any such dewy mornings as those that we look back to in the young days of life? Are there any such warm, balmy, hazy afternoons as those that were new to the fresh glance of the school-boy? Tell me, you that are limping, now, on the sunny side of the city-street, with well-wrapped throats and rheumy eyes, and flabby old cheeks, and hands stiffened to the grip of the accountant's pen and leaves; or you that, in close chariot, behind high-stepping horses and arrogant coachman, hold up a red nose and shift a gouty foot unseen, — were there ever such goings-out as those, after school, to the heart of the woods or the brook-side, forty-odd years ago, before we knew enough to care for bonds and stocks and shares, or to stop even for an instant, on our way, or even to stay the busy blade of our knife to hear the most startling story from 'Change? The breaking-up of camp, with tramping and champing of horses, and clanking of accoutrements, and roll and rattle of drums, and tan-ta-ra, tan-ta-ra of trumpets, and rumble and din and clash, is an exciting scene; and so the sailing of the huge, far-bound ship, with the jostle of luggage and package and crate and passengers, and the driving up of carriages and drays and wagons, and a clatter of block and tackle, and a sound of down-kept might of machinery, and a rush of steam, and a flapping of sails, and a wafting of colors, is a scene of life and bustle; so, too, the sympathy of a listening crowd, with fixed, burning eyes and pale cheeks, or sliding tears or sudden sobs, will draw the speaker out to the larger outlines of humanity; and so the setting-forth, in full dress, with some smell of flowers, and a little stiffness of posture, in lamp-lighted and smoothly-running coach, and with a sense of bustle and glare, as we draw nearer to the house of many shining windows and often-opening door where the ball or evening-party is to be, keeps all the blood astir, if one is new to it.

But to get up early in the morning, with the mists, all waiting for the sun to scatter them; to tramp over damp earth and wet grass, mingling our white breath with the other vapors; to feel, after a while, the slow warmth of the great Heater on side or back; to go, crumbling the rotten leaves and crackling the dry limbs under foot, leaping the rail-fence and stone wall; to come down on one knee at our figure-four traps, to scan and then to climb our sapling hickory; to guess the time from a watch that always acted with a happy independence of every other regulator and keeper of periodical succession, in the universe; to hurry back through all the bright cheeriness and glitter of morning, — this was life at its best; was it not? When, since, has life been better? Now for the boys of to-day.

It was on the morning of exactly such a day — school-life not being yet fairly opened, and there being about one good hour, and that not free of anxious care about time — that Remsen and Brade were going down West Road, while a fog still lay over the face of a deepish valley, just as preparations were going on all over the land for the sun's coming-up. They were not quite so talkative as if the hour were later, but hurried on, speculating a little upon chances, but stopping for nothing. As the day grew brighter, so they, being a part of nature, grew brighter with it.

There had been just rain enough the night before to soften the ground without making it muddy; but that day all was clear.

From what they said, it appeared that, in spite of his being "on bounds," and so, of course, having no leave, Towne had gone down, and Tarleton and Wilkins; and moreover, from the hope which they expressed that no "wolverine" had been along the line of traps, it seemed that there was danger of some ill-minded persons having stolen the "catch."

On the second hill, they met one Phil Rainor, whose reputation was not good, and whose relations to the St. Bart's boys had not been always friendly, for he had, at one time, been thought to make a great many dishonest pennies with the proceeds of his robberies of the St. Bart's traps. Indeed, violent suspicions had, more than once, gone on through the process of absolute demonstration to much more practical violence; in which (beside others) Towne, for his party, and Remsen, for himself, had used arguments more weighty and effective than any that they knew how to make with words.

Rainor was now, professedly, on the footing of a mutual understanding, although the Bartholomæans had not yet made up their minds that he was a changed boy.

This time, at least, his hands were empty, and there was no load in his pockets, or hanging about him. This, the intelligent eyes of the two boys could see, at a glance, almost as far as they could see him. There was something, therefore, almost like cordiality, in their hasty greeting as they ran by.

Phil Rainor, too, seemed more than usually hearty;

for he called after them: "That's your snare (ain't it?) down there by Indian Rock? Well, it's ketched a big white rabbit!"

This news, as may be supposed, put new spirit into every limb of our trappers. Over the first fence they went at such a rate that Brade tripped on a branch of a tree, inside, and went down sprawling with Remsen on top of him; both picking themselves up in the shortest possible time, and in excellent humor.

"Hurt your side, Anty?" asked Remsen, as Brade held a hand to his bosom.

"It's the watch!" answered Antony, showing, when he took away his hand, a lump very large to be made by any ordinary time-piece.

"Don't stop to look at it now!" said Remsen; and on they went.

"He knows everybody's traps, doesn't he?" said Brade.

"Yes," answered Remsen, "and I don't see what he's round 'em for, unless for some badness;" but it was bright morning, and the boys were in good cheer. Besides, they agreed that he had given them good news, and that, if he had had any plunder with him, they would have seen some sign of it. So Phil Rainor went out of their thoughts absolved, for this time.

What they had said about Towne and others being before them was true; for Towne and Wilkins, with Tarleton behind, were coming up before our two had got to their ground. Towne was in luck, too, it would seem, as well as they; for he swung in the air something which their quick eyes recognized as "a big white rabbit." Beasts of that sort were rare; and it must have been a sort of golden shower for Towne to have one, and for them to have one, on the same morning.

They quickened their steps; although they said, as if the same reasoning had passed through both minds, "We've got plenty of time."

Towne added a caution that "they'd better hurry;" a piece of advice which good people are pretty generally ready to give to those later than themselves. Tarleton added, quite as much in the usual style of boys, —

"Ho! you needn't hurry: you haven't got any thing."

Remsen and Brade were already a good way on, running helter-skelter, when Towne's warning reached them.

"We're going ὡς τάχιστα * now," said Brade, like a little pedant, perhaps; but both were in fine spirits, and so Remsen did not object, and Antony enjoyed it. If Remsen did not understand, he was not at the trouble to ask an explanation.

Time was short, and all the way was to be measured back again to St. Bart's. So on they went, so fast that they could not catch breath enough to make words with.

"That fellow's cheated us!" cried one, or both, as they came within sight of their snare, and stood for an instant, looking first at that, and then toward the right and left.

"Hold on!" said Remsen, "let's see! the string's all gone close to the bough! see that bit dangling!" Then, showing a bit of white fur, which his sharp and practised eye had detected, "See here! there's been a rabbit in it, and a white rabbit, too!"

"He's got away!" said Brade, mournfully.

* As fast as possible.

Remsen was a boy of experience in trapping, and he said: " So he might; but," he added, " no rabbit ever got away from one snare and into another, right off! And two such fellows ain't caught in one night, neither. If any fellow'd do that, he ought to be horsewhipped! He ought to be turned out of the school! 'Tain't likely he'd break that big cord we had!"

There was much confusion of persons and things in this speech, as, of course, in his mind; but the wrong was clear, and so Remsen kicked the tree, and threw his hat on the ground, and stamped it with his foot. It was pretty hard, after their cheery hopes, to find worse than nothing, and to have the evidence before their eyes that their snare had had and lost its game! Brade looked cast-down enough, while Remsen thus vented his indignant anger on things in general.

"I tell you what," said Remsen, "there's been foul play! and look at the footsteps round here, — plenty of 'em!" and he turned away. "Well, leave 'em so!" he said. "Don't go near 'em, so's to scrape 'em out."

Brade proposed to make a round of their traps, as fast as they could (for time was short); and Remsen mechanically assented.

They made the round, with little hope, perhaps, but in very short time. They found nothing.

"Well," said Remsen, "we may as well go back;" and they set out for home.

The day came up, not with the thick-springing bird-songs of June or May, to be sure, — not with fragrance of flower; but it came up with splendor of sky and sparkle of earth, and cheery sounds from the farm-yards, and hammering of some carpenter or carpentering farmer.

It might not be true that our two disappointed boys saw or heard much of what was going on; but it was true that their loss did not quite take away all spirit from them, — perhaps because they had morning blood in them.

"Certainly old Towne wouldn't take ours, to trick us," said Brade, "and give it to us when we get up?"

"'Tain't likely," said Remsen. "We sha'n't see our rabbit very soon."

There was a smithy on that road, and, as they came up to it, Rainor came out to meet them, holding in one hand a forge-hammer, and in the other a bit of iron, as if just from the anvil.

"Where's your rabbit?" he asked, looking from one to the other.

"We thought we'd leave him down there for somebody to steal," said Remsen.

"Why! hain't ye got him?" asked Rainor, again, looking very much astonished. Then, as the boys went on, he went on beside them, and kept up his talking. "Ye see Towne's, didn't ye? Well, jest about s'ch another whapper. I tell ye how you'll know your'n: he had his right ear split down quite a ways, an' his right fore foot bloody about the toes. I took p'ticklar notice to him, for I come right down 'cross lots, jest where he was. He was in your snare there, ketched right round his belly. I should jest want to take a look at Towne's, 'f I was you, — white, and a brown spot on his nigh shoulder."

"I suppose rabbits are all alike," said Brade; "but what's his 'nigh' shoulder?" he asked, puzzled by this rustic word.

"Why!" said Rainor, "his left shoulder, of course; but rabbits ain't alike, — not by a long chalk! Not *that* sort, at no time o' year, — nary two of 'em, never." The negatives in this sentence would make a study for philologists and grammarians, as showing the kindred character and habit of two great sister-languages of the Aryan stock, — the Greek and the English. He finished in this way: "an' there ain't two of 'em ketched in a — year, I was go'n' to say."

Here he said "he must go back to the shop," and left them. From this time our friends, though they kept up their rate of going, went silently.

For some while, Antony, still hurrying on, was pulling earnestly at something which he seemed determined to get out of his pocket, but which, for its part, was equally resolute not to come. He bent over, and wriggled his body (still going on), and put up one knee, half stopping as he did so; he worked the thing one way and the other; he pushed down, and then pulled up again, until at length there came up to the light of the morning a large, round, thick thing of silver, — a strange-looking bivalve, with one of its sides obscured by mist, doubtless from the heat of the boy's body.

Nick Remsen wiped the mist off with his cuff; and both Brade and he stopped and studied, confidingly, the dial-face, which now stood revealed in silver, under a crystal dome rounded like that of the Capitol, or (to be classical) like the bossy shield of Achilles. On the broad plain of silver was an outside circle of Arabic numerals, and an inner circle of numeral letters, — the former for minutes, the latter for hours. Other devices, of angels and scrolls, we pass over for the time.

The boys studied the pointing of the two strong arms.

"Only a little over half-past!" said Remsen, wiping once more the glass, which was still smeary. "We'll see Towne before roll-call: there's time enough;" adding, presently, "no Bartlemas fellow'd *steal* our rabbit, of course, — that ain't to be thought of."

As they came into the school-grounds, every thing was quiet, with no signs of life abroad. Remsen led the way over to the gymnasium. A board stood up against the eastern end, on which was stretched, by tacks, the fresh skin of a hare, or, as the boys called it, "a white rabbit." Brade could not yet have got over the feeling of their own loss, and still, so strong was instinct in him, that he began, as soon as he saw the raw pelt, to say something about "Marsyas," whose skin Apollo had flayed off.

Remsen, for his part, was altogether in serious earnest. He walked straight up, in silence, to the board, and put his finger on the green skin, although he hardly needed the assurance of touch to establish its freshness.

"He's carried off the head," said he, after looking about hastily, on that side and on the back side of the building. "There's the Tutor's bell!" he said. "Why, it can't be so late! You saw what o'clock it was."

In spite of the authority of the watch, coupled with the testimony of common sense, the boys hurried over to the storm-house door, Brade saying, as they went, "I thought it was very still all about."

Luckily for them, the boys were quiet in their seats; and the two, as they came inside the hall, could see that something had been going on. They went silently to their places, and evidently were each marked tardy; but it was plain that the roll had not been called, and they were safe for breakfast. Sam Blake looked half across the school-room, till he caught Remsen's eye, and then raised his brows, as if asking a question. Remsen hastily shook his head.

The roll was called, and the boys went out orderly, as usual, to their breakfast. Towne was inclined to be communicative, as he commonly was, on the way,— turning round and saying something to a boy behind, or calling out, in a loud whisper, to some one in front. Remsen and Brade were unapproachable. One thing he seemed to think would prevail with the latter. Turning round and facing him, he said rhetorically, with a good deal of gesture, "PEDICULUM CAPTAVI!" but he produced no effect on the boy whom he so learnedly addressed. In his eagerness to vent his Latin sentence, he probably had not known how loudly he was speaking. Gaston heard it, at some distance in front, and immediately, in spite of rules and tutors, burst out laughing.

"Towne wants to say he's caught a rabbit," said he, "and he says he's caught a —!" The word was whispered in the ear of the next boy, and while poor Towne looked amazed, and presently very sheepish, the communication passed from one to another as fast almost as a message by telegraph, and everybody was laughing at the Latinity which its author had uttered with so much confidence and flourish. The smaller boys could hardly walk for laughter.

"Towne!" said Mr. Bruce, the Tutor, "stand out of the procession." And he took his stand at one side, evidently not understanding things.

"What do you mean by such a disgusting sentence!" asked the Tutor.

"Why, I don't see how it's disgusting, sir. All I meant to say was, 'I've caught a rabbit.'"

"Well, that isn't what you did say," answered the Tutor.

"Why, Gas—, why, sir, one o' the fellows gave it me for good Latin. He told me that's what it meant, and that's what I meant to say," said Towne, with evident honesty.

"Gaston's Latin is well enough," said Mr. Bruce, smiling; "but you'd better take care of people's giving you Latin till you know enough to find out what it means."

"Oh! I don't mean to say it was Gaston" — began Towne, but stopped there, and smiled, too, like the Tutor.

The procession had gone into breakfast, the blessing had been said, the clatter of chairs had ended, and the boys' chatter and the clink of knife and plate had begun. Mr. Bruce wanted breakfast, no doubt, but he had not done with Towne.

"That mud looks fresh upon your clothes, Towne," said he; and it was only after acknowledging that he had broken bounds, a thing which would bring a pretty heavy penalty, that the poor lad was sent in to his fellows, and Mr. Bruce followed.

The boys had gone to the dining-room in very good humor, while the Tutors looked extraordinarily grave and unconscious of the fun. As Towne came in, still sheepish-looking, he nearly set the laughter all going again: even Brade and Remsen could hardly resist the influence; and, as Towne sat down at table, they both looked at him, not savagely. Presently, something happened which changed the condition of things.

A smoking, savory-looking mess was brought in, with much gravity, by the head waiter, and set down in front of Towne. At the sight, his late discomfitures seemed to slip out of his mind, and a look of good-nature and hospitality took possession of his face. With the courtesy customary at St. Bart's, he immediately set his dish in progress, to share his dainties with others. First it went to the Rector, and was duly acknowledged, though not touched. Towne, though a lazy fellow, and sometimes grumbling, was free-hearted and loyal; and as he looked up, blushing, to the Rector's table, wishing to see some of his rabbit accepted by the Head of the School, his plain face was bettered. "You fellows didn't get any thing this morning," he said, across the table, "take some of our rabbit, won't you?" and he set it forward toward Remsen and Brade. It had been served up in style; and the head and long ears made quite a show, separated by a bit of toast from the other members.

The two boys had already lost the expression which they had brought in to the table; and they both coldly declined, — Brade following Remsen. Towne, perhaps, had not observed the distance of their manner, for he pressed his kindness on them, telling them that "there was plenty, and that they need not be afraid to take it."

Remsen went so far as to look closely at one of the ears, while the head was near him; but he put no hand to the dish. The owner was hurt.

"There are plenty more that'll take it, if you won't," he said; a sentiment which was heartily responded to by Arthur Dover, commonly called "Fatty," and by Wilkins and others. The dish circulated, — first to Towne's two partners, then to others, — and came back. considerably lessened, to the hospitable first partner. He showed, by his way of dealing with it, that he understood and appreciated it thoroughly, even though he had not been able to give it its Latin name.

Breakfast passed: the rabbit was all consumed; but with this gathering coldness and storm, which were evident to all the boys in the neighborhood, there was an uncomfortable silence at that part of the younger table; and others after Brade and Remsen were rather awkward in speaking to Towne and his partners. All of them were observed, as if there was a general waiting to know what was to come.

Doubts, suspicions, disagreements, quarrels (it is good that we have to go out of kindly English to Latin for these words) are very serious things with boys, as well as with their elders. Boys of good feelings have not yet brushed through and thrown aside, or trampled down, many estrangements and embittered friendships, and so grown heedless of them.

In a case like this, between Towne and the two other boys, it would be impossible to believe, without overwhelming proof, that any of their own companions could be guilty of downright and low thieving. There are, of course, boys, as there are men, who carry teasing, and what they call "practical joking" to the utmost stretch of falseness, short of making actual gain of it, at last. But to take, and carry away, and skin another boy's rabbit; to eat the flesh and keep the skin, — this could scarcely be believed of school-fellows anywhere; and, of course, of school-fellows at St.

Bart's. Towne, or others, might make themselves exceedingly disagreeable, — they might be even a standing nuisance, as confirmed "practical jokers" always are; but they would not steal, and then lie about the theft.

Yet the thing looked badly, and must be explained.

This would be the natural reasoning of Remsen and Brade.

As things stood, they could hardly get away from the conclusion that he, or his fellows, had taken their rabbit; but they had not asked him "up and down." This, therefore, they proposed to do.

Towne, sitting lower at the table, went out before them; and, by the time they got well abroad, he was already on the gravel, marking out the ground for some purpose, attended by Wilkins and Dover. As Remsen and Brade drew near, he stood up from his occupation, and of himself addressed them.

Our readers already know the bright freshness of that morning, and have felt the spirit and strength which such a day brings up with it.

"What ailed you fellows, at breakfast? Anybody'd have thought our rabbit was rotten, or something, by the way you acted."

This was certainly rather frank and manly.

"I should want to know where you got that rabbit, first?" answered Remsen

"Why, we got him out of the field, like anybody," said Towne.

"But I should like to know whose snare you caught him with," said the other.

"I don't see what that has to do with the goodness of the meat," said Towne.

Remsen made an emphatic gesture with his head, as he answered, —

"A good deal to do with my eating him."

"Why! why ain't Tarleton's trap as good as yours, any day, I should like to know?" said Towne. "I guess that's a noo idea, that one fellow's trap's wholesomer'n another's." He spoke like one that had common sense on his side, but could not see what the other party were driving at.

"And when did you ever know even a common rabbit get caught in an iron trap?" asked the other.

Remsen was growing pale and agitated. Before he spoke again, Brade, who had been entirely silent, spoke, and it was plain that he, too, was very much excited, though in another way, for he was flushed.

"But did you take him out of our snare?" he asked, directly.

"Take him out of your snare!" exclaimed Towne, now, for the first time, showing any understanding of the case, or any real feeling. "No! of course we didn't take him out of your snare! You don't suppose we're thieves, do you?"

Now the thing was brought to a point. The boys suspected had denied, absolutely, that they had done the bad thing suspected.

Wilkins had come immediately forward at the first question, and had stood ready to come into the conference, whenever there should be a chance. Now, then, Wilkins, the instant the denial had been made, supported it by testimony of his own.

"Why, I was the first one that got there," he said, "and there he was in our trap when I got there."

This testimony seemed clear and conclusive: that

very rabbit which had been skinned and eaten had been caught fairly in the other party's trap. What could be said? Remsen, however, was still full of question.

Now, even lawyers, although they are men, and in constant practice, seem sometimes to make poor work of examining witnesses; and Remsen had not the experience of a lawyer. His questions, therefore, were, most likely, not so well aimed or so well expressed as they might have been.

"You didn't know there was a rabbit in our snare, this morning? and his left ear was split down? and his right fore foot bloody, between the first and second claws? and a brown spot on his left shoulder?"

"What are you fellows jawing about? How was I going to know? I never went near your trap,— I, nor any of us, either," answered Towne. "Suppose I *had* known?— what then?"

By this time, boys coming and going had begun to stop, in the way, beside these excited disputants. Indeed, quite a crowd was gathering. Outside of the ring, Alonzo Peters was flitting about, paling and flushing, and sometimes stopping, and seemingly on the point of speaking.

"Let's go off, somewhere else," said Brade to Remsen. "We don't want the whole school round us."

Remsen was too full of his subject to care about surroundings. Towne, too, said that he "did not care how many came round. They might come and welcome, for all he cared."

The bearing of Remsen's question is not, perhaps, obvious to the reader; nor was it, very likely, obvious to Towne. "What have I got to do with your rabbit? Why didn't you bring up your rabbit, if you had one?

What did you do with him?" And Towne laughed scornfully.

Remsen drew his hand out of his pocket, and held up a hare's head: —

"There's something just like ours, any way," said he, showing the ear split down.

"That looks amazingly like mine!" said Towne. "My ear was so."

Some of the crowd laughed.

"I do believe that's my head," said Towne, — "I'm sure of it," he added, gaining strength of conviction, as he looked at it longer.

Of course the chance of an easy joke was not lost upon the crowd; and Tom Hutchins, accordingly, made as much of it as he could, calling out, more than once, —

"Towne's head! Towne says that's his head! Twig the long ears it's got!"

"That's your head if you want it," said Remsen, too much in earnest to see any thing like a joke in the case; "but I want you just to take notice to the way that left ear is split down, — just the way ours was."

"Well, what did you do with yours?" asked Towne. "Did you let it go?"

"Let it go!" exclaimed Remsen: "it's likely we'd let it go, — we never had it."

"Well, if here ain't a pretty story!" said Towne: "coming here, getting angry, and abusing a fellah like a pickpocket! I can't make out what you mean, for my part."

Brade had had very little share of the controversy; but he had stood close up to the two main speakers, with his face flushed and his eyes sparkling, and he joined a good deal of dumb show to the discussion, looking from one speaker to the other, and handling the head when it was brought forward. He now spoke: —

"Rainor told us he was in our snare," he said.

"Then Rainor was mistaken in the place, I suppose," said Towne.

"No, he said our snare, by Indian Rock," insisted Brade.

"Well, then, Rainor lies, — that's all. If he says that rabbit was in your snare, Indian Rock, or any rock, he lies."

"He told us right about the ear, any way," said Remsen; "and he said there was a brown spot on the left shoulder. Dar'st you let us look at the skin?"

Towne turned with some dignity to the gathering of boys before he answered, and having looked hastily round, as if to see what shape public opinion was taking, he said: —

"Of course I dare; but I say, before all these boys, At first, I didn't know what you were driving at; but if you're going upon the supposition that we're thieves till we've proved we ain't, after I've told you we found that rabbit in our trap, I won't have any thing to do with it. I'll leave it out to any fair judges, — to any two monitors, — I say Russell and Lamson."

At this moment the bell, which had not improbably been waiting the issue of the discussion, for its ringer was mortal and a boy, began to roll over and over, and sound its "Ding!" in one direction, and its "Dong!" in another, and the gathering of boys began to move, — some running off immediately to the house, some walking leisurely in the same direction, and even those who did not yet leave the scene of controversy became restless, as if keeping their legs ready to go at the last moment.

"Rainor *is* a great liar," said Brade, who seemed ready to relent and to make up, and who was now impatient to go, and had half started. "I believe Towne."

"But weren't the white hairs sticking right underneath our snare, when we saw it?" asked Remsen; and again the complexion of things changed.

"Here comes Russell, now!" said Brade. "Let's leave it to him and Lamson, as Towne says." And, as Russell, in coming up from the home play-ground, was turning towards the school-house, the crowd, foremost of whom Brade was allowed to go, as being one of the parties, and of the parties the one most impatient to have the difficulty settled, joined him; and Brade and Remsen hastily set the case before him, from their side.

"And you got your information from Rainor, did you?"

"And I say," said Towne, "that that rabbit was in our trap, when we came to it."

"And I say that I came there first," said Wilkins, "and he was there when I got there."

"And you all agree to take our judgment?" asked Russell. "Where's Tarleton?"

"*I* will," said Towne, "if you'll only agree to take time to it, and find out all about it." "And I," said Brade; "and I," said Wilkins; "and I," said Remsen.

"There ought to be some person to watch the traps, till you get there," said Towne.

"Well, the fellow for that is Jake Moody; and he'll

do it, — if you could only get him," said Russell, changing to optative or potential, as he thought how little time they could command.

Before the words were out of his mouth, and without regard to time or season, Remsen went off, like a flash.

"Then you're all agreed?" Russell asked, as they reached the door.

All who were there answered "yes;" and the boys went in, crowding and jostling and pushing, to be in time.

Dover and Wilkins were compelled to give way to every other member of the little throng; and then Eugene Augustus Wilkins asserted himself upon Arthur Dover, who was smaller, and succeeded in getting in before him. Before the last boy was fairly in the school-room, Remsen came, out of breath, but answering the inquisitive look of Blake and others by a quick, affirmative, satisfied nod of the head.

Outside stayed sunshine, on the hills behind; and near the door a small litter of hockey-sticks and other remains of boys. A smothered storm of bitterness and angry feeling had come through the door.

CHAPTER XIX.

SOME FIGHTING THAT WILL DISGUST BRUISERS.

ONE of Towne's comrades in trapping was, as will be remembered, one Guy Tarleton. This boy, by some reasoning of his own, had convinced himself that his party had been "choused out" of the best trapping-ground by Remsen and Brade's party, and had borne an undying grudge. He was counted a thick-headed and rather brutal boy; but, in the opinion of the School, had a sort of instinctive readiness and skill in contriving and working against such lesser beasts as lived in trees, in holes, and in stone fences.

He had been noisy in the few minutes after morning-school, before dinner, over the suspicion which had been thrown upon his partners and himself, and proposed to "make those fellows eat dirt." His bluster had had, at that time, little notice taken of it. At table he had been silenced by the Tutor for loud talking. After dinner, the pent-up current of his anger found its way again.

Towne told him that two of the monitors were going to settle about the rabbit, and went off to some out-door occupation, leaving him unappeased.

In the few minutes after dinner he had found out Brade, reading, on one of the stairs, and tried to pick a quarrel with him, but to no purpose; for Brade told him, pleasantly, that "he was reading about Franklin and the icebergs, and wanted to be let alone; that the monitors' settlement would all be fair, and that he, himself, would have no quarrel;" and so kept on, though not quite unruffled, with his book.

Even the words "cowardly" and "mean-spirited," uttered near him, disturbed him only long enough to look up with a contemptuous and impatient smile, and he was instantly at his book again, only begging Tarleton to go off.

Of course, boys began to gather, for they could not have the stairway to themselves; and things went pretty fast, and a great many words were said in a short time, as usual in such cases.

There were alert and wary bystanders, as usual. "Look out!" said one of these, "you'll have old Cornell after you!"

"No," said another, of the same sort, "he isn't in: go ahead!"

So Tarleton went on to say that he wanted satisfaction from Brade, or Remsen, or Peters, — he did not care which; he was not going to be called thief for nothing. And when Brade told him that they had not called his party thieves, it would have been just as good to speak to a bull or a bull-dog. He then insisted that they should say that they were a pack of liars, and so on, in the usual way of blusterers. "He did not care which it was, — some of them must give him satisfaction."

"Remsen and I are the only ones," said Brade: "Peters isn't a strong fellow."

"Then come on," said Tarleton, "let's have a fair fight!"

"No," said Antony, "I've got a particular reason."

"Oh, yes!" said Tarleton, with the most emphatic contempt. "Cowards always have."

"But I *have*," said Brade, notwithstanding the cowardly sound of the words.

"Royal Highness is afraid, and Remsen daresn't, and Peters is only just strong enough to take a licking," said Tarleton, in a triumphant tone.

"There's the bell!" said some one; but, after a moment's hush, it proved a false alarm.

"Leave out Peters," said Brade, "and you may come at me."

Now the bell struck, and at the same instant a boy came down the upper stairs, to the first landing, at one jump, while there was a general stir of the whole group among whom he came so suddenly, and with such risk to their limbs.

"Clear the way here, fellows! What's up now?" said Phil Lamson, who had in this way so abruptly come down to them; and after shoving the belligerent Tarleton, and one or two others, up into a corner, he seized Brade by the shoulders, and, by his own weight and the force with which he was going, made him run before him to the school-room door.

At the door Brade escaped from him, and, turning back, met the little crowd of boys from the stairs, and called to Tarleton, "Remember! I said I would."

If a fight with fists be not quite so fearful a thing to look forward to as the standing up to kill and be killed with pistols or small swords, there is enough about the looking forward to make the blood run faster, and to lay strong hold of the thoughts of a boy with good feelings. So it must have been with Brade.

The bell was still ringing, when Remsen made his appearance, and Brade joined him, and went a little aside with him, but keeping slowly on, toward the school-room door.

"Perhaps two of 'em together will be able to do something!" said Tarleton, sneering, as he went in.

"I've promised to fight Tarleton, and I couldn't help it. I wish I could have kept out of it, but I couldn't," said Brade to his friend.

"Why, he can't whip you, I don't believe, Anty," said Remsen.

"But I wanted to be confirmed," said Antony.

"Oh, well! I don't believe a fight'll stop you, if you don't kill anybody, or gouge his eye out, or something. If *I* had to fight, I'd fight."

"I used to," said Antony; "but I wanted to leave off."

The bell was silent, as he spoke; and every one hurried into the school-room, and to his seat, for the half-hour after dinner.

The Rector of the School, or "Caput," as the boys more often called him, coming in, as the bell stopped, to read out the inflictions, was generally observed of almost all the young eyes, and was thought by the boys to represent dignity and scholarship and authority very well; for though he was, if any thing, rather short, yet he had thick, curling black hair, and a clear eye and ruddy cheek, and a good strong voice.

When the lines were read out for that day, as everybody had been predicting, in the school-phrase, that "Towne would have to catch it" for breaking "bounds," he sat up straight, like a man of mark, before his name was reached, and exchanged side-glances with Wilkins and Will Hirsett, who was always at any one's beck in the school-room. Brade's five lines for tardiness that morning, being his first, were remitted, as usual in such a case.

Ten lines were read for Gaston, for disorder in going to breakfast; and at this Towne nodded his head, emphatically, to one side, with a smile of much content, as if clinching that infliction for the trick played upon him about the Latin for rabbit. Gaston, before he bethought himself, made a half motion as if to rise and protest on the spot, and sat looking indignant. Presently, however, a happy thought seemed to strike him, and he set himself to writing very fast.

And so the list went on: disorder, tardiness, noise in dormitory, misbehavior at table, received their awards. Remsen had his five lines for tardiness. Tarleton came off clear, this time. Towne got double for breaking bounds, and, with all his accumulation of lines before, was in so bad a plight that he now looked quite chop-fallen. Among his other companions in misery was Wilkins, as usual; and Wilkins's look was one combined of surprise and resignation.

Brade's hand went up, but was instantly dropped again: he looked uncertain.

Gaston's hand was instantly up, after the reading-out of the lines, and stayed up; and by this time he had a smile of inward satisfaction on his face. His name was called, and he stood up with a small paper in his hand, and asked leave to read a plea for a mitigation of sentence.

"Well!" said the Rector.

"'My offence, as I understand it, sir,'" said Gaston, reading, "'was giving one of the boys the word *pediculus*, which means lou—'" ("No matter what it means," said the Rector, "or say 'small beast of prey.'") "'for *cuniculus*, which means *rabbit.* Now, with the boys, a rabbit and a hare are the same thing; so, in taking the word *pediculus* (lous—small prey—) for *hair*, I have only used that figure of speech called Synecdoche, which is 'the taking of a part for the whole.' Most respectfully submitted. Edward Gaston.'"

The Tutor, who had doubtless heard the story of the morning, began to turn over leaves, and to try to smooth his face, so that the School began to smile. When Gaston, being perfectly self-possessed and full of fun, stopped, very meaningly, at the word "*hair*," and then at "Synecdoche," little Meadows began to titter; Thompson Walters, a big boy, to giggle; Hirsett (from sympathy, of course), to snicker; Brade, however unpleasant his deeper thoughts might be, could not help smiling; Blake went down upon his desk in a sort of convulsion. The Tutor gave way moderately, as Gaston finished; little Meadows, Walters, Hirsett, Wilkins, Blake, indiscriminately gave way, and the whole School presently was in a roar, except Towne, who looked indignant.

The Rector exchanged a few words with the Tutor, and then announced that although Gaston had mistaken a little the ground of his infliction, yet, considering the ingenuity of his plea, the same figure of speech should be applied to the penalty,—a part for the whole,—leaving him two lines instead of ten. At this a great many congratulatory eyes sought Gaston's, who handsomely acknowledged the indulgence, and sat down very radiant with his success.

At this point, Brade had apparently made up his mind and held up his hand resolutely; his request he brought up to the ear of the Rector; and it was that, as Remsen had to work out lines for tardiness, his own might not be remitted. This was kindly refused.

Tarleton, whose ears were open to what was passing, fashioned, out of white paper, something which, from its shape and size, might be taken to be a paper-knife, or possibly a white feather, and this he set, for a moment, against his head. It must have been recognized in the school as a conventional symbol of something; for Hirsett grinned, and Wilkins, as well as others, looked intelligently at it during the moment that it was displayed.

After denying Brade's request, the Rector, by way of compensation, perhaps, gave him an outlined map of Cisalpine Gaul to make, while Remsen was working out his lines. This the boy did not accept so cheerfully as might have been expected, and, turning a little slowly away, was just in time to see, as he doubtless did, Tarleton's contemptuous look, and the knowing smiles of some others. He blushed most deeply.

The afternoon half-hour went by: the free boys were dismissed, and the others set about their expiatory tasks. Brade put himself strongly to his map of Gaul.

Remsen had the once honored but now discredited old watch on his desk, where many laughed at it; some of whom, perhaps, had wondered, heretofore.

Meantime, while, in the somewhat restless hush and awe of the school-room, after school, as in the silent Lower Places of the old Mythology, tasks were worked out, and fretful shades sought leave, again and again, of the grim Ferryman (here it was Tutor Cornell) to cross the boundary-stream, great things were doing, out of doors.

As soon as school had been let out, Tarleton had begun to grumble near the door, because he and his partners had been accused of stealing another fellow's rabbit. Remsen and Brade, as we have seen, were both in the school-room; and, of that party of trappers, the only free member was the slight and unpractical Alonzo Peters. This day he was a little late in making his appearance, being among the last boys to come out; and there already was Tarleton, in a group of two or three who had no play or business more urgent than to stop and listen to him proclaiming his indignation. Tarleton was a heavy fellow for his size, and not pleasant-looking; and the expression and ways of dog or cat, or man, or other beast, provoking fight, do not make him look better.

Peters came on, with his head in the air, sauntering and abstracted, and was passing by Tarleton and his surrounders, without seeing any thing strange in them, although the by-standers opened out to each side, with their eyes fastened very meaningly on the unsuspecting Peters.

"They'll have to give us satisfaction," Tarleton was saying. "We ain't to lose our trapping-ground, and then be called a thief for nothing."

Saying this, he walked away to one of the heaps of autumn-leaves swept up to be carried away, and kicked it asunder.

"Here's Peters!" said one of the by-standers. "He's one of 'em, but you don't want" —

"Peters ain't any thing!" said Tarleton, contemptuously. "He wouldn't dare to say his hat was his own;" and he looked at him with scorn.

This free use of his name attracted the attention of the abstracted boy, and he stopped. "Why ain't I any thing, Tarleton?" he asked, in a tone very far from warlike, — indeed, in a deprecating and aggrieved voice.

"You're no fellow to stand up for yourself: if a toad jumped up at you, you'd go over," said Tarleton to the admirer of the institution of chivalry.

"Well, I don't like toads," said Peters, taking this for a serious accusation, whether it had been so intended or not, and half confessing, while excusing it. While he spoke, he resorted to the same pile of leaves, and spread them asunder with his foot.

"Oh, well! I mean you're a coward. There's no use talking to you," said Tarleton.

"No, I ain't a coward," said Peters, holding himself up as awkwardly and absurdly as a dromedary or a giraffe. The boys, who were looking on, laughed.

"I don't believe you'd strike a baby back," said Tarleton.

"No, that's just what I wouldn't do," said Peters. He was looking very pale, poor fellow! and yet it's only for his sake, and certainly not for Tarleton's sake, or for our own pleasure, that we write this part of our story. "And I don't approve of bringing people all up, because one says another's wrong: it isn't the right way. But who's done any thing to you, I should like to know?"

"I don't like to be called thief, just at this present moment," said Tarleton, walking up to him, with his two fists down at his sides, like fighters in drawings, and very likely in real life.

"I didn't call you a thief," said Peters, drawing backward.

It must be said, for the witnesses of the scene, that they did nothing to help on a fight, or, as it would most likely prove, a flogging for poor Peters.

"A pretty fellow you are, to be talking about knights, when they were fighting all the time, and you daresn't strike your shadow!" said Tarleton, as scornfully as Goliath of Gath.

"I don't want to be swollen up, and all black and blue," answered Peters. "What good does *that* do? You know very well it'll all be settled right; and nobody's hurting you at all."

"That's the way you like it!" said Tarleton. "You'd better go, and send somebody else. Brade's showing a pretty big white feather: a little piece of it'll do for you."

"I ain't a bit more afraid'n anybody else, and everybody knows Brade isn't a coward," said the pale, awkward fellow: "but I don't see what good fighting'll do."

"Some of you have got to take back about our being thieves, or else you'll all have to stand up to it. You'd better leave it to somebody else, that ain't a coward," said Tarleton.

"Oh, no!" said Peters, as pale as possible, and with a dampness on his forehead: "if anybody's got to do it, I may as well as anybody. I'd rather do it than get out of the way, and leave it for anybody, as if I was a coward." The boy, judged by his looks and voice, seemed not very far from tears; but his speech was as stout as if he were master of all arts of attack and defence, and ready to use them the next moment.

"Well, what you've got to do is just to say you know we didn't steal your rabbit, and you fellows lied;" said Tarleton, laying down pretty hard terms.

This, of course, Peters, though pale as a sheet, refused. Judged by the sight, Alonzo Peters might have been thought a flimsy fellow; and here he was, a sort of champion for two others.

"Well, come on then!" said Tarleton, setting off up the hill.

Peters went silently along; and the boys, who had already given their time to listen to the preliminary discussion in words, showed great alacrity in giving more of it to the final discussion now proposed with fists.

"Old Wilson will find you out, and you'll have 'The Cap' down on you," said one of these attendants, consolingly, while he walked.

The two principals (if our flimsily-made and almost feeble-looking friend, Alonzo Peters, could be called a principal) went on in silence, Peters a little behind, but now and then, with his quick, uneven steps, getting on close to Tarleton, and then falling back. Neither Brade nor Remsen appeared, and Peters must meet the occasion.

The accompanying boys, leaving the two others to keep silence, if they would, talked pretty freely.

"'Tain't fair, anyhow, Wadham," said one, whom the reader will recognize by his mouth and ears as Hirsett. "Tarleton's twice as big as Peters any day,"—a statement not literally true, if one judged by the eye, for Peters was the taller, though the other might a good deal outweigh him.

"But didn't old Pete stick up for himself? I tell you!" said Wadham, in a sentence of mixed construction. "Who'd ever ha' thought it was in him?"

Certainly the ungainly and almost shambling admirer of knights and their doings seemed a very poor match for the closely-knit, square-built fellow, who was leading the way to a convenient field of battle. Moreover, while they were speaking, Peters might have been heard saying, "I don't see what good there is in banging and beating!"

There was a large oak standing not far behind the gymnasium, spreading over a broad stretch of what in summer was greensward, and was now brown sod, — a favorite lounging-place for the boys during all the time of out-door games. Under this stalwart tree was room enough for all the clothing stripped off for base-ball; and in any bright day of colder weather, when the ground at its foot was fit, it has been still a favorite resort for its summer friends, because it haughtily holds fast its strong leaves against the fury of all winter winds, both damp and dry, and looks like a great shelter, when of its weaker neighbors Dante's simple story has come true, —

> "Come d'autunno si levan le foglie,
> L'una appresso dell' altra, infin che il ramo
> Rende alla terra tutte le sue spoglie." *

Most boys care little for natural objects, which only stand still, and can do nothing for them. This tree was nearer than common trees to the Bartholomeans.

* As by the autumn winds the leaves are lifted,
One after other, from the struggling bough,
Till to the earth all its green spoils are drifted.
Inferno, Canto iii.

"Old Quercus" the boys affectionately called it, out of their books; and, of course, soon, if not from the outset, gave to its surname a twist into English pronunciation, which made two short words of it, and which led Jake Moody to say that "he'd heard himself called a 'queer cuss' a hundred times; but he didn't know what these boys wanted to go and call that tree so for." Near this fine old forest tree was a little group of three or four evergreens, and straight on toward this Tarleton strode, without stopping and without further speech. He threw off, hastily, his jacket under the tree, as he passed, and went straight on, till he got the little clump of evergreens between him and the West Road, from which, though at a little distance, there was nothing else to hide him.

"Now," said he, "if the fellow's got the heart of a mouse as big as your thumb, let him show it! I'm ready for him."

Peters was not yet ready; for he fumbled at the buttons of his jacket, and tried, more than once, to get it off before it was unbuttoned.

"I don't suppose I *have* got one," he answered to his adversary's challenge; "but I guess I've got the heart of a boy, as I ought to have."

"I tell you what," said Wadham, "that chap's got grit in him! — Don't get flurried, Peters! Let me help you;" and he began to unbutton Peters's jacket for him, as the boy's own fingers found it hard to do.

"I don't want to fight a bit," said this self-offering champion; "and I don't see any good in it: but I ain't a coward, — he'll find *that* out. I won't run away, and let others take it;" and he half sobbed as he spoke, while Tarleton seemed as steady as the old tree itself.

"Now," said Peters, moving up, as soon as he was rid of his coat, to the other, who was waiting for him, "what do you want to fight for?"

"Oh! I don't," said Tarleton, in answer to this last appeal, "I only just want to box a baby's ears;" and he gave Peters a very solid slap on the side of the head as he spoke.

Peters staggered, but came back again, facing his antagonist. "Don't do that again!" he said; but without making any assault, or even putting himself in a posture of defence.

Meantime, neither Brade nor Remsen nor any one else came near.

"No, I won't do that again," said the self-possessed Tarleton. "I'll try this;" and he struck him on the other side of the head a heavy blow, which sent the victim staggering in the other direction.

"I told you not to do that!" sobbed Peters, recovering himself, and coming back face to face with the fighter. Then, suddenly straightening himself and throwing back his head, he followed his instinct, rushed forward, and, instead of striking loose, wild blows, flung his long arms round the other boy, who was acting without the least caution and was not at all prepared for any such movement. Immediately, the long arms being locked behind Tarleton's back, held him, like the hug of a cuttle-fish, just above the elbow, so that he could not lift a hand.

Tarleton, thus unexpectedly seized, made a sudden and violent effort to break out of it, but, tripping backwards as he did so, fell to the ground, with Peters on top of him. The on-lookers ran up.

"Don't touch 'em!" cried Wadham, — an injunction

which neither of the others seemed inclined to violate. "Old Peters will take care of himself."

On the ground the fighter struggled fiercely; but the long arms held him fast. "Keep still, now, — you'd better!" said Peters.

"This ain't fighting!" cried Tarleton, from below.

"Why ain't it? It's my way of fighting," answered Peters, whose hands and arms, between the ground and the other's body, must have been hurt in the struggle. "You fought your way, and I fought my way. I showed you I wasn't afraid."

"You daresn't face me!" said Tarleton. "Let me up!"

Alonzo Peters, however, seemed to know what he was about, and answered with spirit, —

"No, I won't! I won't let go till my arms come off. I'm facing you now;" and he set his teeth together, and held on with new strength. The other, being thus grappled, grew more and more indignant and furious to no purpose; and it may be supposed that, all this time, his hair was tangling with dirt and grass and chips, and his neck sharing in the discomfort.

"You shall get up when you promise to let us alone," said the upper one, who, if he could only keep his place and keep the other down, was, to all intents, conqueror, and could dictate his own terms.

Of the three partners, it was Peters who was champion.

Whether Tarleton's writhings might not, by and by, have changed the condition of things, and brought him to the top, is a question; but just now there seemed little chance of this, for Peters, with his teeth set, was exerting more will than strength of muscle, so long as he could keep his wits about him. So far, although the two had worked themselves about on the ground a good deal, and had ruffled the grass and disordered their own clothing, it seemed to have been done chiefly at Tarleton's cost; and, so closely had his grappler clung to him, that he was still bound as fast as ever, and was still as flat on the ground.

At this moment one of the by-standers raised the cry, "There's the Cap!" and all but the two combatants scattered hastily.

"Let me up, you coward!" cried Tarleton. "You want me to be caught," — speaking of himself as if he were the only one concerned, as, in his own eyes, perhaps, he was.

Peters saw things differently.

"I shall be caught myself, shan't I?" he said. "You take that back, and promise not to insult us, nor meddle with us, and I'll do it."

Many an abusive and many a sulky answer came from Tarleton first, and one promise ending in "but —" At length, as solid steps were heard approaching, the promise was given as the conquering Peters dictated it, and with no reservation. Now Peters relaxed his hold, and the two got up.

"I'm your witness, Peters," said a strong, young voice; and Russell, the monitor, appeared, ruddy and tall and muscular.

"The Caput sent me up," he said. "He saw you two fellows."

Russell then quietly helped the two to right themselves, ridding Tarleton's hair of some of its gatherings from the ground, and smoothing Peters. Beginnings of angry words he cut off short.

The conflict was over; and the chief bodily harm

had been done to Peters, both of whose cheeks were swollen, and whose hands were a good deal scratched.

Meanwhile the late on-lookers, scattered just as the contest was very near its end, must have spread abroad their reports of it as they fled; for now, finding that only Russell, a monitor, and not the Rector, had gone to the scene of the battle, a good many boys — some at full speed — were making the best of their way to the spot.

Will Hirsett and Dover, with others, were walking over the scene of the encounter. Not yet were Towne and Wilkins, free from their imprisonment in the school-room, to be found in this gathering, in which they had a nearer interest than most others; nor were Remsen and Brade to be seen. Will Hirsett and Dover were scrutinizing the ground.

"Here's where old Tarleton tipped right over backwards," said Hirsett, beginning to do the honors of the place and share his better knowledge with the less fortunate; "and, I tell you, if old Peters didn't hang on to him!" he continued, in that style of mixed construction in which boys surpass all their examples in the classics. "Look how they scraped the grass up! didn't they?"

"What was it about?" asked Meadows, who brought to the field the curiosity which animated Old Caspar's little grandchild Wilhelmine about the great Battle of Blenheim.

"Why, you know," said the young historian of Quercus-fight, "Remsen and Brade and old Peters said they lost their rabbit, and Tarleton wanted to fight somebody for calling him a thief; and so Peters wouldn't back out, and he took it for all three of 'em; an' he got old Tarleton down" —

"Which beat?" "Which beat?" asked several eager voices. "Yes, which beat?" repeated Meadows, smoothing over with his foot some of the ruffled grass, and having his eyes fixed on the two combatants, while he spoke to Hirsett. "Did Peters give in?"

"No! I didn't," answered the undaunted champion for himself; "ask Russell."

"He was on top when I came," answered Russell, giving the fact in the form least offensive to the other party.

"Oh, well! it wasn't a fair fight: I tripped up," said Tarleton.

"Peters got the best of it, that time," said Russell; and Peters's queer eyes proudly sought the recognition of the cluster of boys who surrounded them.

"It was only chance that I went down. I could flog him, any day: he daresn't try it over again," said the warlike and unsatisfied Tarleton.

"I never wanted to fight," said Peters, as honestly as before; "but I wa'n't afraid of being whipped,—you found that out. I didn't wait for Remsen and Brade."

"Hooray for old Peters!" cried Wadham. "The prince of fire-eaters," added Meadows, who, as the reader already knows, had a studious and literary turn, and had doubtless read The Poets. Then the mixed multitude (half a dozen or so of the younger-form-boys) took up the completed couplet, in chorus, half-laughing:—

"Hooray for old Peters,
The prince of fire-eaters!"

And the whole company began to follow from the field the two late combatants, who were walking away, each by himself, but both keeping in company with Russell.

As the unwelcome song of triumph rose from the boys behind, and urged its quick waves of sound into the ears of the one whom it did not honor, he took it hardly, and repeated his indirect challenge to a renewal of the fight. This time the Monitor took it up.

"Look here, Tarleton!" he said: "we've had enough of fighting. It isn't the way of this School: it isn't Christian. If a fellow's got any wrong, it's easy to get it made right without going to fisticuffs about it. Every fellow, except you, has agreed to leave that about the hare or rabbit to two, to find out all about it, and we've been down already seeing to it. What's anybody going to find out, any way, by fighting about a thing?" he concluded.

Tarleton, without answering, turned as if he had forgotten something, and went back.

CHAPTER XX.

WHAT HAPPENED TO REMSEN'S WATCH, AND TARLETON'S EXPERIENCE.

If the looking forward to a battle brings with it a crowding of the brain and a clanging in the breast, what a change does victory (especially one almost harmless to both parties) bring! What a playing about the casing of the heart by the late stormy and turbid tide of blood! What a happy tingling, all over the body, by things hurrying to get back into their old ways!

The triumphant throng is half-way down the slope toward the house.

Here Peters, the awkward hero of the day, suddenly started forward; for, as they were coming down, they saw in front of them the storm-house-door open, and Remsen and Brade sallying forth. Having hurried a little way forward toward them, Peters then seemed to falter in his purpose, and stopped.

Remsen was swinging, with one hand, by its long chain, what any eye, almost, in the School could recognize afar, the famous time-piece of his forefathers, and apparently threatening to let it go; but the attention of both Remsen and his companion was soon drawn to the unusual appearance of the little throng which was approaching them. The newly made triumphal song was raised with much vigor by the accompanying choristers as the two parties approached each other.

While Brade and Remsen questioned, Alonzo Peters, like a modest hero, had withdrawn a little, as if conscious of having deserved well of them and of the community. The story was told with a little plain web from Russell, and little varied and fanciful bits of warp from members of the chorus. The story, of course, culminated in the unexpected but entire success of Peters.

"How did he get into it?" asked Remsen, looking at Peters in the new character of a hero in single combat, but taking things in a business-like way.

Wadham and Hirsett both undertook to answer, as having had a large share in the encounter by looking on at it.

"That trapping business;" said one. "He said you three were liars;" added the other, leaving the subject of his sentence a little hard to define. "He wanted Peters to confess you were liars."

"What a fool he was, not to wait till we got out! He might have got an awful licking;" said Remsen, as unsympathizingly critical as if Peters were a thousand miles off in space, and further off in spirit.

The modest and withdrawing hero was quick to hear this disparaging speech. "I showed I wasn't a coward," he said: "I stood up for everybody." Having said so much, he began to walk away by himself. Russell looked after him, and said, —

"He's a spunky old fellow, though, Remsen; and he did it for you."

"He's a regular old brick!" said Wadham, not so much seeking novelty as fitness in his phrase. "If you'd seen him walk up!"

"I think *you* ought to speak pretty well of him, Remsen," said Russell.

"Well," said Remsen, smiling not ill-naturedly, and addressing the younger by-standers, "tell him I think he's as brave as Archimedes — or Achilles — and William Wallace, and Robert Bruce."

Meadows, laughing at Remsen's "Archimedes," set off to give the message with much alacrity, as if he thought that Peters would enjoy it as much as himself.

Now that every thing connected with the late battle had been done with, Russell turned to Remsen, who was still carrying the heirloom swinging by its chain, and said curiously, "Oh, let's see the old watch!" and, as Remsen held it up, Russell remarked upon the carvings and lettering of its face, turning the long-time implement round. "What does ἐξαγορεύσατε (*exagoreusate*) mean?" he asked, reading the very word, most likely, which Mr. Don had carefully copied.

"My grandfather told me," said Remsen, "it was out of the Bible, and meant 'redeeming,' or something."

"Ho!" said Will Hirsett, who, though young in years, was already a little advanced in his acquaintance with Language, "twig the old turnip!" and he, too, stared with all his eyes.

Others came up, and there was quite a gathering about the venerable relic.

"Who wants to buy?" asked the owner. "This old thing got me kept in to-day."

He did not add what very likely had touched him more than any thing, that the old thing had become a laughing-stock, that day.

A timid voice from Meadows, already back at the

outskirts, asked what the owner would take for it. Many curious eyes gazed upon the small mass of machinery, incased in glass and silver, which had timed, most likely, many a meal, and possibly some lovers' meetings; had been held to the delighted ear of many a toddler, and allowed to go to his mouth without fear of its getting into his throat.

"Ain't it a buster?" asked Will Hirsett, keeping safely outside of any competition or curious questioning about its market-worth, — perhaps because he had no money, perhaps because he had no faith in Remsen's intention of selling his heirloom.

"Will you sell it?" asked Meadows.

"No!" said Remsen. "Here goes!" And, in spite of several outcries, such as "I wouldn't," from Russell, and "Oh, don't!" "Give it to a fellow!" "Give it to me!" from younger boys, he whirled it out of his hand, and it struck with a thud, and a rattle or jingle, on the bank near the gymnasium.

"Oh, too bad! wasn't it?" said Meadows and others; and a race began toward the spot where the long-valued, but just now dishonored, relic had fallen.

"Let it alone!" said Remsen; and all but little Meadows stopped short of the place. He went up to it, and took a good look at it, as it lay.

"Shall I take it, and get it mended?" asked Meadows; but the owner said, "No!" without giving any explanation of his unwillingness to have any one else own what he himself was willing to throw away.

Such things — indeed, most things — make only a short-lived impression upon boys, even as upon men. The by-standers began to disperse, remarking Remsen's queer way of treating his watch: "If he didn't care any more for it than to fling it away, why shouldn't he let another fellow have it, that would take care of it?"

"I shouldn't think Brade would let him," said Hirsett, "because he liked it so."

"Where *is* Brade?" asked Wadham. "He isn't there.—He *was* there."

"Oh, yes! I saw him there," said Meadows.

But when they looked, with all their eyes, he was not there.

Before this time the famous Peters had come back, looking now contented and restored to every-day life; and the knot of boys, considerate (like men) of the lustre that was fresh on him just now, stopped to give him an account of the treatment of the historic timepiece, and pointed to the spot where it was lying. Thereupon Peters, with his head in the air, walked slowly up to the borders of the little knot, which still stood, of that which had been gathered about Russell and Remsen and the watch, and there stood looking first over toward the rejected heirloom, and then toward the doer of the strange deed, as if to establish some fanciful explanation between them.

When Brade appeared presently, coming from the direction of the gymnasium, Peters ran to him, with much alacrity, and gave him, volubly, such information as he himself had gained.

Remsen, who heard it, laughed at Peters's manner, or at what he said, but did not interfere; and Brade, who could hardly forget with what pride and confidence, no longer ago than that morning, he had borne the long-descended relic in his pocket, ran to the spot, with Peters following, while Remsen and Russell walked leisurely up to join them.

Brade looked at it, for a moment, as it lay in the brown turf, on its back, like a stranded Gallipagos turtle, with his upper shell knocked in. He kneeled and put his ear to it, and proclaimed that it was "all going;" for the stout old thing had kept its honest "works" together, and with a steady ticking was doing its best to bear up. He took it tenderly in hand, and looked it over carefully, and put it carefully in his pocket.

If Remsen had been inclined to say any thing about this disposition of the watch, something even more pressing called his attention.

"What's happened to you, Bradey?" he asked of his friend, who was hot and flushed, and looking as if he might have fallen in the gymnasium. "You're hurt, man! How did you do it?"

"Oh, it isn't any thing. It doesn't hurt: it's only a little scratch," said Brade. "Does it show much?" And, putting his hand to his face, he examined it as if to see whether any blood had come away.

"What ails Tarleton?" Russell asked, while Remsen was occupied; for Tarleton might be seen coming down also, but walking fast over toward the kitchen part of the house, and holding a handkerchief over his face.

Boys' lives have a great many happenings; for boys are almost always trying at one or other of all the laws of the universe, and practising with one or more of the great elements of things. So they are never surprised at what happens to each other.

Russell walked away to meet or overtake Tarleton, and the others took the same direction, at different rates of speed. The by-standers (for we still have a part of our chorus with us) went fast, of course, to be first on the spot. The principals — as Remsen and Brade, and (for the present, at least) Peters — followed more slowly.

Tarleton had stopped at a pump which stood near one of the doors, and was washing his face.

"Let me see, a minute, will you?" said Russell, kindly, coming up and putting his hand under the boy's forehead, and lifting up his face. The poor fellow, what with one or more black eyes, and a nose out of shape, and lips all swollen, and a general smearing of blood, was, certainly, a very sorry sight to see, and our "chorus" looked at him in wonder, and then proceeded to do as Quintus Horatius Flaccus advises all right-minded choruses to do: they began to pity the wretched, and to speculate about the case.

"He's got a bad face, hasn't he?" said Meadows. "Did Peters do all that to him?"

"No, I don't believe," said the conquering Peters, "I hurt him so much as that: I didn't mean to. I don't believe I did. Oh, no! I'm almost sure I never did. It almost makes me sick."

The bruised and disfigured object of their pity here uttered himself, but very obscurely, because the gates of his speech would not open very readily; but he seemed to say, turning to these speakers, "Do clear out!" or "You clear out! will you?" an injunction with which they partly complied, by withdrawing into themselves, and keeping silence.

"I'll get something for you," said Russell. "Don't wash any thing except just the blood;" and, after a moment's disappearance, came back with Mr. Stout, who brought in his hand a piece of raw beef.

"Fell right against two fists, I suppose, and hit just on his face. This had ought to be goose-skin or ass-hide, by good rights," said the head man, not unkindly; and some of the boys, accustomed to his style of satire, laughed. He added, gravely: "but this'll have to do: it's the best I've got."

How Tarleton came to this condition our faithful chorus of intelligent by-standers have not settled, and are still discussing, with many looks at Brade.

Russell, turning for a moment from his attendance, took up the public expectation by announcing the Referees' report, immediately; then wrapped the meat in a handkerchief, and led off the disfigured Tarleton to the house.

Mr. Stout made this reflection: —

"The strangest piece of the business is, that where there's one chap that's met with an accident like that, there's always another, close by, that's just like him, — and mebbe more so, — and perhaps neither one of 'em can tell how they got it."

He had not scrutinized the group of boys, to see whether this general principle would apply to any of them, but, without looking, he said, —

"I see Brade has had a little tumble, too. I suppose there's been some blowing. High winds are apt to bring a good many things down."

Saying this, Mr. Stout took his wheelbarrow and rake, which were close at hand, and went about gathering his fallen leaves, of which one pile, at least, we know to have been disturbed during the wordy encounter of Tarleton and Peters.

"Here come the Monitors!" said the crowd, as Russell and Lamson drew near, followed by Towne. And now all was expectation.

"Fellows!" said Russell, "I see all but Tarleton are here" —

"If he hadn't been a fool, he'd have been here, too," said Towne.

Russell went on: "We've been to the ground. Jake Moody had taken his dinner down, and been there all day. We found Remsen and Brade's track down and back from the fence, — Jake showed it. Then there was one down by their snare, where Rainor says he came, and a track just like it from there to Tarleton's trap, and none the other way. Rainor's gone away. We think none of the fellows ever went to any trap but their own; but probably Rainor knows about it, if any one."

"I didn't believe they ever did!" said Brade, giving his hand to Towne, who shook it heartily. Remsen assented, without shaking hands.

No one could make out why Rainor should have put one party's hare into the other party's trap; but everybody reserved his judgment.

The crowd dispersed, — Brade loitering near Russell, — and soon these two had a clear place to themselves, with no one in sight except Mr. Stout; and he was a little way off.

CHAPTER XXI.

THE CAPUT MEETS BRADE.

When the two boys found themselves alone, as they were left in the last chapter, Russell turned to Brade, and asked:—

"Did *you* do that to Tarleton?"

"Yes; and I feel ashamed of pounding into a fellow; only then I couldn't help it," said Brade, apologetically. "He called me all sorts of names, and abused us all, and said he'd whip Peters or any of us he could get hold of; and at last I had to tell him to let Peters alone, and he might fight me. But he took hold of Peters, you know; and when I went up there, he came at me in an awful way. He gave me this knock before I stirred. I had to hit him; and I'm sure I did not give him more than half a dozen licks before he gave out, and said I 'didn't let him have a chance.'"

"Well, it'll do him good, perhaps. It's his own fault," said Russell.

A new voice spoke:—

"Tarleton's got a pretty hard way o' gettin' a false face,"* said Mr. Stout, who, following his rake, had come near them before they were aware, but who said his say, as if not at all connected with their conversation. "It wouldn't cost much money to buy one, at a

* Mask.

store; and I guess he'd be just as well satisfied, and it would do him just as much good." And Mr. Stout moved on at his work.

"Now, what do you think about it, Russell? I didn't want to fight," said Brade, seriously.

"Oh! I think he won't show it much in the course of an hour or two," said Russell, "and it will do him good."

"But it isn't like a Christian to fight," said Brade. "I know that, very well; and I wanted to be fit to be confirmed! But *can* you help it, always?" Here, after a pause, he shook his head, and added: "you can't, can you?"

He was evidently appealing as to an older and wiser Christian than himself.

"I don't suppose you can always keep out of it," Russell answered. "It isn't Christian to be quarrelsome, or to abuse another fellow, or to be a tyrant; but you may get into it by taking another fellow's part, or you may have to defend yourself; and, if you don't want to, or only do it in self-defence, why I suppose it'll be looked over, — and if you're sorry for it," he added, as if he had forgotten a part of his argument. "You know it's the heart, Brade: it mustn't be in your heart."

"I'm sure it isn't in my heart," Antony said, decisively; "that I'm sure: it isn't in my heart."

"You get a chance and go and ask the Caput. You can talk to him as easily as you can to me," said his adviser.

"But I couldn't tell him about Tarleton?"

"He wouldn't ask you about any boy; but he'll go into it, and he'll tell you every thing."

There was a short silence after these words, while Brade stood thinking. Then he said, "I'll try," and they parted.

Opportunities, in this world, often come very timely to our wants; and so Brade found it now. He had scarcely walked a dozen steps, after leaving Russell, before the Rector of the School came suddenly upon him, and called him by name, as he was slowly walking and thinking.

"Let's go on together," said the Rector.

So here was a chance for the boy.

"Well, Antony, school-life seems to agree with you pretty well. Was it Remsen's family-watch that made the mistake about time, this morning? The hands were caught together? Old fellows (or young fellows) mustn't fold their hands in the midst of things, — at any rate, if they do, people must look to other guides. But, if that's the only fault, it'll be easily set right, in the watch. I suppose trapping, just now, doesn't leave time for the 'Notes on Cæsar'?"

"I found the men's notes were better," answered the boy, with a pleasant laugh, "and so I stopped."

"Well, that's just honest modesty. I suppose the men's notes *were* better, no doubt. Yours were very good practice, though," said the Rector. "I'd keep on making notes upon things as they come, in lessons, and reading, and any thing. Sometimes even boys strike out something good; and, at any rate, they learn to handle things for themselves."

"I always keep a sort of a note-book," said Antony, modestly.

"So do; and tell me about your notes, sometimes," said the Caput, — "will you?"

They had turned the corner of the gymnasium, and had passed "Quercus," and were now on the field of the late conflicts. The spot must have urged upon Tarleton's unwilling antagonist the question that he was longing to ask.

As they crossed the ground on which Peters had won his unbloody laurels, and on which Tarleton had been a second time worsted, not without blood, the Rector's foot slipped on the damp earth. He probably had not forgotten that the fighting of an hour or two before, had been done here, and was not speaking altogether at random, when he said, —

"You haven't read, yet, about Nisus slipping in the gore?"

It was too dark to have seen any thing, unless very showy; and if Brade had thought of it, for an instant, he might have felt sure that any slight blood drawn in his encounter with Tarleton would hardly have fallen to the ground at all, or, if it had reached the sod, would have kept no place upon it; but his voice shook a little, as he answered hastily, —

"I've heard the Fourth read it, sir, about the boxers. It was pretty brutal, wasn't it?"

"Oh! Nisus wasn't one of the fighters: he was running a race, and slipped in the blood of a victim. That fighting was pretty horrible and disgusting work."

Now was Antony's chance, and he used it.

"If that had been now, sir, those fighters couldn't have been Christians?" he asked; and while he asked turned his face over towards the horizon, as if the answer did not concern him much.

"I think not," said the Rector. "We excuse wars,

because nations make their people go into them: they ought to have been done away with eighteen hundred years ago. Mangling and slaughtering honest husbands and sons is too wickedly foolish to think of, quietly. Fighting, for the love of it, or for anger, or for mastery, is brute's work. If you see a beast attack a person, you may fight him; if you see a ruffian attack a person, he's no better; if a ruffian attacks you, you may knock him off."

"That's all I did," said Brade, without thinking, his spirits rose so suddenly. The Rector did not show any consciousness of the slip.

"I should like to be confirmed, sir," said Antony, with a steady voice, "if you think I'm fit," and so brought his timid desire to a head, at once.

To those who serve at heavenly altars; to those who are, by ordination or occasion, ambassadors for Christ to souls of others; to those who love God, or believe in God; to those who have any awe for God's breath of life in the young, a call like this is both holy and touching. It is the seeking of the soul, already, when blind and helpless, blessed and gifted by its Maker and Redeemer, to come consciously into communion with Him. The moments in which this vital work is going on are moments of trembling precaution and hope, and waiting, until the soul, still very new to our manhood, has laid hold, and steadied itself, and is walking in the Spirit.

"Of course, Antony, if you have the right understanding and feeling about it, it's just what you ought to desire, of all things," said his spiritual pastor. "Let's have a very high notion of it. The Christian life is the living in the Spirit, instead of the flesh; and 'the Spirit' is the Holy Spirit. You were taken into God's family before you knew any thing, and now you're to declare openly — being old enough to know — that you choose God's life, of yourself, and want to live in it for ever. That's what you're doing, my young brother; and the Spirit takes part in it, and His part He'll do."

"That's just what I want to do, — whatever is to be done," said Brade, simply. "God will have to help me, I know; and He will do that, of course. He helps everybody."

"Of course He will. It's only through the Spirit that we can live that life; and He dwells in the Church, for ever, to be with those that are living that life. Jesus, our Lord, *is* that Life, and the Raising-up from the Dead; and it's the Spirit that enables us to partake of Christ, in worship, and in self-denial, and in kind doings, and in the great commemorative sacrifice of the Lord's Supper. 'He that eateth my flesh and drinketh my blood hath everlasting life, and I will raise him up at the Last Day.' All that's as high as it can be."

"And what'll I have to do?" asked Brade, as simply as before.

"What *great thing*, to match this great thing?" said the Rector, smiling, as one might judge from his voice. "Just what the Catechism teaches about Baptism, that Confirmation follows: — 'Repentance, whereby we forsake sin, and Faith, whereby we steadfastly believe the promises of God;' and the Spirit works these in us; and we must pray to get the Spirit; and it is He that teaches us to pray. You see that, the moment we begin, He does it for us by making us do it."

They had been drawing nearer, in the dusk, to the noise of the play-ground, though they had walked slowly. The rush of the tireless foot-ball kickers could be seen, as well as heard, through the murk. The Rector changed the subject of the conversation.

"We haven't had any more of the *distinguished stranger?*" he said.

Brade laughed, as he answered, "No, sir. The boys made plenty of talk out of that."

"Well, we've got great times coming, — Mrs. Wadham's party and Benefactors' Day. Every invited boy, with a good record, shall go to Mrs. Wadham's."

Then, sending the boy off happy to his fellows, the Rector kept on in his walk.

CHAPTER XXII.

THE RECTOR OF THE PARISH AND ONE OF HIS PEOPLE.

In the middle of one of the afternoons — a beautiful afternoon — there was driving slowly down what is called West Road one who, if judged by his appointments of dress and horse and buggy, and his way of saluting and being saluted by a neighbor or two, felt himself to be, and doubtless was, a noted man of Eastham. In short, it was no other than Mr. Thomas Parmenter.

As he was just coming to the turn by the wood from which we see out over the valley to the hills and the one mountain-top beyond the Gap, a gentleman bounded over the rail-fence at that place to the bank above the road, startling the horse, and bringing him to a stand-still. This gentleman was tall, large, — a little solid and heavy, perhaps, but strong and healthy, as his action and figure and cheek and eye all showed. His dress was that of a clergyman, ending in good thick-soled shoes, now pretty dusty.

If both parties had timed the meeting, they could not have met more exactly; but the walker apparently had his thoughts upon the landscape; for, in coming over the fence, he turned toward the open West, and it was only after a steadfast look to the hills and sky that he became aware of horse-hoofs and wheels, and the man's voice; then, turning to the driver, whose horse seemed to be recovering himself from a short fright, but was now only backing on his legs, and starting with pricked-up ears and moving nostril, saluted him cheerily and apologetically: —

"Oh! Pardon! How are you, sir?" he said, lifting by the rim a soft felt hat, and showing dark, auburn, curling hair. Do you see that atmosphere? (I wish we had a good English word.) It's happiness to breathe it, isn't it? And only look at those hills! as if they were just standing still to enjoy themselves! That's for my little cripple, Billy Carnes" (showing his coat-pocket full of what, from shape and sound, might be supposed to be nuts), "and this" (opening the breast of his coat, and showing fern-leaves) "is for poor Mrs. Rainor."

Whatever might be the reason, there was no corresponding flow of kindliness from the other party to the meeting, who was pretty evidently in a graver humor; nor had his blood been wholesomely stirred up and warmed like the parson's. After exchanging salutations, he had listened patiently while the clergyman uttered his cheery speech, assenting with "Very fine, sir," to that part about the landscape; and, when it was done, said, smiling rather ironically, "You're quite an athlete, sir (I believe that's the word). I don't know what our friend Mrs. Weatherbee would say to such agility. — She's a candidate for Confirmation, I believe?"

"How do you mean: 'What would she think?'" asked the clergyman; then added, good-naturedly, "You mean, How would she like to do it herself? I can easily conceive of her objecting."

The other explained himself: —

"I didn't know whether, with her habits, she might consider the Rector altogether clerical."

"What!" asked the active parson, with look and tone of amused astonishment. "Pooh!"

"She's been brought up an Orthodox,* you know," answered the driver. Then, after a preparatory smile, he said, "I believe she thinks Mr. Manson's *sermons* are so short she can't make head or tail of 'em. She's more critical, perhaps, than old Church people."

"Mr. Manson must look out," answered the Rector again, good-naturedly; "but I think Mrs. Weatherbee and I'll get along pretty well together."

The parishioner had not yet said all that he had in his mind.

"The *Church Post* is quite satirical, in its last number, I'm told," he said, touching his horse with the snapper of his whip; making him start, and then holding him in. "You know, of course, better than I can tell you. You know every thing that comes out in it, I suppose. That's the understanding, I believe."

"Of course, I'm supposed to, and bound to, and do, generally," said Mr. Manson.

Mr. Parmenter continued: —

"The article I refer to is upon influential laymen, I believe. The title is not very elegant, — 'Lay-popes and Nincom-popes,' or some such word, though not very choice language, I should think. Perhaps you've read it, sir?"

"Certainly," answered Mr. Manson, smiling.

"I should think it might be somewhat unwise to assail the great lay-body, which supports the Church,

* In New England, "Orthodox" means Trinitarian Congregationalist.

and furnishes the means for all its work, and all its growth," said the objector.

"I should think so, too," Mr. Manson answered, still smiling.

"Laymen don't like to be called asses; and the great business-men of the country consider themselves as having some judgment, and being fit to exercise some influence."

"To be sure," said Mr. Manson; "but you don't object to asses being called asses? and you don't object to silly actions being treated as silly, do you? I don't know what a paper would be worth, that could not tell the truth?"

"Then I understand you to approve the sentiments of that article?"

"I wrote it," said the hearty priest, laughing; "but, Mr. Parmenter, let's understand one another: attacking abuses or wrongs isn't attacking the laity, — it isn't attacking persons at all. Only, if you fired at offences that nobody was doing, you'd waste ammunition. Sometimes a man's so close to a thing that he gets hit with it, to be sure: that can't be helped, and there's no reason to be sorry for it. It'll do 'em good."

"Sometimes no pains are taken to make distinctions where laymen are using a legitimate influence," said Mr. Parmenter, "and the public are apt to look upon it as a personal attack."

"But you speak as if you'd been hurt: you don't feel personally aggrieved, do you?" asked the cheery Rector-and-Editor, upon whom Mr. Parmenter's steady gravity and tone of grievance began to make impression.

"I can scarcely suppose that the Rector of this parish

would make an attack on *me*," said Mr. Parmenter, with dignity. "The parish would all take it home to themselves, if the attack *was* made, — as one man."

The cheery priest easily recovered his equanimity. Here he laughed, as he answered, in a jesting tone, —

"There *is* only about one man of them, altogether, to 'take it home.'" Then, with a good-natured attempt to overcome Mr. Parmenter's gravity, he added, in the same strain, —

"Happily our constituency isn't very large, — counting the six men that don't yet come to church, with the two that have begun to."

Mr. Parmenter seemed to be in no humor for jests upon so serious a subject. He answered: —

"That's rather a strong way of putting it, I think. Our parish is growing: the soil is uncongenial, but the growth is steady. I don't know what the result of the last year or two has been; but it was counted a very respectable parish when it was put into your hands. A parish that contributed, if I recollect rightly, last year, one hundred and eighty-seven dollars and over — forty-three cents, I think — to diocesan missions, isn't insignificant, I should say."

This answer seemed to be dictated by a wish to show that the parish was doing as well as could be expected; that possibly it might do better; and, if so, better work was needed from the Rector.

"Oh, no! I was only in fun," said Mr. Manson. "*I*'ve brought in a family or two, thank God! If we had an enrolment of bona-fide names, I fancy we could make the *beginning* of a list. But let me tell you about that article on nincompoops. It was made upon communications from half a dozen different places, and not out of my own hand at all."

"You seem to have made it your own, pretty well," said Mr. Parmenter; then added: "That is, I judge so, from what I hear."

"Certainly I went against the abuses full tilt, as usual."

"So I suppose," said the other, with grave civility. "Are you going my way, sir?" Mr. Parmenter continued, drawing up his reins before starting.

"Thank you, no," said Mr. Manson, jumping from the over-hanging gravel-bank as he spoke; but taking care, this time, to alight behind the carriage.

So, with mutual salutations, the Rector and his "influential layman" separated; Mr. Parmenter rumbling rapidly away, and raising a dust as he went.

CHAPTER XXIII.

A YOUNG REPROBATE.

The Rector-editor followed, for some distance, the same road with the buggy, which soon went out of sight. Before long, unmindful of Mrs. Weatherbee and of Mr. Parmenter, he crossed the bars by a leap, as before, into a pasture where a dozen or more of fine cows were feeding.

As he walked, with a quick, steady step, across the field, turning his head from side to side to look it all over, a figure of a boy rose from behind one of the cows, a good way in front of him, and, turning away, walked, as steadily as he, down toward the wood, in the hollow. Mr. Manson did not quicken his pace; but he called after the boy by Christian and surname.

"Philip! Philip! Rainor!" he shouted, not with much effort, but still loudly enough to be heard by any intelligent ears. The call was altogether unheeded: the boy neither quickened nor slackened his steps, but walked straight on. The gentleman, smiling, with a shake of the head, walked steadily after him.

At the rate at which the two were going, the distance between would never have been shortened; but the boy scarcely entered the wood, and, passing behind two or three of the outermost trees, was seen immediately coming back,—not exactly over the same ground as in going down, but aslant; and now it might be seen that he was carrying a book, which he seemed to be closely reading, in such a way that his voice was heard, now and then, through the still air of the afternoon, as also was seen the emphatic accompaniment of his hand as he read.

The clergyman smiled at this exhibition, and said aloud, so that he might have been heard a good way off, "Um!" then turned a little from his own course, so as to bring the two paths together. As they drew near, the boy, at the sound of footsteps, looked up from his book, and, like one that had been taught manners, bowed his head, and said, "A good evening, sir!"

Our readers will remember this boy's encounter with Brade and Remsen, on one bright memorable morning. He was a shabby lad, with ragged clothes and shoes, and a sun-burnt cap hanging at the back of his head, with the visor half-ripped off. His face was pale, surrounded by straight, light-colored hair, and opened by watery, bluish eyes, and a watering wide mouth, partly open, showing large teeth.

This was the boy whom the reader has already met, in the matter of the traps.

Mr. Manson returned a kindly greeting, and, as he spoke, held out, in such a way as to be readily seen by the other, a squared, even, and apparently unbroken package of paper "currency," from which an outside paper-wrapper was turned back.

A change flitted over the boy's flabby face, and, by a sort of instinctive motion, he put his free hand to his trousers' pocket, while he fastened his eyes upon the package of currency. The pocket seemed to be a pretty full one.

"I want to have a little talk with you, Philip," said the clergyman.

"I've got to drive Mr. Bancroft's cows home," answered the boy, but standing still, with his eyes upon the package, and with a very wakeful look.

"Would you rather meet me by-and-by, or stop now?" asked Mr. Manson.

"Well," said the lad, "I dono's I care about doin' ary one of 'em."

The healthy-looking man who was talking with him seemed in no way surprised or disconcerted by his ungracious tone, and answered gravely and decidedly, —

"But I must have a talk with you; and, as it wants some time of sunset, perhaps I may as well do it now."

The boy answered in a surly way, "I dono's the's any 'must' about it;" but he stood still, nevertheless, and, with stealthy glances at the parcel of currency, proceeded, deliberately, to put a grass-stalk into his open book. Then reading aloud, "Page forty-eight: 'and that was the last of him,'" he shut the book, and put it away into a jacket-pocket. Another grass-stalk he put into his mouth, and chewed diligently.

"You and I may differ very much in our ways of looking at things," said the clergyman, with a large and confident kindliness, which seemed to take for granted that he could interest the boy; "but I'll tell you what I go upon: I'm sent out with a message to anybody that's going wrong, to try to bring him right."

"You can preach that in church, can't ye?" asked the boy, looking away: "I don't belong to your church, nor yet no other church."

"That's just one part of it," said Mr. Manson; "but I've got just as much tó say in a sitting-room, or in this field. You needn't hear, if you don't choose to; but that doesn't make any difference to me about *my* duty."

"Don't it make some odds if I don't choose to hear ye?" asked Phil Rainor, but yet without moving to go away.

"I'll try it," said the other, still holding the package before him: "I want to help you to be a good boy."

"S'pose I want to be such a kind of a boy 's I please, hain't I got a right?" asked the young good-for-nothing, pulling and chewing a second grass-stalk or two, with much seeming indifference.

"If you mean whether I can tie you up, and"—

The boy interrupted:—

"I guess you'd hev' to ketch me fust, f' one thing," said he, shying to one side, to show how he would escape, if an attempt were made.

"Yes, yes; that I shan't try to do: all I want is a very few words," said Mr. Manson, waiting and giving him time; and, after hearing him, going on, quietly and patiently, "There's a right and a wrong."

"Who says so?" asked Rainor, who seemed likely to permit no common ground to be established between them, even upon truisms which had been accepted ever since the world began.

The moralist allowed time for this interruption, though he took no notice of the question, but repeated:—

"There's a right and a wrong," making a good pause. "A man that does right goes on well."

"Yes, Jim Fiske, that made so much of other folks' money," said the boy.

"He was murdered by another man as bad as himself," answered the clergyman.

"Wall, Stokes, then, that murdered him," said the young vagabond, readily, but not looking at the respectable and kindly person, who was listening with all patience, and who now answered, —

"So far he hasn't gained, and he hasn't got through yet. Well, now it's *you* that I want."

"You shall hev' me if ye can get me," said the boy.

"So I suppose; and that's just what I expect to do. Now, Rainor, did you ever feel ashamed or sorry for any thing that you'd done?" asked the moralist, beginning from a new position a direct assault upon this thoroughly entrenched young outlaw.

"I dono but what I have. Pooty sure I must have, when it didn't turn out the way I wanted it to," Rainor answered, promptly, from his (imaginary) fortress. "I've felt 'shamed 'nough 'f other folks, sometimes."

"Why, I know better of you than that," said the beleaguering moralist, heartily. "I've heard of your having been a leading scholar in Sunday school."

The boy answered both bitterly and contemptuously, chewing faster, and pulling and thrusting into his mouth new grass-stems: —

"Plaguy sight o' good goin' to Sabbath school done me. To hev' a teacher come along, 'th kid gloves, right afore the class, when ye'd got your lesson all perfict, an' was the best scholar 'n the class, 'n' look fierce, 'n' say, 'ye'd ought t' look better'n that, to come to Sabbath school;' 'n' I'd been half 'n hour fixun up, a-purpose, 's happy 's could be."

The kindly man who was listening attentively threw

up his head in a mute gesture of sympathy, and was just about to speak, for the boy's lips quivered, and tears actually showed themselves on his lids; and there he was — this hopeless-seeming young rascal — showing good feeling, and proper pride, and worthy ambition, and a very serviceable regard for the opinion of others; but there was more yet: —

"I never went to Sabbath school agin, an' in two-three months they sent me round a one-legged doll, or something, f' my Noo-Year's present; 'n' a tract roun' it, — 'Let not the sun go down 'pon your wrath!' — I made a hole 'n it, and stuck it on our old sow's tail; an' she thrashed round, an' lay down on it, an' mashed it, an' trampled it all into muck, in no time."

The listener, being a parish-priest, may have known from experience that there are a great many Sunday-school teachers (one-third, two-thirds, occasionally three-thirds of them, in a given school) who have no training, or calling, or liking for their work: at any rate, he did not, in any way, undertake the defence of that Sunday-school teacher, or of the race of such teachers. The little confidence which had been just brought about by the sharing of this painful experience in the boy's life promised much easier work in the establishing of a common understanding between them than had at first seemed likely. As moisture, whether spread through miles of earth or air, or rounded into a drop, is a good conductor of heat and electricity, so is it of feeling; so it was with these tears of Phil Rainor. But if the package of "currency" was the subject to be come at, they seemed to be no nearer, and getting no nearer, as yet.

"But then, I suppose, somebody called, to say that there'd been a mistake, and to make it right, and to see after you?"

"Oh, yes! ever so much! 'N about three weeks, teacher come to the door, 'n' stood a-talking 'th mother on her bed, inside there, 'n' I was a-doin' chores, in the yard, close by, 'n' said, 'Th' object was to teach the children self-respect, 'n' respect for teachers'" — ("But respect for God, first," suggested the listener.) "That wa'n't it, fust n' last, nary one; the' wa'n't no r'spect for Him about it; 'twas all 'bout the teachers and scholars, an' that 'the' was a good many nice-dressed children there, an' a fullah hadn't ought to be shabby 'n' dirty' (I wa'n't dirty, 'f I was shabby"), — here was a little spasm of feeling and stoppage of speech, — "'an' the' hoped I'd show a proper sperit 'n' be p'lite 'n' 'umble;' 'n' about a peck 'f apples come round to mother 'n' a bottle o' rawsb'ry vinegar."

"There's where you 'felt ashamed for' your teacher, I suppose?"

"I guess I did," answered the boy, with a peculiar "rising inflection," as elocutionists call it, at the end.

"I don't wonder, and I can't say that I blame you: you weren't well dealt with. Well, now I know where you felt ashamed of *yourself*, — when you left your mother, and the neighbors came in and saved her."

A dark turn came over the boy's face at this; and, glancing at the sinking sun, he repeated what he had said at the beginning, that "he must be looking after Mr. Bancroft's cows;" and he was turning off, accordingly.

"Stay!" said Mr. Manson; and then, adopting the

boy's vernacular, repeated the synonyme, "Hold on, boy! — that isn't all of it. Do you remember how faithful you were, when you came back, and how she said 'there wasn't such another son in Eastham'?"

"That wa'n't nothin'," said the boy, not yet fairly turning away, and even looking almost, if not quite, bashful, under the effect of this commendation. In a moment, he even came nearer than this to the fellowship of good morals and good feelings within which stood the respectable person who was now dealing with him, and toward which the respectable person was trying to draw him. Of himself he offered an explanation of the dark-looking place in his history, which had been just brought up.

"Why I left mother that time was 'cause she took part against me, and pretended to scold me for not bein' careful 'nough 'bout m' clo'es. I went off an' got a place to work, for next to nothin', 't fust, an 'hev' my clo'es an' board. I was goin' to giv' 'most all I earned to mother, an' do her chores; an' the' wa'n't no danger 'f her dyin' nor nawth'n like it, no time; the' wus al'ays plenty o' neighbors comin' in, an' hangin' roun'."

Whatever was in Mr. Manson's mind, he made no attempt to interrupt or divert the boy from his story: it seemed to suit his purpose very well. He helped him on in it by asking, briefly, —

"Did you stay in that place?"

"No!" said the boy, with a strong emphasis; and there followed something which seemed like a choking in his scrawny throat, and something which seemed like a heaving of his chest; and these, with his turning-round and kicking at a tuft of grass, showed a deeper up-stir in his bosom than any thing yet.

This unwilling show of feeling was not meddled with, and there was a dead silence.

"B'cause I had a little sore," Rainor began again, after a while (and over-dainty and even delicate readers must put up with the mention of the not-nice ailments of their poor fellows, if they wish to come near them and do any thing for them). Then there was another pause and a dead silence.

"I couldn't help it; an' I done the best I could about it." (This came out piecemeal.) "I kep' it washed out clean, an' put in a plug o' cotton-wool,— an' done the best I could," said the poor fellow, repeating himself, while he handled his unsavory subject with as much delicacy, perhaps, as he knew how to use. "The' said 'I wasn' nice to hev' roun';' said 'the' was sorry' (teacher'd ben givin' 'em a little moral 'dvice about me)." Here, with a last definite kick at the tuft of grass, the much-broken explanation ended. The thing had touched him deeply, and the hurt was rankling still.

"*That* was all!" said his sympathizing hearer cheerily. "Well, you'll do yet, Philip, never fear." The voice brought Rainor round again; and he looked up also before he was aware.

"Now, look here!" said Mr. Manson, holding out the package of scrip, upon which the boy fixed his eyes, as he was asked to do, but with a very unintelligent look at first, so much was he still occupied with the painful thing just laid open. His look was, for a while, as unrecognizing as if he had never seen any thing of the kind before, or did not know enough of it even to desire it.

This expression, however, did not last very long, and

was followed by a look of something like confusion, and then by a smile, which seemed as separate from the rest as one of the little side-scenes on the stage is separate from every other, however often made to combine in order to some desired effect. There the smile was; but the face was not made up into any definite expression, and so the smile was unemployed.

"You dropped this, and I picked it up. Now don't let's lose the good understanding we've gained. Let us keep on understanding each other" (for he might not be sure that the boy was not sinking back again into the saucy doggedness from which he had, with a little timely and skilful help, just scrambled out).

"If you say I dropped it, I s'pose ye're goin' to give it to me," Rainor said.

"No, I'm not, at all," said the clergyman. "I suppose you know that one of these bits of paper would send a man to the state's prison? Now, don't say a word yet; for I'm going to keep on the right side of you. I'm a friend; and I'm perfectly willing to have you know it. — Now any one of a hundred of these bits of paper would send a man to state's prison, by the law of every country on earth."

"Some of 'em haven't got no state's prisons, nor yet no money, neither," said the boy, proposing a correction, with a smile.

"Stay!" said Mr. Manson, shaking his head. "No mocking, now, my boy! I'm going to keep you on your best side. Remember that we understand each other: I know your discouragements and mortifications. You remember your geography, from school? Do you remember the name of any of those countries?"

"Over'n Afriky, I s'pose, somew'e's, — f' *one* place."

"Savage? or civilized? (I'm glad you recollect.)"

"Oh! savage, I s'pose: I shouldn't say they was very civilized."

"Yes: all civilized nations make a great crime of passing counterfeit money; in some, the punishment is death." (The boy began to grow paler, even, than was natural to him.)

"I hain't put off 'n atom 'f it. But what's the odds?" he exclaimed: "it's jest exactly 's good 's any the' is goin'. 'Tain't none of it real money: they called it merchandise." (This reference to third parties he seemed to make unwittingly.) "It's wuth jest 'xactly 's much as folks 'll take it for. What's two-three inches o' paper wuth, any how?"

"Now, stop! — that'll do," said Mr. Manson, very quietly. "Let's try to speak truth to each other. Have you passed any counterfeits?"

"No, I hain't; but I know 'bout it."

"Well, don't talk to me as if you thought I hadn't common sense, or didn't know how much you knew. That's nonsense. You know, very well, that this is wicked stuff, and the men you got it of wouldn't dare to acknowledge it. It's only in the dark, and under lies and cheats, that a man can pass them off." (All this time Rainor looked agitated.) "Now, you've got yourself into a very bad position, and it's hard to get you out of it. If you were a man, you'd deserve to go to state's prison for having those on you."

"Who says I've *got* any on me?" asked the boy, looking half-up, askant.

"This parcel's enough," answered Mr. Manson.

Instantly, as suddenly as if he had been preparing for it, Rainor sprang toward the hand that held the fatal package, and made a snatch for it. Quick as he was, however, he did not find this good-natured gentleman off his guard. Not only did the spring and snatch accomplish nothing; but the man, quicker than he was, putting one hand in front and one behind, laid the boy on the ground almost before he had made his spring.

"It wouldn't be hard to search you, you see," said the conqueror, putting his hand quietly at his throat, with just effort enough to keep him down.

"No, ye don't pick none of my pockets!" answered the young prisoner, trying to speak and act like a desperate fellow, and drawing a pistol from inside his jacket, where he had kept one hand.

"Pooh! pooh!" said Mr. Manson, with a laugh: "you don't think you can frighten me, do you? That thing isn't loaded, and, if it were, you wouldn't use it." The boy said nothing, and certainly made no formidable demonstration with the weapon, which was, apparently, an old, six-inch smooth-bore of the cheapest sort.

The unwilling captive, however, began to squirm upon the ground; and, as he writhed about, another package, like the first, found its way out of his trousers-pocket.

"Come, come!" said Mr. Manson, taking possession of this booty: "I'm not going to hold you or hurt you. Get up, and put away that silly thing."

The late would-be ruffian, looking rather sheepishly, obeyed; but, as he got up to his feet, he said, glancing at the hand which now held two packages, —

"You hain't got any right to pick my pockets."

"Now, Philip," said the clergyman, in a patient, kind voice, "this wicked stuff is no more property than the runnings of small-pox are property. I'm only your friend: I'm not a constable, and I want to help you out of trouble. You're worse than I thought, — some people would say you were too bad to do any thing with, — but I see you're not very far in yet."

"Pooty much 's they say, I guess: I s'pose they wouldn't give me a trial," said the boy, answering one part of the sentence.

"No, I think there's plenty in you to go upon: we must make something of you."

"Not much, I guess," said the boy, not yet facing the eyes that were looking steadfastly and thoughtfully at him.

"You wouldn't have gained any thing, by getting these," said Mr. Manson.

"You wouldn't have had no proof," interrupted Rainor.

"You're mistaking fearfully. But we won't argue; and time's going. You'll have to drive your cows shortly." (Philip looked, as if mechanically, toward the sun.) "I want to get you out of this ugly business, — out of the men, and out of the thing."

"I haven't said nothing about no men," said the boy.

"I mean the men that sold you this vile stuff, and called it 'merchandise.' Don't talk. Let's consult as friends. I want to get you out of this first, and then make an honest boy of you. You're pretty deep in this," he said, gravely and thoughtfully; "but there must be a way of getting you out, and then I know you're not lazy, though, I hear, you've been a thief and a liar, and I don't know what else."

"I hain't lied to *you*," said poor Philip, "'n' I guess the most stealin' ever I done was I took a St. Bart's trap I thought they'd left. An' I put it back; but they wouldn't hear to no reason." Then, with a look of satisfaction, — "Got into a squabble, though, 'mong 'emselves, t'other day; but 'twan't the right ones, 'xac'ly."

"Was that something between you and the St. Bart's boys, lately?"

"About the trap, was quite a spell ago; but I played a trick on 'em, jest to show 'twan't so easy, all'a's, to find out. I meant it for Remsen, there, 'n' Towne; but two-three others got into a tussle about it. I wouldn't 'a' done it 'f they'd ben any ways reas'nable 'bout the trap; nor I didn't want to set 'em fightin' nuther."

"What was it that *you* did?" Mr. Manson asked.

"Changed a white rabbit over from Remsen's snare into the other fullah's trap," said the boy. "I wanted Towne 'n' Remsen t' have a jaw over it, an' try an' find out; 'n' then not be so quick to think they knoo all about it, an' another fullah didn't know nothin' an' was all lies, to boot."

Ridiculous as the thrusting-in of bungling machinery like this into the workings of the moral universe might appear, Phil Rainor's story had the appearance of truth.

"We'll have a better way than that, next time," said the clergyman, smiling. "Do the boys know yet?"

"I told Tarleton, — one that fought about it."

"Well, I'll see that all made right. Now, we must keep you out of state's prison."

"There's a plaguy sight o' smart fellahs, by all the talk, gets" —

Mr. Manson caught him up: —

"A set of thieving, lying, gambling, swearing, fighting, house-breaking, murdering, defiling villains! You must have done with all that sort of thinking, or the One that I act for won't help you."

"'Taint Tom Parmenter?" the boy asked, making free with the name, as country people are apt to do, about any one who has grown rich among them. "My gran'ther picked his'n" —

Mr. Manson, with little curiosity to know what might have happened between these ancestors, — whether one, more lucky, had picked the other's metaphorical pin-feathers for him, or had picked him up where he had fallen, or whether for an honest wage that one had picked the other's peas or apples for him, — cut short the story: —

"No, it isn't Mr. Parmenter," he said: "it's God. — Your father was respectable. — Come, I'll walk with you, while you gather your cows."

"My father worked himself into a hactic, an' went off, 'fore I ever knoo him."

"Well, we must try to get you up to something respectable; but we've got to go on with it, — no thieving, no cheating, no lying, — we're to stop short off, and start from where we are."

"If I say I will, I will," said the boy. "I'll keep to it, 'f I die for't."

"I'll trust you," said his friend.

He paused as if to give Rainor a chance to meet him half way; but the boy was silent. Suddenly he broke out: —

"Sh'll hev' to do it m'self, — 'n' I tried once and failed. 'Tain't 's if I had any friends, or en'thin' to go 'pon. Who's a-goin' to git me a place?"

"You'll have to take your chance for that," said the adviser, quietly; "but to be somebody, and not a villain or a scoundrel, is worth all risks. You'll have to stick fast. You're looking at it in the right way: only, if you do go at it yourself, there's One to help you that you don't believe in yet."

They walked on silently for a few steps, down the field.

"You'd better give me that currency," said Mr. Manson, decidedly. "Of course I shall see that not one bit of it ever passes."

"I give cash for that scrip," said Phil Rainor; "but I s'pose I must lose it."

"Yes, that's a loss I can't help: you'll have to bear it. If you waked up, you know, with walls of fire all round you, you'd jump through, though you might lose some of your clothing, and get scorched, too."

Here was a pretty strong obstacle to meet, at the outset, with a subject to work upon whose habit of well-doing was so fresh and unstiffened as that of this lad; but his befriender left it just as it was.

Rainor, without another word, began emptying his pocket. The vile stuff Mr. Manson received with an expression of disgust. Then, having longer and larger experience of human nature, and of how things go in it, he said (and pretty much in the boy's own vernacular): —

"Perhaps you won't feel better right off;" then, as he handled the wretched stuff, — "Enough to make an honest fellow sick, to look at it!" and he read, from the wrapper of one of the packets, "'Patent Exemption Matches: open the other End;' and a counterfeit Revenue Stamp!"

All this, except the first few words, might as well have been an aside, as far as Rainor was concerned. He seemed to have heard only those.

"Yes, I do, though," answered the poor scapegrace, who had really made a very heroic move for a boy like him, and might have been excused, if he had felt, as yet, pretty much like one who has had a loathsome tooth wrenched out, and has not got himself back quite, and therefore does not quite know how he feels. "I feel better, an' plaguëd glad I be I didn' git any further into it, though one thing you can tell 'em, — I never had a mite 'f it 'fore this; an' I hain't put off an atom o' this."

"Remember we're on the way upward: we've made a start," said his adviser.

As he spoke he took a penknife from his pocket, and then, laying the packets, of which there were five, on their edges, in one body on the ground, he slashed deeply into and across them, in several places, and then said, as he lifted himself up: —

"Now, what we want is a match, to get rid of these things on the spot, and put them out of the way of doing harm."

Upon the word, Rainor, as such boys always can, produced a match from his pocket, and Mr. Manson, thus supplied, broke every package, and stirred the whole pretty thoroughly up into a loose heap, inside the newspaper in which they had been wrapped; and then laid the parcel upon the bare top of an imbedded stone, repeating, as he did so, a line which, though of course lost upon Rainor, doubtless brought some satisfaction to himself: —

"'Lustramurque Deo, votisque incendimus aras.'" *

Then, setting fire to the easily kindled mass, he formally took off his hat, and said to the boy (what he could understand): —

"Now, Philip, may God accept this as a little sacrifice!" and he fanned the flames with the hat, till a bright, strong blaze had got possession.

The boy must have both understood and sympathized pretty well; for he, too, took off, a little sheepishly, his hard-worn cap, and applied himself to pushing together the fast-burning pieces of paper to make sure that nothing should be left of any of them.

The very last bit of paper was, before long, burned into black and brittle uselessness, and was ground under Mr. Manson's heel, and then scattered with his foot to the air and the earth.

"There, Philip," said he, "you've done the first thing well. There'll be plenty more of it for you, like the rest of us, if you live long enough. Doing right, after wrong, will be hard, sometimes, and cost something; but it's the only thing. You'll hear from these scoundrels and their 'merchandise,' very likely, and you'll have to be strong. Mind you, Philip, no giving-in, a hair's breadth! Let me tell you. Tell them, at once, that you've burned their vile stuff, and that I know all about it. Will you? Promise me!" (holding out his hand). "On your honor!" (as Rainor promised). "That'll do. God bless you!" and he left the boy to his cows.

* Æn. iii. 279: "We purify ourselves to God, and with vows we kindle our altar fires."

CHAPTER XXIV.

A BREATH OF FRESH AIR.

The elements of which this world is made up are, happily, very different; and as our healthy priest, with every reason to feel thankful and happy over his work, left the field and took the road, the musing stillness of nature was broken only by his own quick and springing footsteps; while before him was the broad waste of the sun's abandoned gold which the clouds were decking themselves with.

Before long, there came up from some turn below a very clear voice from a girl, as separate and free as steam in cooler air, —

> "A little rose peeped through the fence
> To find the golden sun;
> But careless fingers plucked it thence
> Before the hour was done."

Mr. Manson quickened his pace; and soon, turning into a cross-road, came upon a bevy of young people, of whom one was our friend Kate Ryan, and three others he addressed, in returning their salutations, by three different Christian names with the one surname of Bemis.

He complimented Kate cheerily on her song, and, failing to draw from her a second stanza (for, as she said, "she knew no more of it"), applied a little moral of his own, that "peering after 'golden suns' was dangerous business," he gave his voice decidedly with those of the Misses Bemis, that no one could so well as Kate represent, at Mrs. Wadham's party, some character, whatever it was (from which, as it would appear, she wished to escape), and received sudden thanks from a voice which had not before spoken for itself, and to which he returned some pleasant compliment to "Mrs. Ryan."

Then taking leave of them, after this momentary encounter, which must have given a pleasant waft to his spirits, he went on; gladdened with the present of nuts little Billy Carnes, the cripple, who was sitting at a window, watching the not very abundant life upon the road; and ended by finding Mrs. Rainor waiting, and a little impatient, for Philip's coming home. Very naturally, as soon as a footstep was heard near the door, a weak and rather peevish voice called "Philip!" But she was glad to see her visitor.

Her room showed many little contrivances in carpentering, — as shelves for flowers, and book-shelves, and the like.

Poor Mrs. Rainor was not alone as the clergyman entered; for a pleasant-faced neighborly-looking woman, to whom Mr. Manson's coming in seemed to give much satisfaction, was sitting in a corner.

Mrs. Rainor had already set in motion her intelligent consciousness and appreciation of her forlorn condition, and they were expressing themselves in words. Mr. Manson's strong, healthy nature could not only meet and neutralize a great deal of this, but also give back far more of cheerful and hopeful feeling. He listened attentively and respectfully, with well-timed monosyllables of sympathy, while Mrs. Rainor, in a sharp, plaintive voice, was giving a faithful account of "that old trouble she took in the spine of her back the February that father died; and then this one, that come on her at the pit of her stomach, and from that straight to her right side." Then, as the thought of supper (perhaps a little later than usual) grew strong to her, she explained that "the way with her was, she would have a good appetite, and think she could eat hearty, and enjoy any thing; and when it come to the scratch, 'twa'n't there, and every thing went against her;" and, as she added plaintively, "she *was* a woman that did set a great store by her victuals." This appeal to a character which, if nowhere else recorded to her credit, was doubtless cherished in the memories of her friends, seemed to bring some relief, — comfort, perhaps, could not be expected.

Mr. Manson got the conversation turned to her son, of whom the mother seemed to have formed a pretty impartial opinion: that "he was thoughtless, like boys, and yet for all he was pooty thoughtful, and, no doubt, he had considerable to try him; but he meant to be good to her. There was a time when he and the St. Bart's boys didn't seem to get along very well together for a spell; but she didn't hear no complaints now. Poor old 'mother,' she expected, was a burden; but it was about as bad for her as anybody else to be layin' there; for, *you* know, Mrs. Weatherbee" (to the neighbor in the corner, and in a high, wailing tone, which contrasted strongly with the energetic vigor of the words which it faltered forth), "when I was any ways myself, I used to flax round lively, — I tell *you*."

The Parson was just showing, to Mrs. Weatherbee's admiration, as well as to the quiet gratification of Mrs. Rainor, his gathering of ferns, taken up with little clumps of earth. They were very insignificant-looking in their winter state; but he was setting forth the beauties of a green forest under glass, for which Philip should make the frame-work, with Mr. Manson's superintendence.

The son came in while he was speaking; and he considerately interrupted himself at once, and took his leave, after giving Philip notice of the job in store for him.

CHAPTER XXV.

SOME BOYS VENTURE ON THE FAIR SEA OF PHILOLOGY.

THE days of boyhood, as we need hardly tell those who ever went through them alive, are days in which we are sure that there is a world close by us, and open to us, in which are Greatness and Glory and Beauty; into which world we shall, some time, go to get them. Those are days in which hope is stronger than any thing it meets; in which, without consciousness of our own riches, we have hold of a share of eternity, because things past, — the achievements of the race, men of the furthest ages, — their words; the stands that they made; their daring, their indignation, their endurance, their faithfulness, their chances, failures, triumphs, — are not gone out of being, but are all there.

The wondrous tongues of Greece and Rome are great to the boyish fancy, because, as boys, we come, through them, into a sort of common nationality and relationship with all the wise and great who breathed the earlier air of our earth. Latin and Greek live yet, and thrill from mighty brains and hearts within the same nature with ourselves.

Now there were boys of fancy at St. Bartholomew's School; and at least one current of ambition was setting, at this time, toward discoveries in LANGUAGE. We have heard already of "Notes on Cæsar," and have heard the friendly encouragement to Brade. Now it was understood in the School that a couple of Bartlemas fellows were doing what probably had never been tried by any boys of any school: Brade, of the Third Form, with help from Gaston, of the Fourth, the foremost scholar, WAS MAKING A BOOK ABOUT GREEK AND LATIN!

Such boys as had mouths most ready to open, as Will Hirsett, for example, were open-mouthed about this forthcoming wonder, but doubted whether the Caput knew of it. Hirsett said "he knew that Brade had an awful heap of paper to write it on" (which is certainly one step toward book-making), and Ransom, or somebody, "had seen him looking out ever so many words in the dictionary, — Greek words, — when he wasn't learning his lesson, and writing them down."

To questions asked directly of himself about this great work, Brade answered, with a very natural look of satisfaction qualified with mystery, that it was not any thing yet, but perhaps it would be; and Remsen, when he was appealed to on the same subject, had said that "Brade had got a notion in his head that would astonish the world, as he (Remsen) thought. He did not know exactly what it was himself; but it was a very bright thing."

Mr. Hamersley, the new tutor, in whose recitation-room was the largest table of all, had given Brade leave to take his books into that room, for the purpose of this work, for two hours, every other afternoon; and certain specified boys were to be allowed to go into it with him.

On the second of these afternoons, there were seated in this room Gaston and Brade; and on the great table were two or three large books (like lexicons) lying open, and a good deal of writing-paper, and an ink-stand and pens. All this looked like a preparation for business; but the two, like other boys, were as yet engaged in conversation, and both looking at a transparency in one of the windows which seemed not like a part of the regular furniture of the room. This was a copy of Collins's admirable painting of the "Sale of the Pet Lamb," from Mrs. Howitt's story. It had all that exquisite and wonderful shading which is characteristic of fine specimens of that sort of art-work, and the boys were duly impressed.

"It's too bad, isn't it?" said Gaston. "Do you suppose they did really let it go? That girl's pushing the butcher's boy. — She couldn't do any thing that way!" he continued, with the wisdom of a boy a little older than the girl, and who had sisters at home, and knew by experience their faults. Then he laughed, as he saw a new part of the scene.

"Look at that youngster pointing off into the woods; proposing to carry the lamb off, and hide it, isn't he? But they couldn't do it: they'd have to bring it back," said he again, after a pause. "No, they needn't, though. Why couldn't they keep it off in the woods, somewhere, and carry food to it?"

Brade was silently watching the picture (if we may so call a thing which is without color, but which represents most faithfully a scene of many-colored life), and said, —

"I don't know what they did do: I only just got it to-day," and he looked a little longer. Then he said,

"But there's the mother; and the butcher is paying down the money. If they sell it, they'll have to let it go. They're poor, and they can't keep it: poor people have to sell their things. It *is* too bad, isn't it?"

"Well, I'll tell you what it is," said Gaston, smiling, "a fellow mustn't *be* poor. If you get money, you can take care of yourself, and have what you want to."

"But there are a good many poor," said the other, "and they can't help themselves."

"Well, all I say is, you mustn't *be* poor. If a fellow can learn his lessons, he can learn a profession, and then he can make his way."

"It would be good if we could stop the poor from losing their things," said Brade. "That's one thing Peters is after, isn't it? He's always talking about helping people."

"Peters has got some smartness in him," said Gaston; "but he hasn't got any gumption. I don't believe it'll come to any thing. I'll tell you, you'll have to get rich yourself first: oh, *you are;* but *I* ain't. You won't have to do any work, if you don't want to; but I shall. And my father always said, 'Work earns pay; and good work earns good pay.'"

"I mean to work all *my* life, just as hard as I'm working now," said Antony, with quiet determination. "Every man ought to work."

"If you don't work any harder than you're working now," said Gaston, laughing, "I don't think it'll amount to much;" and then, without further words, but laughing, Brade gathered the papers toward himself.

"I'll take it down now," he said, "and then we sha'n't look at it;" and he went toward the window.

"You won't have to do that, though," said Gaston. "We needn't look at it."

"We've talked about it long enough," said Brade; and so he laid the transparency down on the table.

"What do you think we ought to call it?" he asked, his mind now full of the other subject.

Gaston seemed as full of it as he, and answered readily: —

"My father always says, 'You ought to have something steadily in your mind, and keep to it;' but he says, 'It don't matter about naming a book till you've got through;' and he's written books. He's written several books."

"Wouldn't 'Analogy of Languages' be good?" Brade asked. "Analogy means that, doesn't it?"

Here there was a knock at the door; and after a parley, to make sure who it was, Remsen was let in.

"Yes, I should think that would do," said Gaston. "Well, how much have you got, so far?"

Antony was busy writing down the name, which he read, as he finished, "The Analogy of Languages." "You can't say Greek and Latin, can you? because there'll be others: there'll be English, and others."

"Why, there's Sanscrit!" exclaimed Gaston, "that everybody's making so much of: my father says 'they'll find out every thing by that,' and he knows a great deal about languages."

"Oh, yes!" said Brade, eagerly, but modestly, "I think I've thought something about that, that I can't find in any book I've got."

"Yes!" said Remsen, "he's made a discovery, I do believe."

"Don't you suppose," asked Antony, glowing with

his expectation, "that it was called 'Sanscrit' because it wasn't written?" — He was a little nervous, as he spoke.

"I don't know," said Gaston: "I've thought of that; but I never remembered to ask my father. I've heard him talk of it, many and many a time. Let's see: '*sans*' is French for '*sine*, without,' — that we know. How do you make '*crit*'? Let's see: 'écrire' is French for '*scribere*, to write,' — '*sans-écrit*.' If it's French, I should think everybody would know it," and he was evidently puzzled. Presently he assailed it again; "'Sine scripto,' — 'sin-script,' — 'san-scrit,' — it might go so, couldn't it? and then people would forget what it came from, perhaps. — There's a word," — he continued, thoughtfully, — "look here! 'tisn't the one I was thinking of; but there's '*doubt*' with the '*b*'" —

"Look here!" exclaimed Brade, triumphantly, "'*manuscrit*' is French, — with the '*p*' left out."

"So it is!" cried Gaston, slapping the table. "Good. In '*doubt*' you don't pronounce '*b*,' but then you write it."

"Hooray!" said Remsen, beginning to dance, for his part. "What have you got to now? Isn't it fun? St. Bart's School is going to be heard from."

Our philologists must have made more noise than they were aware of; for a giggling was heard at the outside of the door, which showed that there were more persons privy to the gratifying discovery just announced than were contained within the walls of the room. The faces, however, of the successful scholars, radiant with joy, showed little concern about the promiscuous crowd of nameless plodders in the ways of learning who might be loitering on the other side of the secure fastening of their own retreat. They said no word to them; and Brade, in the full flush of the achievement, occupied himself with making a record of it, in enduring ink, his face all glowing with enthusiasm.

"One trouble will be that we don't know all the languages," said Gaston. "We know," he continued, confidently, "Greek and Latin and French and English, and you know German. How many is that?"

"Six," said Remsen, like a ready reckoner.

"Well, that's a good many, ain't it?" said Gaston. "As far as it goes, you know, it'll be good. Come! let's go on!"

"Shouldn't you like to take it up to the Caput?" asked Brade.

"Yes; but let's get some more down first," said Gaston.

Antony began pulling forth with his forefingers, from his waistcoat-pockets, little rolls of paper, which he proceeded to unfold, one after another, spreading them out upon the table. Gaston seemed disposed to depend upon his own head: at least he made no show of producing memoranda.

"I've got a few," said Brade, and he began to read.

"Here's a queer one," said he, laughing in anticipation, "'Σμώκω:'* in Greek that means to *chew*."

"Now, how do you suppose that ever came?" said Gaston, with the eagerness of a scholar. "The curiosity of it is that a fellow that smokes don't generally chew, and a fellow that chews don't generally smoke:

* "*Smoko*," if our readers will allow us to put it in English letters.

I've heard my brother say so. There's a change that, I suppose, might come round in the course of ages. Chewing, probably, comes before smoking. They used to chew, now they smoke. I wonder if there's any Latin word like that. Look out *smoke*, or any thing like it, in Andrews. I'm pretty sure there isn't."

Remsen entered into this very readily, and turned over the leaves so fast as to get beyond it, each way, before he hit the place; but then he proclaimed that "there was nothing like it there. There was 'smaragdus'" ("Oh! that's Greek," said Gaston, who had a quick ear), "and 'smilax' and 'smintheus'" ("We all know that's Greek," said Gaston), "'and smyr —'"

"But there's nothing like 'smoco,'" said Gaston; "but I'll tell you, — we had something in our French, to-day, '*s'moquer*'"— (Antony looked up from his papers, at this new 'analogy,' if that is the name; and Remsen was tilting backward in his chair, awaiting, with much equanimity, the progress of science. Gaston went on), "'*s'moquer*,' to laugh at a fellow; when you find him out, when you '*smoke*' him" —

"But that's short '*o*,' '*moq-uer*,'" said Brade, learnedly: "in Greek it's 'omega.' Besides, it's two words, — *se moquer*. Oh! you're only joking. We mustn't have any thing but what's pretty solid. I know the German: it's *schmauchen;* but in German it only means 'smoke.' We've got German and Greek and English," he added, summing up complacently. "There's another word I don't suppose we could bring in, — that's '*schmuck*,' dress. You see 'smock' 's the same word, I'm pretty sure; and farmers wear 'smocks;' but then there's some kind of a woman's dress called that, too. If it wasn't for that, we could bring it under 'smoke,' couldn't we? You see it's very light: they could make tinder of it, and that's a sort of smoke."

"I shouldn't wonder if you could bring it in so," said Gaston.

"If it wasn't a woman's dress," said Brade, doubtfully. "Well, here's another!" and he smiled pleasantly again, in anticipation, as before his first word, and showed no trace of that excessive irritability which seems to belong to men of words, but was apparently happy in the harmless rewards which science herself gives, "'*Σκώρ*' (scōr): that means 'dirt,' 'filth.' That's just like 'SCOUR,' isn't it? I could not find any German for that" —

"They don't have any filth in Germany, perhaps," said Gaston, laughing.

"Or they don't have it *scoured up*," said Remsen, who, as it will be remembered, comes of Holland-Dutch stock.

"There's French, I found, — '*scorie*,'" said Antony, resuming.

"Hah! from the Latin!" exclaimed Gaston, promptly; for Gaston, as we have seen, has a sharp nose. "Isn't it Greek, too? Where's the Lexicon?" looking to Remsen, apparently content with head-work for himself.

"Haven't you got enough?" said Remsen, to whom the manual and mechanical part of science seemed to come much like what would be drudgery, in any other department. "*I* can't find Greek."

Brade hastened to fill the gap: "Yes, yes, it's the same thing as '*Σκώρ*:'* it's from that."

* Pronounced "score."

"*Haven't* you got enough?" asked Gaston: "that is, for a beginning?" Then, himself suddenly feeling the breath of science, he was carried away. "Oh!" said he, "do you suppose our word '*score*' comes from that, because it's put down in black?"

"Come!" said Remsen, "now let's stop!"

"Oh! not yet, not yet! a little more!" said Antony, disappointed. Then, with a generalship suggested by the occasion, as Quintus Horatius* says, and possibly some other people have said, a leader's genius is displayed, at a pinch, he secured Remsen's patience. "I've got one of Nick's coming directly," he said. Gaston, though restless, had enough of a turn for philology to make him sure, for a while.

"There are not a great many," said Brade: "'τεμνω' (temno), I cut; Latin, '*temno*,' I despise; for despising is very *cutting* to the feelings, you know" —

"Ho! look here!" burst out Gaston, laughing, "if you despise a fellow, you *cut* him, don't you know you do? Yes, put that down! put that down!" and it was evident that Gaston's interest in the work was blazing up. "What's Remsen's?"

"'Δίψις'" (*dipsis*)," said Brade, "Greek, '*thirst;*' Remsen found that. He says '*dip*' is the same thing; for when you're thirsty, you *dip* up something to drink."

"Is that for fun, or serious earnest, Remsen?" asked Gaston, smiling.

"No," said Remsen: "why shouldn't it be, if there's any thing between Greek and English?"

"Well, what next?" asked Gaston: "that's not bad for Remsen. Put it down."

* Satirar, II. viii. 73.

"Here's one," said Brade, hesitating. "I don't know about it: I don't feel quite sure."

"Give it to us, and let us judge for ourselves," said Gaston.

"Well," said Brade, "it's 'χεῖμα' (Hheima*), Greek, 'winter;' '*hiems*,' Latin, 'winter.' — What I was thinking of was," continued Brade, hesitating, modestly, over a venture of his own, in language, "'heimat,' in German, means 'home:' now, a man cares more for his home, in winter, when he wants fire, and to be warm and comfortable."

"Pretty good!" said Gaston. "Besides, perhaps their houses didn't amount to much, except in winter: I don't believe they did. And there was one time, I suppose, when they dug their houses in the snow, — that would be their home, — winter-quarters, you see."

With all this, time was going by, and the light was lessening, as Remsen reminded them; so even Antony seemed inclined to hurry. He turned over, hastily, his scraps of paper, and put away one or two of them in his pocket again. Then, turning to Gaston, he asked for his contributions to the stock.

"I thought of one," said Gaston: "'πειθω' (peitho), to '*persuade:*' the stem of that is '*pith*' (πιθ in Greek). Now, isn't that just like it? A fellow that's got *pith* in him is the fellow to persuade."

"Come, fellows," said Remsen, "ain't you ready to stop yet? You've got enough to carry up to the Caput, and show him what you're doing."

* The double H will represent, perhaps, to English readers, as well as any thing, the strong aspirate of this word, and leave its shape as Brade had it.

"Would you put that in?" asked Brade of the author of the last contribution.

"Well, I don't know," answered Gaston. "Do as you please. What hard work those Ancients must have had, in thinking, when they'd got to turn it all into Greek and Latin, in their heads!" he added, showing by the words a glimpse of boyishness rather surprising in one who learned like a man, and often thought and talked like one.

"Why couldn't they think as easily as we can?" inquired Remsen, in a matter-of-fact way.

"Why! ain't it harder to think in Latin and Greek than it is in English?" asked Gaston, with smiling assurance.

"But it was their own language, you know, just as English is ours," said Brade, — "except us Russians," he added.

"Well, but I appeal to you: ain't Greek or Latin harder to think in than English? Take '*νομίζω*' (nomizo), to '*think;*' you've got to have '*think*' in your mind first, and then '*νομίζω*'; but in English it's all one thing, isn't it?"

To this ingenious and well-put argument, neither of the other boys answered, — perhaps not seeing their way well through it; but Brade, setting up again his transparency in the window for the entertainment of his friends, while he should be occupied, professed his own purpose of writing out, very carefully, what they had got already, in order to carry it to the Head of the School.

"You've got that about the Sanscrit first, haven't you?" asked Gaston; and being assured that that was at the top of the page, and should be made very plain, he turned slyly to Remsen, as if leaving Brade buried in his work, and therefore not capable of hearing or seeing any thing besides.

"Look here!" said he, aside, laughing. "Let's get up a little more by ourselves. Yŏu write, and I'll tell you what to put down. First say, —

"'Greek'" —

"I can't write Greek," pleaded Remsen.

"Well, there!" said Gaston, taking Remsen's pencil, and writing, —

"'*Μῶσαι*' [*Mōsai*], the same as '*Μοῦσαι*' [*Mousai*], the Muses; from *μῶσαι* [*mosai*]'" —

Here, notwithstanding his being so busy, his brother philologist, Brade, slackened the steady working of his pen, and was evidently listening in spite of himself. Gaston went on: —

"This verb means 'to seek,' or '*mouse out*'" —

As he got so far, Brade's pen went on again; but the smile on his face showed that he had been allured before he detected Gaston.

"Oh, don't!" said he. "You put me out."

"You put yourself out," said Gaston. "You've no business to listen. Here, Remsen, let's have one more" (Brade kept himself hard at work): —

"*Σκέλος* [*skelos*], Greek, '*leg:*' Neuter, Third Declension, Genitive (old) *skelesos*. *Skelus*, Latin, '*wickedness:*' Neuter, Third Declension, old Genitive *skelesis*, — '*is*,' in Latin, answers to '*os*' in Greek, in the genitive. Wickedness is *transgression;* transgression is *walking over:* with the leg you walk over. That's the way it came to mean 'leg' in Greek, and 'wickedness' in Latin."

"Now, Gaston, stop, please!" said Brade, "and let me write."

At this request, made with much urgency, Gaston abandoned active exertion in philology, and now proceeded to examine again and remark upon the transparency.

"Isn't the little sister pretty, kneeling down and giving it milk?" asked Remsen.

Brade, busy as he was, looked up, as if he did not hear, but still turning his silent and abstracted look toward the subject of Remsen's criticism; then, without saying any thing, looked down, and busied himself with his work again.

"There!" said he, in a few moments, rising with a smile of satisfaction, and laying down his pen with so little thought that it rolled off the table and was picked up by Remsen. "Look here! 'Sanscrit: the name probably derived from having no writings.'"

"That's as plain as printing," said Remsen.

"Do you suppose we *can* be the first that found that out?" asked Brade. "I hadn't any book to look it out in exactly," he said, with some appearance of apprehension because of the importance of the thing which was at stake. — "Oh, see!" he said, as he caught sight of one of his scraps of paper which had escaped being put into his pocket, and had fallen to the floor, "I didn't know whether I ought to put this in or not: '*Limn* (Latin, *illumino;* French, *enluminer*), *to draw, to paint*, particularly in water-colors.' I think that might come from *Λίμνη* (*limne*), a lake, — don't you think it might, Gaston? — because a lake reflects every thing, just like a drawing. What do you think of that? I haven't put it down yet, because I don't want to put any thing down that we're not pretty sure of."

This wise regard for the necessity of having all evidence weighed, and judgment and deliberation used, in whatever they did for a science so exact as philology, met Gaston's approbation, too, who said at once, "Oh, no! it wouldn't do." The conscientiousness of our young friends will be gratifying to men with the true scholarly instinct, who know what Gaston and Brade perhaps never thought of, that the happiness, if not the lives of some hundreds of persons (philologists) is depending upon that science's being not hastily nor easily developed.

"Water-colors! water-colors! Has that got any thing to do with it, do you suppose?" said Gaston. "It can't, though, can it? That only means mixed in water."

"Come, Anty!" said Remsen, with a tone of good-natured indulgence, "don't find any more; and when you've been up, and got through, we'll go out."

The papers were gathered together, the books shut, the transparency taken down, and then, apportioning a load for each, they went forth and locked Mr. Hamersley's recitation-room, the scene of hopeful and successful work, behind them.

"Perhaps, some of these days, they'll say it was done in there," said Brade, as many a discoverer or inventor has said, with his lips or in his heart. "You'll go, too, Gaston?" he asked, taking Remsen's going for granted; and Gaston assented, only insisting that Brade should be spokesman.

As the little procession approached the Rector's door, Antony's heart began to feel more and more strongly, perhaps, the greatness and the boldness of their venture, for he began to lag. Gaston, however, showed no apprehensions, and after a word or two, to keep his more bashful comrade up to the purpose, went straight up to the door of the Rector's study, and knocked.

There was no answering sound. He knocked again: there was no answer, still. Gaston began to laugh, Remsen to caper, and Brade, raising his head from listening, came forward, and Remsen followed.

"The Captain isn't in," said Nicholas. "Now, let's be off."

Gaston, who was at home in any circumstances, flung out his arm, and took an attitude. "'No hope of gilded spurs, to-day!'" he said, like an orator; "'O spem falla—!'" when suddenly the study-door opened, and the Head of the School stood smiling at Gaston's attitude and the expressions of the group, and then invited them in. This introduction took off a good deal from the solemnity of the occasion, but it also put Brade at his ease; and Brade was not only the bearer of the treasures of learning and intelligence contained in their papers, but was the chief author of them.

Gaston was not a bit abashed, and at once mentioned the purpose of the party, beginning with an explanation of the circumstances in which they had been found at the moment of the opening of the door.

"We thought you weren't in, sir," he said, smiling as he thought of it, "and so we were just beginning to express ourselves"—

"Pretty well done, I thought, so far as I heard and saw," said Mr. Warren; and, having seated them comfortably, asked, "And what now?"

"Brade," said Gaston, continuing to be spokesman, "has got something he wanted to show you, sir. We boys talk over the meanings of words sometimes, and we thought we'd found out a few things that looked right to us. We wanted to show them to you before we did any more."

During this speech, Antony may be supposed to have been sitting in a state of trembling eagerness and apprehension also; and, as the Rector turned to him, he got up, and modestly offered the manuscript. There was no great deal of it as yet in amount; but it was evident, to a glance, that what was there was made very plain upon the paper, in clear, fair letters.

"Some more of our Greek, Antony?" the Rector asked, as he took the paper.

"All sorts of languages, sir," said Brade: "I mean different languages we're learning, — two or three."

"Oh, ho!" said the Rector, "we start with Sanscrit, do we? That's pretty far up."

Neither Antony nor Gaston offered a word, leaving him to inform himself, as he would in a moment when he began to read.

Mr. Warren read, and, as he read, he smiled. Gaston began to smile contagiously. Antony began to blush all over. The Rector looked up.

"Did you ever see Dean Swift's fun about Greek," he asked Gaston, "where he says that 'Andromache' was the daughter of an honest Scotsman named Andrew Mackay, and kept his name; and 'Pygmalion' was really Pigmy-lion, because he was a wonderfully brave little fellow; and so on?"

Gaston, who, as we have seen, had a turn for those things, and was not altogether blind to fun, even where it made against himself, pricked up his ears at this, and laughed, while he confessed that he had never read Dean Swift. As for Antony, his face showed a mixture of feelings; for, while he smiled for 'Pigmy-lion' and 'Andrew-Mackay,' he looked as if he did not yet know whether his own house of words had been blown down or not, and was not quite content.

"I think you've got some pretty good things here," said the Rector, encouragingly. "You've made a capital beginning." Then, seeing the expression of Brade's face, he added, "Why, beginners in science pick up pebbles and clam-shells. You've done better."

"Some of it was half fun," said Brade, "and some of it" (looking round at the others) "we thought might be something, possibly. — We didn't know."

"Well, I'd keep on with it: it's very good practice. There's one thing you didn't think of here. Sanscrit, you know, is a written language" (Brade blushed more than ever, and his head went down a little, in spite of himself; for, as the reader knows, the boys' definition of Sanscrit was one of their strongest points; but a smile came out at the corners of his mouth); "in fact," continued the Rector, "as thoroughly written up and written down as any language ever was: but, while you were about it, trying to make something out of the name, I wonder you didn't get in 'Sanct-script, sant-scrit, san-scrit,' because it's the sacred language of the Hindus."

"Is that it?" asked Gaston. "We didn't think of that," said Brade; but both looked encouraged, as if they had been feeling in the right direction, after all.

"No: I believe it means 'perfect,' or polished,' or something of that sort, really," said the Caput.

"That dishes our definition, sir, pretty well," said Gaston.

"I hope to see something more of you, in this line, yet," said the Rector: "as any thing turns up in your lessons or in the lexicon, put it down, by all means."

So here the philologists took their leave, and brought away their papers. Once fairly out of hearing, they stopped to consult.

"We weren't so bad, after all, were we?" said Gaston. "Live and learn. I'm rather proud of that 'Sanscrit:' the Cap did something like it, that wa'n't much better. I think we've come off pretty well for a beginning." And now three pairs of nimble feet were skurrying downstairs.

CHAPTER XXVI.

A FIELD-DAY OF THE TRUSTEES.

St. Bartholomew's School had no endowment but its buildings, most of which it had paid for itself already.

This fall, an announcement had appeared in the papers "that Thomas Parmenter, Esq., of Eastham, had begun a system of graduated endowment" in St. Bartholomew's School in that town; and, as he wished to benefit by the wisdom and experience of others, he would be glad of communications from persons familiar with the subject of higher education and the operation of endowments. This piece of information was worded in much the same way in different papers in which it appeared, as any inquiring man, who read different newspapers, could easily assure himself. It was, in substance, taken from a sort of circular letter which the originator had sent to faculties of colleges, to heads of schools, and to eminent literary men and scholars.

Of course, this publication and Mr. Parmenter's action were early known in Eastham. In the first place, the Trustees of St. Bart's School had been officially notified of the munificent disposition of their fellow-member, and had convened at the School, in unusual numbers; Mr. Parmenter's carriage having gone ten miles to bring Judge Pearson, who was hard to get. This meeting had received an explanation of his plan from its author in person; his purpose being, as he explained it, to endow by instalments. "For this reason," he said, "he had used the word 'graduated.' There were dangers in too sudden inflation by very large endowments; and there was, at least, safety in endowing by degrees or step by step, as he believed (in deference to classical scholars who were present) the word 'graduated' implied."

At this appeal to classical scholars, Mr. Manson said, in an aside, "I'm afraid that word 'graduated' *often* implies *very* partially endowed, — indeed, chiefly endowed by their *degrees*." The members of the Board generally smiled; and Mr. Parmenter, having accepted the interruption with a smiling bow, began again: —

"It wouldn't do for him to question the attainments of college-men; he took it for granted that they were all learned, — as Shakspeare, he believed, said, 'all honorable men.' Possibly, too, the Trustees would pardon in him, as a man of business, a natural anxiety to see to the operation of his own plan, and to help in the administration of it."

Mr. Parmenter then informed the Board that "Mr. Don, who was one of their number, would, he was sure, do him the favor to furnish any explanation which might be desirable for the action of the Board, while he himself withdrew, in order to leave their consultation quite unembarrassed. He was aware that the question of endowment was not perfectly simple. There were evils to be guarded against. Endowments sometimes checked the spontaneous flow of liberality, were sometimes a hindrance to life and progress, and occasionally furnished incentives to extravagance. Perhaps he would be pardoned for using an illustration from his experience in the country. The Trustees were aware that he had devoted himself a good deal to the interests of the country, and, among other things, to the development of agriculture, — indeed, from early life, he had been more or less practically familiar with agriculture. Now, he had had occasion, in connection with agriculture, to use guano, as well as other kinds of manure; and he had observed that, while the manure helped the development of good crops, it helped the development of weeds too. He would here leave the matter, — asking the indulgence of the Trustees for having occupied them so long, and referring to his friend Mr. Don for any information which might be needed in his own absence."

He then took his hat, and withdrew; and the Trustees had the matter before them, after a grave set of vibrations from different members of the Board in returning Mr. Parmenter's parting salutation.

There was the very moderate-sized and large-mannered Dr. Farwell, with one long-necked, sober-looking, white-cravatted man; one short and squat man, in white cravat; several respectable gentlemen not noticeable for their dress; and one perhaps as likely to catch the eye of a stranger as any, the hearty, wholesome-looking Mr. Manson, who, partly behind the capacious chair-back which rose above Dr. Farwell's head, was reading, and with a pencil making notes. The life of this organized Board soon began to show itself after its manner.

"The first motion in order, I suppose," — said the long-necked serious clergyman.

"I think, myself," said the Reverend Dr. Farwell,

beginning in a tone, slow, measured, and important, which implied keeping on, "that we have arrived at an important era — I think we may, perhaps, fairly call it AN ERA — in the affairs of this School. The communication which has just been laid before us, as a Board, strikes my mind — I don't know how it may strike other members of the Board, but, I confess, it strikes my mind — as what may be the inauguration — I will use the word 'inauguration' for want of a better — the inauguration of a GREAT DAY!" (This last expression was pronounced with strong emphasis.) "The general question of endowments — *particular* endowments, *profuse* endowments — I am not at this moment prepared to go into myself; but I think we can't be mistaken in regarding this benefaction as an accession of just so much power and force to this School."

"Yes," said a gentleman opposite with a face somewhat like that of a reflective racoon, though with much more solid whiskers: "five thousand dollars is five thousand dollars;" and he relaxed the gravity of his face, with a smile, for that expressed the thing, and implied that the speaker knew more than that.

"I agree with Mr. Pettie," said the short and stout clergyman, as if he, too, understood that thing about as well as anybody: "five thousand dollars is five thousand dollars."

"There is more involved in this case than that," said a thoughtful gentleman, taking off gold spectacles and holding them in his hand. "I don't wish to interfere with any expression of opinion, or the offering of any motion; but, if agreeable to all the members of the Board, I should like to call upon Mr. Don for an explanation of the plan proposed."

The President bowed, saying that the suggestion seemed a very reasonable one.

Mr. Don assured the meeting that "it would give him much satisfaction to comply with Judge Allen's request;" and the general silence indicated that everybody present agreed with him. Dr. Farwell, seeing an occasion to give to that silence fitting expression, said: —

"Undoubtedly — he spoke for himself — it was eminently proper, before any action was taken, that they should have the case in its length, and in its breadth, and in all its dimensions, before them, that they might act understandingly."

When Dr. Farwell had thus put himself in the proper attitude to the business, Mr. Don began: —

"It had been (he believed) the intention of Mr. Parmenter — until diverted, perhaps, by a suggestion of his own (the speaker's) — to give a full explanation of his plan to the Trustees in person. The suggestion referred to was one made by himself, without premeditation, — a mere thought of the moment, — that the Trustees would like to testify by some action their appreciation of his liberality. This was simply his own natural feeling. Mr. Parmenter's explanation to himself had been brief. As he understood Mr. Parmenter, the plan was to endow with five thousand dollars now, and, after an interval, with five thousand dollars more; after another interval, five thousand dollars more; and so on. How long it was to go on, he could not say."

There was a pause, and, in the silence, a gentleman who had not yet spoken, but who seemed as if he had a good deal to say, inquired: —

"Do we understand, then, that five thousand dollars *is* already presented, is already in hand? That is part of the statement, I think? — I wish simply to put the thing into shape."

"Certainly, sir," answered Mr. Don; then, being familiar with propriety and parliamentary usage, turning to the President, he said, "If I may reply to Judge Pearson," and received a bow from the presiding officer. Then he proceeded, "I should say, in the absence of the Treasurer, that that amount, or its equivalent, is in the Treasurer's hands."

"It is in the Treasurer's hands, sir, at this moment?" repeated Judge Pearson, blandly.

"Yes, sir, so I understand, — some days ago," said Mr. Don.

"That seems to be conclusive, upon that point," said the Reverend Doctor Farwell.

"Then I should like to inquire — if there is no objection, and if I'm not taking the place of any other gentleman," said the Honorable ex-Judge Allen, — "for the purpose of laying the subject still further open, — whether the principal or the interest is available for the School."

"The interest, sir," said Mr. Don: "the principal is part of a permanent fund."

"Then," said the Reverend Doctor Farwell, who had a faculty for knowing just when he ought to speak, "the case, as I understand it, is in this way: The principal of five thousand dollars — or five thousand dollars — is in fund; is, to all intents and purposes, the commencement of a fund, which fund is to be increased. The interest of the five thousand dollars is to be used for the School, as it comes in."

"Will the gentleman," said Judge Allen, as soon as Dr. Farwell had put things into a shape satisfactory to himself, "pardon my asking one farther question: I wish to know the conditions attached to the donation; or whether the interest is placed unreservedly at the disposal of the Trustees."

"As I understand," said Mr. Don, in answer, "there are no conditions whatever, except the general condition that the interest of the fund shall be devoted to the payment of the teachers of Saint Bartholomew's School."

"That seems to settle the matter," said the long and serious-looking clergyman, who had not sat impatiently under the interruption of Dr. Farwell and the rest, but had entertained himself partially, in the mean time, by side-talk with different persons near him till his time should come. "Whenever the Board is ready for my motion, I am ready to put it."

"It will be proper, I suppose, to accept the endowment formally, and to thank the donor," said Judge Allen.

"Without passing judgment upon the plan of occasional endowment, which is only partially before us," said Judge Pearson.

"What we've got, we've got," said Mr. Pettie, with a smile.

"But expressing our willingness to take a few more of the same sort," said Dr. Buttonn (whose name we write with a second 'n,' to suggest its own pronunciation).

"My motion" — said the clergyman, who had waited so long.

"I cannot feel willing," said Dr. Farwell, sententiously, "I am decidedly unwilling to allow this subject to pass to a vote without" —

"We haven't any thing to vote upon yet," said the mover. "My motion" —

"I will wait for Mr. Merritt's motion," said Dr. Farwell, "of course."

"My motion is," said Mr. Merritt, reading, "'That the Trustees accept, with much satisfaction, the munificent gift of T. Parmenter, Esq., one of their number, and place upon record their grateful appreciation of the same; that the Clerk be directed to forward a copy of this resolution to Mr. Parmenter,' — simply a formal resolution of acknowledgment. We can now consider the matter, and take such action as we may see fit."

"Whatever action the gentlemen may take will, of course, be agreeable to me," said Judge Allen, putting on his coat, which he had left on a chair. "I shall be obliged to excuse myself."

Judge Pearson, too, "had engagements, and would be glad of Judge Allen's company;" and so the two ex-judges took their leave.

"I was merely going to say," said Dr. Farwell, begining another speech, with something of his large manner, and gaining more of it as he went on, "and I am glad to have an opportunity of giving expression to my decided conviction that this day may prove a turning-point in the history of our School. Already, without help, and under the excellent management of the Rector of the School, we are paying our way, and more, — we are more than paying our way, — I suppose I might say, we are prosperous, — without endowment. Now we shall be able to do more" (emphatic) "than we could before" (emphatic).

This was a good place to stop at; and, at this place, Mr. Manson, who had kept himself quietly occupied with his book and pencil until the judges, by going away, had left the burden of debate and deliberation to be borne by fewer members, said:—

"Verse again: 'Do *more*, Than we could *before*.' That's like your rhyme upon the Trustees."

Whether Dr. Farwell would have taken with perfect equanimity this obstruction to the flow of his speech, if there had not been in it the reference to his former success in a still higher department of letters, we will not say; but, as it was, he at once, with a wave of the hand, disposed of the rest of his speech:—

"That was all that I think it necessary to say;" and then turned, smiling pleasantly, to his neighbor, and said,—

"This, of course, was nothing: that was an accident, and was entirely unintentional,—unpremeditated. I wasn't conscious, at the time of making that rhyme (there it is again), that I was saying any thing more than plain prose,—the plainest prose. You know, of course, I didn't mean to call that poetry; but (you're a literary man) did it ever occur to you that poetry might not be confined to a few, the *Sacra Vates*, (what was it we used to learn in our Horace?) but was rather appropriated to certain states of mind" (with a very definite emphasis, for the doctor had thought these things over),—"states of exaltation? So that we're poets, just as we're eloquent, under what you may call an exaltation of the faculties. You're a poet when you feel lofty emotions. You're an orator the same way. I don't know whether this ever occurred to you so; but it seems to me often that I could be a poet,—that I wanted only 'the divine afflatus,' the breathing."

"It seems very probable," said Mr. Manson. "As an editor, I should say that was all that was wanting with most of our contributors."

"I never tried it on a large scale," continued Dr. Farwell, sententiously, as usual; "but I suppose that a man does it when he's in the state to do it. You put water into one condition, and it freezes: you put it into another, and it boils. You put a man into the condition, and he's a poet." (Here the vote was taken, and Dr. Farwell interrupted himself long enough to say "ay," and then continued.) "That idea struck me so forcibly that I wrote a sermon on that subject once, — 'All Scripture is given by inspiration,' — first showing the general meaning of 'scripture' (writing)."

"Mr. Don is coming with a proposition," said Mr. Manson, and so lost (if he had never heard it before) a summary of that discourse; for the speaker recovered himself easily from his flight, and alighted in silence among the discussions of the Trustees of St. Bartholomew's School.

"I had in mind, sir," said Mr. Don, who had not been in the Legislature for nothing, "that it seems proper to make some substantial recognition of the liberality which has been announced to us, — something more than a passing vote of thanks. I know that it is not uncommon to do it, in a lasting way. There's the Hemingway Classical Institute and the Phillips Exeter Academy, and others of that character."

"How would you propose to do in our case?" inquired Dr. Farwell. "'Parmenter's St. Bartholomew's' or 'St. Bartholomew's Parmenter's' would be a little harsh, wouldn't it?"

"Somebody else may give us five thousand dollars,"

said Dr. Buttonn, with a smile. "I don't object: I only think that we may be put to inconvenience if we undertake to name the School after every donor. I don't object."

"Couldn't we make it understood," asked Mr. Merritt, smiling, "that we'll adopt anybody's name that'll give us so many thousand dollars, and put the sum pretty well up?"

"Of course," said Mr. Pettie, "a prospective endowment isn't an endowment in hand."

"Suppose we adopt a system of graduated naming," said Mr. Manson, "at ten thousand dollars a letter,—or twenty thousand,—beginning with the Christian name?"

"All this perhaps, which is only intended for fun, is very well," said Dr. Farwell, with a genial smile. "I should be sorry to check the flow of fun: it wouldn't be good for boys, it wouldn't be good for men. I'm inclined to join in it, I'm inclined to make it at proper times; but it is not business. As Beauregard, or whoever he was, at Balaklava, said of the charge of the Six Hundred (I'm no Frenchman; indeed, I'm pretty much an Englishman about French): 'Say magnific, but non la gare,* — it isn't war.' Is there any further business? If there is not, I think we may as well be going about our own business."

Mr. Merritt, during Dr. Farwell's modest utterance of his quotation from Balaklava, had slyly remarked to Dr. Buttonn that "what was not French in it was pretty good English, which was probably better than their Mr. Sabot-Roquelaire would have done."

* A sentence much like this of Dr. Farwell's, in sound, is said to have been uttered by Marshal Canrobert: "C'est magnifique; mais ce n'est pas la guerre."

This criticism Dr. Farwell overheard, and answered good-naturedly : —

" Don't you meddle with my French ! it's the French of the Academy."

" Yes, you'd have learned better, in College," said Mr. Merritt, facetiously.

While this little by-play was going on, other members of the Board were engaged in conversation. There was by this time a general readiness of the Trustees to adjourn, when Mr. Don, saying that he saw the difficulties about the name, suggested that there might be some other way in which the Board could testify its appreciation.

" You've voted to thank Mr. Parmenter," said Mr. Pettie. " That's a beginning."

" If you do too much for one, you'll never be able to encourage anybody else," said Dr. Buttonn ; " but I don't object to any thing, — I only make that suggestion."

" As I understand it, sir," said Mr. Don, holding faithfully to his purpose, " Mr. Parmenter is beginning a series of endowments " —

" You might combine two things in this way," said Mr. Pettie. " The boys have a 'Pro-St.-Bart's-Day,' in December, because St. Bartholomew's comes in Vacation : you can have something special, on that day. Mr. Don tells me Mr. Parmenter's birthday comes about that time. You might put 'em together."

" That would be a very proper subject for future consideration," said Dr. Farwell, and, with general assent, the Trustees rose and adjourned.

CHAPTER XXVII.

MR. DON CALLS UPON MR. PARMENTER, ON BUSINESS.

NEAR the top of one of the most eminent hills, and just in the middle of Eastham, commanding a wide view in all directions, was a large and very architectural-looking house, which, as any one could tell you, was Mr. Parmenter's. This gentleman our readers have already met; and to this house we shift for a while the scene of our story, because Mr. Parmenter is not only a great man in Eastham, and has a good deal to say and do in town affairs, but also, as has been seen, carries great weight in the affairs of St. Bart's School, and influences, moreover, the fortunes of our Antony Brade. It is in the forenoon of one of those fine days that make the fall in New England the loveliest season of the world's year.

A flag-staff went up from the top of the roof into upper air, from which was commonly flying, in the latter part of the day, a red flag, with an angular device of some sort, which the neighbors differently explained. "Old Uncle Nat Burrows," at the foot of the hill (very often to be found, in pleasant weather, leaning on his stick, at his front gate), would say that "Tom Parmenter was jes' like a boy about that: 's quick 's ever he got home from his store, he set to work an' histed that thingumy, to let folks know he was there, — the way they did at the State House;" but what device it bore neither he nor any one near him would pretend to say, with certainty, — most of the neighbors having settled it that "it was some nonsense;" and Mr. Chambers, the carpenter, who had done "a sight of work in that house, first and last," saying that he "didn't know, but had always thought it was a square."

A short way went straight and steeply up — in some places by stone steps let into the sod — to a little flat, in front of the house; while a carriage-road wound up, with easy and leisurely bend, to the same place. The house had a great arch-way through the middle, from front to back, and had plenty of windows in front, and chimneys atop.

On both sides of the archway were verandas whose floors were continuous with opposite platforms inside the arch, on each of which opened handsome doors, — one from its size and style, evidently, the main entrance.

Up the side-path to this house, that day, the reader's friend, Mr. Don, had climbed, with some loss of breath and weariness of legs, if one might interpret his attitude and gait, as he stooped over, with his hand at his side, after getting to the gravelled flat before the house.

"'Ah! — who can tell — how hard it is — to climb —
The heights where Fame's proud pinnacle'" —

he uttered, as he could catch breath.

"Allow me to correct you, sir," said Mr. Parmenter, who was opportunely in front of his archway, at the moment: "'The height where Fame's proud *temple* shines afar.' I'm familiar with that stanza, for I print a very large edition of it every year, you know."

"No: you surprise me, sir," answered Mr. Don, recovering his wind, and speaking a little like books of the last century. "I wasn't aware of it, sir. I remembered the verse (or stanza), from the girls speaking it, at school, when I was a boy. You publish, then?"

"Yes, in connection with my business, I publish a large edition of "Standard Selections from the Poets."

"Certainly a very desirable thing, sir, to have your productions associated with the flower of our literature. As I frequently say, I can compare your situation here to nothing but a lord of the manor; that is, just about my ideal of what a lord of the manor would be."

Mr. Parmenter loked very modest at this compliment, and, turning, instinctively glanced over the front of his house, architectural and capacious, and answered, with befitting self-depreciation: —

"In a small way, only, sir, I'm afraid. We can't have the reality, here."

Mr. Don had followed the direction of the owner's eyes, and in looking upward caught the slow waving of the emblematic flag (of which, indeed, if he had known or remembered the habits of great families abroad, he might have made good use in the carrying-out of his comparison of Mr. Parmenter's position to theirs), and found in it matter for conversation and compliment.

"That flag is a great convenience. I had a little business, and I knew I should find you at home. One of your neighbors, sir, with whom I was talking as I came, asked me what that figure was on it. I couldn't tell him. It had never occurred to me to ask. If you were a druggist, I should say a hand and a pestle, sir. Connected with 'Melitrech'? A very good device (or whatever it's called): 'Melitrech' helped to build the house, I suppose?"

"No: that comes from a different source," said Mr. Parmenter, seriously. "My relation to my neighbors — and the town — and Saint Bartholomew's School — is such that there may be a little curiosity to know some circumstances about my family, — a little more than just '*he lived and died!*' There has been a proposition to secure my portrait by Rose, the eminent artist, for the Town Hall" ("I'm not surprised at it, sir," said Mr. Don), "and," continued Mr. Parmenter, "I suppose I shall be obliged to yield to the pressure, ultimately. That's the result generally, I believe, in such cases. I believe we generally yield."

This plural pronoun which he turned off so lightly might represent the human race at large, or that upper rank of it, — the heroic, — a sight of whom or of whose photographs so many long to see.

"I'm assured that the name is of some note: French, I think, in very early times, — Parlementer. You see the French, — 'parley,' 'parlez-vous,' 'Parliament,' 'Parmenter.' Mr. Merritt knows French, and has taken some trouble about it: I haven't given much time to those things."

Mr. Don's face had assumed an expression of good-natured amusement, which gained strength, and became more and more pronounced, as the speaker went on; but when Mr. Parmenter stopped, and looked inquiringly at his smiling visitant, Mr. Don hastened to remove any thought of incivility: —

"Pardon me, sir," he said. "I was thinking you might well say your pennon (if that's the word) was not '*pestle-lential;*'" and it was evident that it was only the fun of this joke, within him, which had put him into such merry humor, in spite of himself.

His host accepted the explanation, pleasantly, explaining that the device was one which Dr. Farwell had found in a book, and was a hand flourishing a scroll; and this gave Mr. Don an opportunity to use that vein of ready wit and compliment which is seldom at a loss in this world: —

"Every thing flourishes with you, sir, I believe," said he.

"That might be a little too much to say, perhaps," answered Mr. Parmenter, modestly; and here, like a man of business, he left off his dissertation on the probable eminence of his family, among the early French, and turned to other things: —

"Oh! I see," he said, "about the flag. Yes: I didn't go to the city. I was contriving a little improvement here." ("I think you're never satisfied without perfection," said Mr. Don.) "I want," continued Mr. Parmenter, "to put something in the style of a platform-balance here, that will throw up a draw-bridge, under the arch, when a carriage comes upon it." ("Very ingenious, truly," said Mr. Don: "we can always learn something, by coming up to Mount Fairfield.") "Then, you see, with my draw-bridge down, anybody can walk across from one side to the other, without being obliged to touch the ground at all. Then, when a carriage drives up, it comes upon the platform; the draw-bridge is lifted and caught by a self-acting hold, or spring. — Walk in, sir," and, leading his visitor up stone steps under the arch-way, he ushered that polite person, who made several bows, and uttered several compliments, in undergoing the treatment, into the chief door of what the proprietor called, as he opened it, "Fairfield House."

"It wants a lady of the manor, sir, does it not, to make it complete?" said Mr. Don, modestly, though possibly not for the first time. "There are some charming housekeepers, I understand, in Eastham, and of course plenty of them in other places. I did hear that Mrs. Osborn was likely to be the favored one."

"Perhaps they wouldn't come," said Mr. Parmenter, smiling serenely around upon the furnishing of his house.

"I've no fear of that, sir," said Mr. Don. "You have but to ask, I think." Then, without impatience to press the "business" which he had mentioned, he left the subject of a lady for the house. "I believe, sir, I never come into this room without thinking of some of the apartments in the noble mansions abroad. This was always a particular favorite of mine," he said, setting himself before a picture on the wall, in which was a hooded face, with a good deal of blue and some dark-red drapery. "It may not be finer than many others in your — gallery, I call it, sir, I don't know whether I am technically right, — but there's a religious repose, to my eye, about this" —

"That's counted very fine, sir; though I have several as fine, or finer," said the owner, letting his eyes wander over the richly framed treasures on his walls. "I think I've often called your attention to this," waving with his hand, and leading up to a corner of the room, where heavy silken cords and tassels were arranged, as he showed, to draw and draw back a heavy silk-damask curtain, so as to let in more or less light upon a fresh-hued painting in which some pretty beings — nymphs, or sylphs, or fairies, — merry and roguish-looking — were blowing, with fanciful and be-ribboned bellows, on rosebuds and buds of morning-glories, which were opening, at the breath. A good deal of really life-like and comely drawing and coloring had been put into this fanciful extravagance.

"A very happy conceit, sir, you observe, It's called 'The *Blowing* of the Flowers.'"

"And yet I think (if you'll allow me, sir) you're not *conceited*," said Mr. Don, emphasizing just so much, and smiling just so much as was becoming to a man who felt that he could, and wanted others to feel that he could, make a very neat joke without any appearance of effort. "I have often admired this painting, sir. I think, with you, that it's a very happy conceit, all but the word 'blowing,' which strikes me as a little ordinary. Doesn't it strike you so?"

"WORCESTER, sir, I believe," said Mr. Parmenter, like one who could quote authorities.

"I should suppose '*bloom*' was the more elegant English," said Mr. Don, like one who, for his part, had a choice in such things, and knew how to use our tongue.

"It's Worcester, sir. Mr. Merritt objected a little, too; but I satisfied him."

Now Mr. Don saw a favorable opening for his business, and mentioned it again. Mr. Parmenter accordingly led the way to a smaller room, which he pronounced to be his 'Study.' He did not, however, omit to say, as he passed a tall rosewood stand, on which, in the middle of a purple-velvet cushion, lay a very black and somewhat odd-looking fiddle. "This is probably the gem of my collection, — a genuine Stradivarius, — a Cremona of the sixteenth century, one of the only five known to exist in the world."

"I'm aware, sir; but it's all lost upon me, I'm sorry to say. I've no music in my soul, sir. Somehow, it was left out. — The business on which I came," continued Mr. Don, as they seated themselves near a large desk in Mr. Parmenter's "study," in the presence of an inkstand, a broad, open dictionary, an illustrated almanac, a Prayer-book, and a Bible, which gave a literary cast to the room, "is partly public, and partly personal to yourself. — You mentioned, if you remember, the custom of having some public recognition of those who have made great endowments; and you thought it might be as well, in your case, to wait for the future, — till after your demise. I found myself unable to agree with you, sir; and the more I have reflected on it, the more it seems to me eminently appropriate that it should be done now. The living example, sir, to my mind, is a great thing; and I think you should be willing to waive personal feelings for the sake of principle, as I make no doubt you would."

"I'll do any thing that's thought best, *if I approve of it*," said Mr. Parmenter, in a business-like tone; and he looked into the blaze of the fire. Then he turned to Mr. Don, with a smile, and added: —

"I won't do any thing I don't approve of."

"What I should propose — and I think it would meet the views of the other Trustees — would be to have a celebration by the School, on some particular day, — your birthday, for example" —

Mr. Parmenter sat, not as if taken by surprise, although

it seems always possible, in such cases, to take great men by surprise.

"How does the suggestion strike you, sir?" asked Mr. Don, after waiting for some expression.

Mr. Parmenter left his abstraction.

"I think," said he, "a proposition of that sort will keep;" and he smiled pleasantly. "There's no hurry about doing me honor;" and he stroked his face with his broad hand.

Mr. Don was not to be easily moved from his purpose.

"That's your way of looking at it, sir: I must take leave to differ. It isn't every day that a man gives five thousand dollars to endow tutorships in a school, — at any rate, our school has never had any such benefactions. The question of a proper name, or title, has been raised," he went on, as if the first point was by this time pretty well disposed of: "how would 'Patron' do?"

"Oh, no!" answered Mr. Parmenter, decidedly: "I should object to that name, as unpopular and invidious."

Mr. Don was embarrassed, but not long. He made another proposition: —

"It's proposed to call that fund 'The Sustentation Fund:' how would 'Sustentator' do? A little too unusual?"

"Too Latiny, ain't it?" asked Mr. Parmenter, who occasionally fell to plain English. "How do you spell it?" and he drew the open dictionary to himself. "There is no such word in 'Worcester,'" he added, after searching.

"An idea occurs to me, which might need further development," said Mr. Don, by no means at the end of his resources. "We have an American word — suggested to me by the circumstances of your position" — and here, sitting up straight, and looking earnestly into the fire, he thought vigorously.

The idea was, perhaps, a little crude as yet; for Mr. Don's active mind labored with it in silence for a moment, and then put it forth diffidently: —

"'Patroon' was the word which I had in my mind, sir. Your position, here, makes it natural. A patroon, as I understand it, is the chief man in the neighborhood, and owns most of the land there. That corresponds very well with your case, sir, I think."

"We never had any thing of that sort in this part of the country," said Mr. Parmenter, rising, but not as if he must absolutely reject it on that score: "do you think it would go down?"

"I put it forth as a suggestion: we can take it into consideration," said Mr. Don, rising too; "and I shall feel it my duty to bring up that subject of a demonstration on your birthday, at the next meeting of the Trustees. You haven't heard any thing more, I suppose, about our mysterious boy, since the Stranger's visit, the other day? You were going to make inquiry at Weston, sir."

"Yes: there was such a man there, with a letter. He'd been at Wale, Leavett, & Co.'s. Mr. Wale read his letter; but couldn't recollect his name. He said it was some sort of a jaw-breaking name" —

"Has he got the letter?"

"No; and he can't remember who it was from, whether it was from the Governor, or Lieutenant-Governor, or President of the Senate, or Speaker of the House, or who. All he can remember is, it was from some 'big bug,' as he said."

"We might inquire of every one of those, if it was important; but they wouldn't be likely to remember."

"No, sir; and we shouldn't want to make the matter too public by pushing it too hard. I wouldn't recommend being apathetic, like Rector Warren, — he made it almost a personal matter, you know, sir, — but I think we can afford to wait;" and, after this hopeful forestalment of the future, he took his leave, as courteously as he had entered.

CHAPTER XXVIII.

THE ROSICRUCIANS.

WHILE affairs, in the busy circle of the boys of St. Bart's, and in the wise counsels of its Trustees, were in this condition, there happened something to give a little new interest to the every-day life of the School, and concerning Brade and some of his friends.

Secret societies, which have come to the playing of so important a part in many of our colleges, and which have found their way into some schools, were forbidden here, as not being open and manly. Perhaps the Rector's eye and the practised intelligence of tutors may have been now and then eluded for a while, and some transient and timid organizations may have had two or three stealthy meetings, at long intervals, undiscovered; yet every thing of the kind was pretty thoroughly put out, and it might be said that no lasting combination of that sort existed here.

Of this halcyon state of things an invasion seemed now to be threatened.

A certain mysterious handbill, over copies of which small groups of boys had talked and wondered, was read by several tutors, and was made the subject of a little comment, even among them. It was a printed bit of paper, on which the first thing to draw the eye was a red cross. Above this were the letters "B. R. C.," and underneath it, "Rosicrucians. — This Brotherhood defends the widows and fatherless, provides for the poor and needy, and encourages each other. — No initiation-fee required. One black ball excludes from admission. — Per order G. M."

These — though not arranged as on that paper nor printed in the same type — were the contents of the handbill. The younger boys discussed it, when first found, as it was, in several of their rooms, remarking upon the cheapness of it, and "where they got money from, to do all their works, if their members didn't pay any thing;" and so dismissed it. It appeared again; and then the boys, having ascertained that the wording was just the same, and the printing just the same, began to wonder "what fellow was sticking these things about?" Towne applied to it a witticism of his own, which made no one laugh but himself, although it was about as good as the average of boys' jokes. "The Rosy-crutchers!" he said: "who'll be a rosy crutch?" Wilkins uttered another, about as good as this: he called the name "Rosy Christians." Sam Blake, coming along while several boys were making their comments upon it, said it was just the thing that he wanted; for he "had been obliged to leave a disconsolate widow and several fatherless children behind him, when he came to get an education, and he wanted them provided for." Peters, though he read the paper, with the others, made no comment; perhaps because of his general sympathy with chivalry. Brade had as many of these thrust into his alcove as any one.

Night after night these things found their way into the dormitories, and always into the same rooms, one of which was Brade's, another Remsen's, and another

Towne's. Where they were made, or how they were distributed, no boy could tell. Several printing-presses were owned in the School, and, except the red cross, more than one of them was competent to do the printing of this strange bill; but then none of these presses had done the work. Of course, if the printers had put their name at the bottom of the paper, it would have been a simple matter to read it; but no such help to discovery was there. There was the name "Rosicrucians," and there were the letters "B. R. C." and "G. M;" but these gave no information, and were, in themselves, mysterious.

If the scattering of these handbills had happened only once, all interest in them and curiosity about them would have died out with the first reading, and with the application to them of the usual amount of comment and discussion and witticism; but, coming again and again, as they did, they kept discussion astir; and, of course, the Tutors very early, and in time the Rector, became aware of the strange fact. Meanwhile, as much in fun as in earnest, one of the base-ball nines called itself 'Rosicrucian,' by anticipation of the next season; beginning so early in order to secure the name. This, as may be supposed, was not of the older boys, for they had attained to too much gravity and dignity to apply to any organization of theirs a name from a mere transient occasion; but the "Rosicrucian" Nine was not the youngest, nor the worst in the School; for it took in Brade and Remsen and Hirsett, and Albert Wadham and Towne, and others of less note. Tarleton had been in it; but had withdrawn, on finding the general feeling to be strong against him, and Peters half-filled his place.

In adopting the name, the Nine adopted the device of the red cross, to be worked upon a blue lozenge, or, as they called it, " a diamond," on the shirt-front.

This adoption into the life of the School ought, perhaps, to have satisfied the unwearied originators of this handbill; and it showed that, whatever unexplained mystery there might be about it, there was, at least, no apprehension of it, or scruple about meddling with it. Still, at short intervals, the production of the papers went on, and there was added, at the foot of them, in print, " Seek the Association."

" Who can be doing it ? " everybody in that dormitory asked, and " What's it for ? "

When the new words appeared, a gathering of boys discussed the subject in Brade's alcove, three of his visitors occupying places on his bed, and the rest sitting and standing as they might.

" It's the way fellows get people to attend to 'em," said Tom Hutchins, — " by keeping on. It's the way with advertisements. Why, look at Parmenter! Do you suppose anybody'd ever hear of Melitrech and that other stuff if he didn't advertise 'em ? He sends thousands of advertisements away out West (he don't care who sees 'em out there), and puts rhymes to 'em. Blanchard told me so. ' A man out West Thought he would test A better thing than honey: He drew a check For Melitrech, And found 'twas worth the money!' That's the way he does it."

" You made that up, Tom Hutchins," said Towne, who was within hearing.

" No, I didn't, fact. Blanchard out here told me. You ask him, sometime. He's got some prettier than that, — real poetry. I shouldn't wonder if he kept poets. They're poor, and don't have any thing to eat. Look here!" and then he began to repeat, "'The south-west wind'" —

"You've got it wrong!" said Blake, as Hutchins stopped. "Let a fellow try it, that's got a little poetry in him;" and, having sniffed, as if he were drawing in some fragrance, he repeated, in a dainty voice: —

"'Of all the scents that load the air,
Where'er the zephyr blows,
The sweet wind leaves the others there,
And bears off Aqua-rose.'"

Blake left off, with his face and eyes lifted up, and his right hand spread aloft, heedless of the "Encores" which greeted this recitation.

"Well, but what's this fellow going to sell?" asked Leavitt. "He hasn't got any thing to sell, unless it's red crosses."

"Well," said Hutchins, who, as we know, is something of a reasoner, "I tell you this chap's got deep thoughts. He wants to *make* out of it."

"I don't believe it's any thing but trying to fool us," said Remsen. "What do you say, Brade? Don't you believe it's just trying to fool us?"

Brade laughed: "We haven't got any widows and orphans," he said.

"Yes, we have, too," said Alonzo Peters, in an awkward sort of way. "My mother's a widow, and there are ever so many widows and orphans in the world."

"Oh, well!" said Remsen, "the orphans are to take care of their own widows. Everybody hasn't got to take care of all the widows and orphans."

"But who's going to look after the orphans, your

way, Remsen?" asked Tom Hutchins, who has encountered Remsen before.

"I tell you," said Peters, fortified by this unlooked-for support, "people have got to join together, to look after 'em, and the poor: the Church is for that."

"Gentlemen," said Towne, taking from his mouth, and holding like a cigar, a bat, which he was pretending to smoke, "you're wandering from the subject. What's this fellow printing these things and putting 'em in here for?"

"Oh! it's some *fellow* that's doing it, of course," said Remsen, giving, as the Chinese do, by his emphasis, an entirely different meaning to the word emphasized.

"If we don't take any notice of it, he won't do it,— you see if he does," said Hutchins. "'Tain't worth making a fuss over, any how."

To this they generally agreed, and dropped the subject. In the School at large, it was not talked of, now.

A night or two passed by, and then the printed things appeared in a new guise, in the same rooms as before. This time, there was a triplet printed below, in which "land," "holy band," and "heroes stand" rhymed together, as well as they rhyme in high verse like "Hail Columbia;" perhaps caught from that fountain, perhaps original with the author, or some one else.

As this came soon after the talk of the different visitors in Brade's room, and Tom Hutchins's rhyme, quoted from Mr. Parmenter, had not yet been forgotten, and as this doggerel appeared so soon after, the boys began to say that it was a joke of Hutchins's, and not a very bright one. Hutchins denied it, entirely, and said "they must not put such stupid stuff on him: if he was going to make any thing, he'd make something better than that."

The mystery, therefore, such as it was, had kept itself mysterious, up to this point. Here a sort of jog was given to it, which changed the condition of things.

There had been a foot-ball match between the Great Middle Class, as the Third proudly and facetiously called themselves, with the Fifth, on one side, and the rest of the School on the other. Towne had kicked hard enough for any three: every one had done his best. Once Brade had run the ball up among everybody, till Russell got a chance at it, and followed it nearly out, when Lamson had gone at it and kept it, in such a way that he ran it all the way down again. Gaston had done wonders; Wadham, the elder, had distinguished himself; Burgess had done as well as ever; Peters had run the risk of personal harm, in an astonishing way. Hutchins, Remsen, — who had not done honor to themselves, and worked hard for the victory?

In short, the field was manfully contested; and all who were engaged got hot, and pretty tired, when at last the challengers (the Third) with their allies, the Fifth, came out the conquerors by two out of three. Gaston and Hutchins happened to leave the ground together, and happened to be followed by Brade, whom Peters joined himself to. It was not yet late, and the greater part of the boys stayed where they were, for more play.

Gaston and Hutchins had taken a short run, to try their speed, and so had got a good way ahead. They reached the house, while still the other two were so far off that Peters's voice could not be perfectly heard, as he discussed the varied fortunes of the afternoon. Already, though it was not dark out doors, some lamps were burning in the house, and as they stopped not far from the back-kitchen door, which stood ajar, and indulged their curiosity by looking in, as they passed, they saw the cook, to be sure, in the inner room, and other women, too; but they saw something nearer, which drew all their eyes.

"Ain't he too handsome to be lying there?" asked Gaston.

Now, though the reader may be too old and wise to care, or may be impatient to see the connection of all this with the Rosicrucians, we must linger a moment here. This beauty, which delighted the clever Gaston, lay not in wholeness, nor in symmetry; for that which had been a full-fleshed, evenly browned bird of the mid-day board had been impaired a good deal in his integrity. Much of his mighty breast had been cut off, and one of his stalwart thighs. A broad, steep-sloping smooth of white stretched down from his breast-bone — which Gaston, learned fellow, while he stood there, with grinning face and watering mouth, twice told Hutchins was his "sternum" — under his strong pinion. About a fourth part as much of a gray, mottled substance stretched out, in like unbroken smoothness, beyond this white, to where the neck, cut off, bounded the view. Under the pinion, squeezed against his breast, — "the way a fellow carries a book," as the bookish Gaston reminded Hutchins, who, all this short while, was talking only with his eager eyes, — was a stout gizzard. Such was this sight; and in such a state of incompleteness was this once-splendid roasted bird, when seen by these two hot and hungry boys.

"There!" said Gaston, who could not keep his learning down, and who, perhaps, having nothing better to do, thought he could wear away a little time, while still enjoying, with the sight, a feast on which his more substantial senses were forbidden to make inroad, "there! that stuffing — just that sort of mixture of colors — is what the Greeks called 'ποικίλος' (poikil'os). It's a sort of" —

"I should like to try whether it would 'kill *us*,' I know," said Hutchins, for the first time breaking silence, and not only taking patiently his companion's learning, but taking the trouble to make a play of words on what he said. "Well, it's no good standing here: it only makes a fellow hungrier and hungrier."

Gaston, however, was not so minded.

"Hold on a minute!" he said. "Let's show it to these other fellows."

Upon the word, the other boys drew near, of whom the fantastic Peters was the most heard, discoursing of the doughty deeds that had been done that day.

"Somehow," he was then just saying, "you don't care when you get into it, do you?"

Gaston nudged his companion, and repeated aside his request: "Hold on, now, Hutchins!"

"We're waiting for you fellows," he said to Brade and Peters, as soon as they were near enough to hear him in his common voice. "Now's your chance! You haven't been in, yet. That's for the conquerors," (Peters and Brade, as the reader knows, were both Third-formers, while Gaston and Hutchins were of the Fourth), and, drawing back, he left room for them to come between him and the coveted sight.

"What do you mean?" asked Peters, looking

through the chink of the partly open door, and seeing, of course, that dainty dish which stood upon the table. "That ain't for *us?*"

"*We* didn't open the door, really: did we, Hutchins?" said Gaston. "*They* opened it. Now, you've just got to go right in, and ask for your share. There's Mrs. Porter; and there's Christina: they're all there, ready to wait on you."

Brade, whether through wisdom and wariness, or whether because he happened, at the moment, not to have what healthy boys are hardly ever without, an appetite at any time, for any good thing, and for almost any amount of it, said that "he was not hungry, and did not want any thing."

This statement Gaston treated with contempt.

"You don't know what you're talking about, man!" he said. "Look there!" and then poured forth a polyglot profusion of exclamations, as "En tibi! *ἰδού*! Voilà! There you have it!" and he pointed to the turkey.

Brade still declined; but Peters said "he guessed that he'd go in: he felt pretty hungry, for they'd worked hard."

"That's sensible!" said Gaston. "I wish I had your chance. Only be quick! There isn't much gone yet; but there'll be plenty of fellows here, before long;" and he looked up the road that led by the gymnasium to the play-ground.

"Come, Brade!" said Peters, not stirring yet: "you come with me, won't you?"

For some reason or other, this seemed not to be according to Gaston's plan.

Before Brade could answer, Gaston "took the word," as Frenchmen say.

"He'll come right in: she likes one at a time best. I want to ask Brade a question."

So, pushing Hutchins to one side, and drawing Brade by the button to the other, while the often-abstracted Peters seemed about lifting his foot to enter, Gaston addressed his captive thus: —

"Look here! What do you suppose 'turkey' is in Latin?" (Peters still lingered, but with his queer eyes fixed hard at the temptation: "Go on, Peters! don't be too long!" said Gaston, by way of parenthesis.) "Don't you suppose" (to Brade, again) "they had a" —

"But they didn't know about turkey," said Brade. "It's a new thing, isn't it?"

"The Romans must have known!" said Hutchins. "The Turks are a big people."

"Don't you suppose," Gaston continued, without changing the character of his sentence, "they had a word 'dindo'? You know the French — (Rush in, Peters!)" Gaston's voice trembled with the excitement of the occasion. Then to Brade, again: "It sounds like Greek *Διν*" (din—). Peters was slowly, and with a very uncertain hand, opening the door a little, when the cook, whose ears were good, looked toward them, and Peters started; the other boys keeping themselves out of sight, at each side.

Peters went, with his usual wavering and unsteady step, across the floor of the back kitchen, and presented himself, awkward and hesitating, to the authorities of the inner room.

Peters began to speak, and immediately there was a laugh of scorn from within.

"I won't leave him," said Brade.

"No," said Gaston, whose plan now seemed to admit of a change. "Go in and bring old Peters off!" and he made way, and Brade went in. "Now, Hutchins!" said the chief speaker: "there's a towel!"

Brade went in to the relief of the undaunted Peters, and found, when he got to his side, that that boy had not succeeded. The cook was just saying, with the utmost downrightness, to the applicant, "that it would be a pretty thing for her to be giving a bit of turkey to every boy that played foot-ball;" and one of those attendant women, who were to have been so ready to help in the distribution of the reward to the conquerors, craftily advised that "the turkey should be looked after, where it was." Things therefore gave little hope of rewards to the strenuous victors from the play-ground.

The cook sent an assistant to bring the great fowl in, and to begin cutting slices for the table; and Brade and Peters turned to go from the fruitless errand, when suddenly there rose a cry from the assistant that "the turkey was gone! there wasn't sight nor sign of it!"

Then was there running and crying out, among the maid-servants of St. Bartholomew's School; and, as may be supposed, the two members of the victorious Third were given to understand, in very plain English, that their room was better than their company; that "the Rector would find it out, and then they'd have to take their deserts; that if boys went on in this way, there would be no living at St. Bart's;" and as much more of wise thought and earnest exhortation, as half a dozen excited and indignant women could put into words in the space of a minute.

It was to no purpose, of course, that Peters rather indignantly denied any business but just the honest one of asking for a bit of turkey; and said that he had not got even that. All eyes, his own included, although they were different from other people's, could see that where a turkey had been was nothing now but a large empty dish, on which were a very few and slight, however savory-looking, traces of the great roasted bird which a boy could not look at without wanting.

Brade assured the cook that "Peters was perfectly innocent, and that he himself had only come in to keep Peters company, for he did not want any turkey."

The cook's answer to all this was, "Of course not; what would he want turkey for? Boys didn't eat turkey, — oh, no!" and another less angry, but not less indignant female explained that "these two were only blinds; and, while they were talking, others were carrying off the fowl. That was the way of it."

Brade's face, as we know, was a very sympathetic and communicative one; and at this explanation it went through sudden conscious changes. He had too much presence of mind to call out to their late comrades at the door; and, after insisting upon giving his word that they knew nothing about it, he hurried away the unpractical Peters, who wished to stay and clear himself, and got him out of the door.

Strangely enough, their troubles seemed only to have begun within the house; they went on worse, as soon as the boys set their disappointed and indignant feet upon the great earth that holds up every thing.

Just by the door, apparently attracted by the turmoil, were Tutors Bruce and Hammersley, who had been down at the play-ground when the match was played. Gaston and Hutchins were no longer to be seen.

The women, who had been so hard when talking to the boys about the punishment that they deserved, now, when they saw the Tutors, drew in, or threw away, a good share of their hardness. "The turkey was gone," they said; "and it had been stolen. Orders had come, express from the Rector, to have some for the boys' supper, and it had been standing right there, upon that dish, in open sight. The cook had seen it, and Christina had seen it; anybody might see it, up to the time these boys came in, five minutes ago, or less than that. Then these came in, asking for a bit, because they'd beat the foot-ball, and while they were standing there the bird was gone, — just the way it was then;" and here two of the speakers pointed to the sad emptiness of the dish; and one, to make the expression stronger, took the goodly-sized and shapely piece of stone-china between her two hands, and showed how light and how utterly empty it then was. It was the opinion of the cook and her chief associates that "the Rector ought to know how high-handed the boys were getting."

The Tutors, without expressing any opinion, set up a preliminary court of inquiry on the spot; and the two boys told their story, leaving out, of course, all other names than those of one another. Peters came nearest to mentioning a third party, when he said that "they told him that any of the Third and Fifth could have some turkey, by only going in and asking for it. That was all he did: he just asked civilly, and they told him he could not have any." The reader knows the story.

"If boys tell you, up and down, a thing, you must believe 'em," said Peters.

"It ought to be so," said the Tutors. "Did you believe them, too, Brade?"

"I didn't ask for any, sir," said Brade. "I didn't want any. The girls were all laughing at Peters, and so I went in, to stand by him and bring him out."

This story furnished a very imperfect explanation of the turkey's disappearance, for it left that point untouched: it accounted for the doing of these two boys, supposing it to be true; and a boy's word, at St. Bart's School, was always taken to be true, unless overwhelmingly contradicted, which seldom happened.

So Brade and Peters, coming home as victors from the well-fought field, are caught suddenly in unsuspected toils. They had nothing to do with the carrying off of the turkey: they can fancy how it went, but cannot open their mouths, except to assert their own innocence.

The Tutors go in before them, and Mr. Bruce turns off (as the boys can easily understand), to report to the Caput.

"Well, don't let's tell Gaston and Hutchins about the Tutors," said Peters. "It'll serve 'em right, for playing us such a trick."

To this Brade readily agreed, laughing at the prospect; but soothing his aggrieved companion with the assurance that "those boys did not mean to get them into trouble"

CHAPTER XXIX.

THE TURKEY FOUND, BUT NOT THE SECRET SOCIETY.

MR. BRUCE went straight to the Rector's study, and, being admitted, found Mr. Wilson, the Head-Tutor, already there.

"Something more about the Rosicrucians?" asked the Rector. "Mr. Wilson has just brought one bit of information," and he handed to the last-comer one of the now long-familiar cards of the "B. R. C." and the Red Cross.

"Turn it over," said Mr. Wilson to his brother-tutor; and on the back appeared "Cœna Lux. Reg. ap. Hol. XXIV. Hor. 8½, Hod."

"It would be astonishing," said the Rector, "if a secret society, with feasting, could have been going on under our noses, and with our leading scholar in it. I'm told that Gaston calls his room 'Holworthy 24,' after his brother's in college; and this looks like a notification to supper, there, to-night."

"And there are only two boys in School that use Greek or Latin that way, — Gaston and Brade," added Mr. Bruce.

"Our two philologists!" said the Rector, with a shake of the head.

"And I've got something about Brade," said Mr. Bruce.

The Rector looked rather blank at this announcement, as if the clouds were unexpectedly thickening; and Mr. Bruce proceeded to tell his story about the pillage of the lordly turkey, during Brade's and Peters's visit to the kitchen.

"There's something much wholesomer in it, from its all being under our own roof, at least," said the Rector. "Then Brade and Peters say that they went in to ask?"

Mr. Bruce explained their story, that Peters went in, because he was told that he might, and Brade to bring off Peters.

"Then you'll accept this invitation," said the Rector to Mr. Wilson, "(it's at First Bed-time) and we'll wait for further developments. They'd better be allowed about three minutes to get comfortably together; but not more, for they'll be quick."

This arrangement having been made, the council broke up.

At tea, Gaston and Hutchins, whom the reader will remember to have been at the back-kitchen door while the turkey lay on the dish, ate their supper like other boys; and certainly, if they had any consciousness of a coming feast, they did not, by way of preparation, spare the sliced turkey on the table.

After tea Gaston and Hutchins used the few minutes of free time as industriously in play as any of the boys. School went in, and time went on, to first bed-time. Then Gaston and Hutchins went quietly out with the lower-form boys.

There was no disorder in entry or room: the younger fellows had their own subjects of conversation, among which, as may be supposed, Brade's adventure with

Peters, and its probable consequences were discussed, with much prudence about pronouncing any other names than those of the two.

Among the rooms of larger boys all was quiet; and about Gaston's room, or "Holworthy 24," all was particularly still.

Within a few minutes Mr. Wilson quietly made his appearance in the passage-way; and then, if any heads had before been appearing now and then at doorways, if any occasional missile had before been hurled now and then from one room to another, all sight and almost all sound of boyish life was gone.

In this state of things, the Head Tutor walked silently straight to Gastón's door, and without formality entered. Two lamps were burning on the bureau; but, by a contrivance familiar to boys, the unusual light was hindered from making a more than usual show by barricades of books.

Four boys — Gaston and Hutchins and Towne and "Ultimatum" Blake — were standing with their backs toward the door, or rather with all their faces toward the well-lighted top of the bureau. Towne had "got himself up" in what he perhaps considered a holiday rig; for not only was his hat turned inside out, as we have seen it before, but he had managed to put on his coat upside down, with the tails falling like a cape down his back. Hutchins and Blake were in their usual dress, — Blake at one end, where half of his face could be seen drawn into a very comical expression, but intensely silent, and with his eyes fastened unwaveringly. Gaston had on what may have been meant for a priestly garb from old Rome. His chief garment was a sheet fastened about his neck and trailing to the ground, except where one foot, in a stocking, was thrust out behind. About his head he had a band of twisted cotton-batting, and round that a purple neck-tie whose ends hung down at the back. His face could be seen in the looking-glass which hung over the chest of drawers; and it was overflowing with satisfaction. The glass also showed, what the shoulders of the boys otherwise hid, the ample remains of a huge roasted turkey.

"Gentlemen," Gaston was saying, in a voice narrowed down to the necessity of the case, "I bid you welcome to this auspicious feast! Under the nose of Wilson, most vigilant of observers; between the hands, as you may say, of Bruce, most sagacious of tutors, *per tela, per hostes*, have I, with the help of Hutchins, borne this bird. Time fails. Draw swords, and march into the beast, as I do!" and thereupon he cut a thick slice of breast and stuffing, and three knives more assailed the savory meat.

There was a hurried noise of cutting, with a glad murmur of voices and then a general munching of the festive viands, all in a moment, when a new voice was heard: —

"I've come upon this invitation," said Mr. Wilson, showing the card, while, before he had spoken three words, the four feasters had faced about to any quarter but toward the bureau. Gaston, whose eyes had taken in the card and the Tutor at once, still kept a good deal of the merriment in his face, with his cheeks stuffed full of turkey. Blake increased the drollery of his look at this unexpected diversion. In one hand stretched out, he held his knife; in another a large piece of unbitten flesh from the great fowl.

"I'm authorized to invite the whole company to the Rector's study," said Mr. Wilson, "with the turkey. Gaston, you'll lead, with the turkey in the napkin; and all of you follow, just as you are. I'll come behind, with one of these lights."

In this order, therefore, the procession set forth; all but Gaston following Blake's example, in eating most diligently as they went. Gaston's hands were so occupied with the larger burden that he was denied that comfort. Towne, having a leg and drumstick, could hardly hope, even with the most frantic efforts, to make his bit much less conspicuous by the time he reached the Rector's presence.

A strange-looking company they were; but the Rector maintained his gravity.

"So these are some of our Rosicrucians, are they?" he asked. "And who's the head of your society? You, Gaston?"

"There's no society, sir," said Gaston. "I happened to have a turkey" —

"Yes, I know the history of the turkey," said the Rector. "First explain that card," — pointing to it in Mr. Wilson's hand. — "Put all your bits of turkey here," he added, spreading several thicknesses of newspapers on the floor, on which they all made their deposits. "Now, Gaston, explain that card, if you please."

"This side of it is my side," said the boy. "I don't know any thing about the other. This is just one that I picked up."

"Read and explain your own side, then," said the Rector; and Gaston read and explained, a little awkwardly: —

"'Cœna regalis luxus, apud Holworthy Viginti-quatuor, hora octava et dimidia, hodie,'—a supper of royal luxury, at Holworthy 24, at eight-and-a-half o'clock, to-day."

Amid the discomfiture of the feasters, this glowing announcement fell absurdly.

"Now for the other side of the card, — this stuff about the Rosicrucians, — who can explain it?"

Here Blake spoke: —

"Nobody knows any thing about that, sir. That's a sort of ghost: none of the fellows know any thing about it."

"None of you know any thing about it?" asked the Rector.

To this question all gave so definite and evidently honest an answer in the negative as to make it clear that Gaston's entertainment had nothing to do with the Rosicrucians or any other secret society, and that the "B. R. C." and the Red Cross were as much mysteries as ever.

The boys looked down at the booty on the floor.

"A liking for turkey's not a bad taste, Edward," said the Rector; "but a liking for turkey that isn't yours is."

"Blake and Towne hadn't any thing to do with getting the turkey," said Gaston; "and Brade and Peters. They didn't know any thing about it. — I don't believe they do yet," he added, smiling at the thought.

But the end was come.

The little company of revellers was dealt with, first of all, by ordering them, just as they were, down to the kitchen, to restore their stolen food. Their proper punishment was to come in due course the next day.

CHAPTER XXX.

MR. PARMENTER MORE THAN EVER ACTIVE.

PEOPLE with a strong turn for being busy have their times and seasons, like other things and beings, and sometimes are stirred up to special busyness. Our Mr. Parmenter had his busier times. If we might use a poetical figure about a man who was not poetical, we should say that that strong sea-swell which had floated on its bosom the grand project of "Graduated Endowment" broke itself up into many wavelets of lesser activity, before sinking back to the common level of the sea.

The noise of the fights had reached the alert and active ears of Mr. Parmenter, and not less the story of Gaston's and Brade's ambitious adventures among Words and Languages. The turkey, stolen and recovered, had occupied his attention; the traps, and Rainor's supposed connection with them, had not escaped him; he knew of the Rosicrucian mystery.

In all these, Mr. Parmenter interested himself, and with an amount of bustle unwonted even in him.

About the traps he satisfied himself from boys of the School; as to the turkey he made, in passing, personal inquiry at the scene of the marauding; complimented, with dignity, the cook and Christina, in turn, on their carefulness and skill, — receiving, in his face, a smiling expression of satisfaction at being appreciated, and in his back, when he turned it (alas! cooks are not choice in their English) the comment that "there were some would be always sticking their noses where they thought there was a hole: couldn't he leave the Rector of the School to look after his own kitchen?"

He had convinced both Mr. Don and the Rev. Mr. Merritt that they ought to go (as they accordingly did) to ascertain whether discipline had been wisely administered in the case of Tarleton and his two unwilling antagonists.

Lastly, he came himself on a friendly visit to Rector Warren's study; and, after a preliminary compliment, as he looked round with a sort of salutatory wave of his hand and hat to the books and other ornaments of the room, that "he always felt awed, in such an atmosphere of learning and taste," went on to speak of the various happenings and doings in such a way as to show his familiarity with School-topics, and his never-flagging interest in them.

"The Trustees felt," he said, "that the School was in able hands. He regretted that a *secret organization* seemed to baffle the authorities, — that sort of thing had been too much for former Rectors."

Then he smilingly changed the subject to Brade's treatment of Tarleton. He "supposed that some people would recognize Brade's conduct as high blood showing itself, — a flashing-out of the diamond. He didn't attach much importance to those things; but there was no knowing how strong blood was, that might be said to have filtered for centuries through pretty choice clay. And then, he supposed, it wouldn't do" (this he said by way of parenthesis, and with very evident embarrassment) "for people who had some pretensions that way themselves to be hasty in saying that old blood was not a very powerful instrument. He himself, perhaps, was drawn by his descent to French manners and tastes."

To this, of course, the Rector of the School, being a well-bred and sensible man, assented, and said that "it was very possible." This gentleman, as we have already seen, was not enthusiastic on the subject of Brade's mysterious birth.

Mr. Parmenter enlarged a little: —

"He was glad to find that Brade's abilities kept pace with his future station, — in this or any other country" — (a difficult figure, but boldly managed), "and that he was going to turn out an honor to his position. Mightn't it be well," he asked, "to put a boy like that, — like Gaston and Brade, for example, — forward, without spoiling them? There were not many public occasions, to be sure; but a classical speech assigned to two such boys as Gaston and Brade, for instance, on some public occasion, might be a good thing; for their scholarship was creditable to the School.

There was a tone of recommendation through all this, that, very likely, did not make it more pleasant to the Head of St. Bartholomew's School.

He answered simply, "Yes; very likely."

Mr. Parmenter, with much definiteness of purpose, went on: —

"There was one thing which, he thought, it might be well to mention. Not many things, generally, escaped him; but he had observed Brade particularly, at Church, for the last Sunday or two, because (he believed) Brade was a candidate for confirmation. Now, of course, his behavior was always like a young gentleman; but Mr. Parmenter had observed one practice, which, perhaps, might be corrected at once. All through the prayers, Brade appeared to have his eyes shut, while his lips were moving. Now Mr. Parmenter did not know what might be the custom in *foreign churches;* but it would not do to make exceptions or allowances here. St. Bartholomew's was a Church School, and it must be understood that whoever came to it must conform. The rule of the Church was to follow the book with the eyes open, was it not? Mr. Parmenter thought it might be well to speak to Brade privately. There were other things, about the deportment of different boys at their prayers, which he would reserve for another time. He thought Brade's case important as a candidate for confirmation, and brought up, perhaps, in another way."

The Rector of the School, as we should expect, having seen him through former visits of this sort, had sat impatiently under the latter part of this speech, and had risen from his seat before it was finished.

He answered a little unceremoniously: "He thought very well of encouraging Gaston's and Brade's scholarship; but the other suggestion he could not accept. He must take leave to be guided, in such matters, by his own discretion. There was no question about indulging foreign habits. The boy, he believed, had never been inside of any place of worship in his life but one sort; and he was going to be confirmed just as he had been brought up. But the boy was singularly truthful and earnest, as sensitive boys were apt to be; and in spiritual things must be treated with great reserve and delicacy."

Mr. Warren spoke hastily; but his visitor, with only a slight change of countenance, accepted the difference of opinion. It had not been without moral benefit, probably, that he had had the practice, for many years, of managing his temper and manners, in dealing with customers from behind a counter. His control of himself, now, was just about of the same sort that we have seen him apply to his horse, and with the same apparent consciousness that what he was doing was the right thing, and done just rightly.

"He was sorry that their views did not entirely coincide," he said; but then, by a sort of transition that seemed habitual with him, changed the subject, and congratulated the Rector of the School on "having so good a set in his kitchen." He finished, in his usual handsome way, by saying that "he had observed a vacant place for a statuette" (the word seemed familiar to him): "might he be allowed to present a mate to the figure of a martyr, in the corresponding place?"

Mr. Warren thanked him, but declined: "the place was already provided for."

The visitor departed ceremoniously, and in the hall was probably unconsciously rehearsing the interview; for, with hat in hand, he was in the midst of an elaborate bow to the emptiness before him, when the cheery salutation of Mr. Manson, from below, interrupted.

Mr. Parmenter recovered himself; and, having ascertained that his pastor "had a few moments' leisure," led the way to the outside of the house, and there addressed himself to the Rector of the Parish. To him he represented the propriety of exact conformity by the boys of their School, when in Church; and testified, from his own observation, to sundry discrepancies.

"How do you manage," asked the parson and editor, "to keep such a strong eye to earth when you're praying? I couldn't for the life of me. I think the boys behave very well; and it isn't a good thing to meddle too much."

"It's as well to have things right, I suppose?" said Mr. Parmenter.

"Oh, yes! but meddling too much is what I'm talking about. Here's one of the leading places in this country: its Dutch neighbors, in Colony times, for always trying to domineer, called it Boss*-town, and the name's stuck to it ever since,—just as the thing has too, for that matter."

"I don't quite see the connection," said Mr. Parmenter: "you can hardly call doing your duty 'meddling,' I think."

"I'll tell you where to begin, though," said the parson. "Begin at the older people. There are some of your Trustees that kneel in a very trusteeical way when they're here,—with nothing but their heads. There's a missionary field for you to expatiate in. You'd better go at them. It'll do 'em good."

Mr. Parmenter was grave and in earnest:

"The cases are not quite parallel, I think, sir," he said. "The boys are under our control, to be brought up as they ought to be. We can hardly apply the same rule to grown-up people, who are their own masters."

* To be exact as a philologist, Mr. Manson ought to have given the true Dutch form, "Baas" (pronounced *Baws*), and not the American form of it, "Boss." The Bostonians show the force of traditional habit, in pronouncing the name "Baws-ton," to this day.

Here Mr. Parmenter, by an easy diversion, changed the subject a little, changing his mind also.

"You're aware that there's to be a meeting of the Trustees on Thursday, sir?" he asked; and having given this turn to things, and received Mr. Manson's answer, he courteously left him to pursue his visit to the Head of the School.

As the visit does not directly concern our story, we leave the account of it untold.

CHAPTER XXXI.

THE TRUSTEES MEET.

The meeting of the Trustees had been called to occupy Mr. Parmenter's house on an evening during a three-days' absence of the owner.

The day had been rainy, and the night was so; but the room was bright with chandelier and candles, and a quiet blaze of cannel coal from a long and very low and open iron basket, laid across a pair of handsome andirons.

A majority of the Trustees came. The Judges were absent. Counsellor and Law-lecturer Pethrick had been made sure of.

Dr. Farwell was bland to a high degree. Dr. Buttonn twirled his thumbs, while he awaited whatever action might be proposed. Mr. Manson was not, this time, reading and pencil-marking, but apparently indulging himself in absolute leisure; talking, listening, keeping silence, as might happen. Mr. Pettie wakefully held his place, looking out from under his eyebrows, and entered into little conversation, as if afraid of delaying the opening for business. Mr. Don was in a condition of grave importance, as having been the chief occasion of this meeting, and likely to have a chief hand in the furtherance of its action. Mr. Merritt was in a state corresponding to that of Dr. Farwell:

where the Doctor was more than commonly spreading and wise and beaming, the other was, perhaps, more than usually quick and to the point.

Between Dr. Farwell and his friend a by-play had been going on, in which more than one familiar, and therefore inoffensive, joke had been let off by familiar hands. The younger divine had been already called, with emphasis, a Merritt-orious trustee, and a Merry-ttorious man, and also an e-Merritt-us officer. Very likely even then the reverend Doctor had not emptied his quiver of half the bright-tipped weapons with which he wore it loaded.

The meeting was called to order; and Mr. Merritt retaliated by saying, as he leaned over, "And now Farwell, a long Farwell, to all thy brightness!"

Dr. Farwell entered upon business in the happiest state. His eyes twinkled at each side of his nose like lighted windows in fishers' cots nestling at each side of a jutting promontory. (There's a pretty figure for our tasteful readers!) He sat there, ready to do justice to every thing in turn, and to carry all, if needful, along with him. His last private act was to call Mr. Manson's attention, aside, to the artistic taste and beauty of a pair of andirons, of gold bronze, on the hearth, and which represented furnace-men, shielding their faces with mittened hands from the heat.

The minutes of the last meeting having been read, and a pause ensuing, Counsellor Pethrick employed the empty time in laying out the business, as "it seemed to divide itself naturally, into two parts, each of which was capable of further subdivision: I. Shall the Trustees institute commemorations of benefactors? *a.* Shall individual benefactors be recognized in their several capacities? *b.* Shall Mr. Parmenter be so recognized? II. What shall be the character of the commemoration? *a.* Shall it take the shape of a School holiday? *b.* What shall be the character of the public celebration?"

This systematic treatment of the subject had an effect which it often has, of making everybody ready to proceed to the immediate consideration, and, if possible, the speedy settlement of the business. Dr. Farwell felt that it was his time to give that direction to things. There was in him now no trace of pleasant levity: he was all himself.

"We have heard," he said, "the matter well laid out, — laid out with the largeness of scope and accuracy of definition of a legal intellect. It was proper — it was fitting — that it should be so laid out. He had no doubt that every one present felt, as he did, the eminent propriety of the thing. The word which he [Dr. Farwell] had in his own mind to say was that, as there were moments for reflection and deliberation, so there were moments for action. It seemed to him that the time had now come for action."

At this point his friend Mr. Merritt "moved that, in order to bring the subject in a tangible shape before them, the propositions which they had just heard should be reduced to resolutions and acted upon separately." Mr. Pettie offered a ready pencil to the mover for this purpose.

The subject was now open for discussion, in the consideration of the first resolution: *Shall the Trustees institute commemorations of benefactors?*

Upon this point the opinions seemed already pretty well made up. Dr. Buttonn, smiling, said that "those sort of things tickled benefactors, amazingly." Mr. Pettie "saw no objection: people when they give like to be recognized." Dr. Farwell "did not know that there was any objection: people give, because they have got something to give. There is the broad fact. The question is, Shall the fact be recognized? Well, Shall the sun be recognized? Will you recognize the rain? Then, as to a *public* recognition. We are *a public body;* the world looks upon us as *a public body:* we can't hide ourselves, — we can't put ourselves out of sight, — as *a public body.* We" —

Mr. Merritt "thought that, if the Trustees were ready, the first resolution might be submitted to a vote;" and Dr. Farwell, falling back into his armchair, expressed all the rest of his sentiments, as well as his concurrence in the general tide of opinion, by a wave of the hand. The resolution was adopted.

Upon the second resolution, about recognizing *individual* benefactors, a great deal of good sense and discrimination was shown. Dr. Buttonn expressed a large truth when he said that "there were but three hundred and sixty-five days in a year, and if you have three hundred and sixty-five benefactors you may have three hundred and sixty-five holidays; and then you'd have no time for school."

To this Mr. Manson answered that "each might take his turn — one a year — for three hundred and sixty-five years."

A difficulty was apparent here. Mr. Manson's proposition could hardly be intended seriously to meet it. Dr. Buttonn inquired whether "you could set a certain stent, and say all who came up to that stent should have a day?"

It "struck" Mr. Counsellor Pethrick "that this arrangement might be inconvenient; for, unless you set your mark pretty high, you would not obviate your difficulty, and, if you set it high, you seem to cut off Mr. Parmenter, who (as the Counsellor understood it) was only giving five thousand dollars."

"Excuse me, sir," said Mr. Don, for the first time taking part. "I understand Mr. Parmenter to be giving five thousand dollars at a time: he may give ten times five thousand dollars, or he may give twenty times five thousand dollars."

"But five thousand *at a time?*" said Counsellor Pethrick, "and not more than five thousand, *yet?*"

"Suppose we lump 'em all together, as I believe was proposed last time," said Mr. Merritt, "and that'll settle two of your resolutions" (looking at his paper). "You'll recognize individuals, and you'll recognize Mr. Parmenter, who is your first benefactor;" and he moved the adoption of a resolution to that effect. It was carried.

It was now proposed that the Counsellor's second head, with its two subdivisions, should be disposed of in the same compact way: "There shall be a School-holiday, with such arrangements for the celebration as a committee may determine." The resolution was adopted, and Dr. Farwell, Mr. Merritt, and Mr. Pettie were appointed the committee.

Every thing seemed to have gone well. The evening was rainy: the Trustees were all to sleep in Eastham, — there was no hurry. Instead of adjourning, therefore, when the business was done, the members stayed together, talking; the chairman of the Committee, Dr. Farwell, remarking that, "in making their plans, the

Committee would have the advantage of hearing an expression of the views of the Trustees."

"The Committee," said Dr. Farwell, "are establishing a precedent for posterity, — for all time. They will want to have large views. They cannot prevent their action from being scrutinized ages hence, — it's one of the conditions of their office. Posterity will say, 'Here was a committee, composed of such and such members, — why did they make this arrangement? We see the name of one Farwell here. What was the determining consideration in his mind? What was the ground of his action?'"

Mr. Manson suggested that the chairman of the Committee might leave on record, for posterity, an account of the processes of his mind, in coming to a conclusion. Dr. Farwell, acknowledging that this might be done, thought that it would be better to have their action explain itself, so that it might be said, "Here was such a one (Farwell or any other): his course is a track of light."

"Suppose we talk it over," said Mr. Merritt. "What is proposed? You want something that the boys can take part in."

"It occurred to me, sir," said Mr. Don, modestly, "that a procession, with some decorations, — perhaps some exercises —. There are two boys, — Gaston and" —

"You must remember you've got winter," said Mr. Merritt.

Dr. Buttonn, who had seen the inside of trade himself, said: "It'll be a pretty good advertisement."

"Suppose it is," said Mr. Pettie: "it's all fair and legitimate."

"Oh!" said Dr. Buttonn, "I don't object at all. I wouldn't object to any thing that's proposed."

Mr. Counsellor Pethrick, the moment it had been understood that the Board was going to relax a little of its order and stiffness, and be informal, had lighted a cigar, and stretching out his legs, and resting his head on the back of his chair, was comfortably and reflectively blowing slow and long streams of smoke up towards the ceiling. Acting on his suggestion, the Reverend Doctor Buttonn had cloven a huge lump of cannel coal, and brought forth a blaze of light and warmth.

Out of his serene infolding, the lawyer spoke: —

"Parmenter's made a wonderfully good thing out of that 'Melitrech.' Who gave him the name?"

"One of the results of having a classical school at his elbow," said Mr. Manson.

"And now he wants to have a Latin speech, on the *Great Day*, eh?" asked the lawyer.

"You'll have to have your 'exercises' in-doors, if the weather isn't good," said Mr. Merritt. "It's proposed, I believe, to give a Latin speech to one or two of the best scholars, — Brade, the Great Unknown, and Gaston" —

"There is *something* about that boy, *isn't* there?" Counsellor Pethrick asked. "Mr. Parmenter went at the guardian, or agent, Bates; but Bates got his funds through other people, and when Parmenter tried that string he found there was a lawyer at the other end, and it wouldn't come. Is he Russian? or what?"

"I don't believe he's any more Russian than I am," said Mr. Manson. "He's quick at languages, — you've heard of that funny paper Gaston and he got up, — but doesn't know a word of Russian. By all accounts, he's a fine-spirited, generous-hearted fellow."

"I shouldn't like to dismiss the subject too hastily, sir," said Mr. Don.

"Talking of a turn for languages," said Mr. Merritt, drawing from a pocket a scrap of paper, crumpled and soiled, "can anybody make something out of this?—*You*'ve seen it before," he added to Mr. Don, who, after eying it sharply, said,—

"The same document that was picked up, I think, sir?"

"Yes: 'Ekat Nryai,'" said the possessor of the paper, reading, with some grimace, and handing it to his next neighbor, who happened to be the Rector of the Parish and Editor of the "Church Post." "There's one curious thing about it, certainly: '*swa*' is a good Anglo-saxon word, I find, in the books."

Mr. Manson did not keep the paper; but having glanced hastily at its front, and then at its back, put it out of his hand. "Yes," said he, in answer to the last speaker, "I believe there is such a word as '*swa*' in Anglo-saxon."

The Trustees, in one way or other, gave more or less attention to the paper; Mr. Pettie scrutinizing it closely for a few moments, and handing it on, without comment; Dr. Buttonn holding it long enough to say that "he could understand the arithmetic, but wasn't any hand at languages;" Mr. Pethrick eyed it only from his comfortable distance as it traversed the circle; Dr. Farwell, with a face of happy blandness, read some of the words, with emphasis and gesture, and called upon the company to say how it compared with the Classic Tongues, but hoped that he might not be asked to commit himself to a judgment. "There seems," said he, "to have been some little doubt about the spelling, here: 'gaterrapin,'—no, it's 'gatrapin,' first with two *p*'s, and then one scratched out." He turned with a knowing look to Mr. Manson, sitting at his right: "you know something about this,—I saw you smile."

Mr. Manson disclaimed all knowledge of it, and "had no opinion about it at all."

Mr. Don, as the attention to Mr. Merritt's paper flagged, produced one of his own, containing a single word, of which no one present could make any thing.

"We shall have to make ourselves into an Inscription-society, if this goes on," said Mr. Manson. "Where did this last come from?"

"I copied it from a very ancient and curious watch, belonging to Brade"—

"That old silver watch?" asked Mr. Merritt. "Oh! I know all about that: that isn't Brade's, it's Remsen's. It never was Brade's; only Brade had it. There's one thing more about that other paper," he continued, returning to his own, after having dismissed Mr. Don's, "It's written in a girl's hand.—That 'swa,' I think, is rather curious."

"So you're going to have the celebration, and speechifying;" said Counsellor Pethrick, who had taken no active part in the examination of the papers. "You've settled that?"

"That's a sudden *pop* given to the Committee;" said Dr. Farwell, condescending to a familiar word capable of a sudden emphasis, which he gave it, with his lips, in uttering it. "Shall we resume our deliberations?"

"I'm getting a little sleepy," said Dr. Buttonn, who

was a solid man: "there's a general understanding. We can trust the Committee. Suppose we adjourn."

No one was unwilling; and gathering itself up again, from its relaxation, into an official body, the Board formally adjourned.

"An informal Committee-meeting at Mrs. Wadham's party?" asked Mr. Pettie, of the Chairman, as they shook off the weariness of sitting. So it was agreed, it being understood that one or two others of the Trustees were likely to be there.

CHAPTER XXXII.

MRS. WADHAM'S PARTY.

Mr. Greenwood, as we have already heard, had been away, just when his help was wanted, in correspondence with the Russian Ambassador. He did not, however, stay away for ever, and had, some time since, come back, ready (and perhaps a little more than ready) to lend himself to the carrying out of the projected party, and all that belonged to it.

Yet weeks had gone on into the Uncounted Past, since the first forecasting, in Mrs. Wadham's parlor, and still the party had not come. This delay could not have been owing to any fear of expense, for, as we have seen, the lady was not niggardly. It was not owing to the want of Mr. Greenwood, for Mr. Greenwood had for some time been upon the spot; yet already all the almanacs had counted into December. The Trustees had appointed "Benefactors' Day" to come on the Fifteenth.

The truth was, that Mrs. Wadham herself had been away, on a short visit to the city.

Before going down, she had expressed to Rector Warren her sympathy for "that young motherless-boy that they called a Russian," and had got leave for him to come to her house to dinner. She had had him all by himself; had had a most excellent chance to impress upon him, with delicacy and good judgment, the loneliness of a boy who had "no mother to come and tell his little secrets to, and lay his head on her bosom;" and then, when doubtless his heart was tender, she had adroitly touched upon languages, and asked him how many he knew. To this Brade, like any reasonably modest fellow, and also a free-hearted boy, as he was, had answered that he supposed he did not know any one language really, but he was learning; and so he gave her a short list of the tongues which a boy commonly learns at school, in fitting for college. Russian was not among them.

In making his answer, it may be, indeed, that he recalled to his mind, with some tenderness, his late work on "The Analogy of Languages;" and he may have been even more tenderly conscious of his share in the authorship of a whole Language; but his list took in a couple of old-time tongues, and a couple of those of to-day, and there it stopped.

Mrs. Wadham had drawn things very skilfully to this point; and, now, to get one step further! This she did also skilfully, by saying that "there were some fine languages that they did not teach at St. Bartholomew's School," and then suddenly, but with great delicacy, springing upon him the word "Russian."

For an instant, Brade looked as if he thought that she was making fun of him; but presently he laughed, and confessed that "he ought to know Russian, but he did not." And when she asked him slowly, — not with "archness," which was not her style, but with broadness and massiveness, lightened by a smile of intelligence, — "'*Smis nryai*, isn't it? *Smis nryai?*'" then, as she would have said, she "had got him." As soon as he fairly took in the two cabalistic words, he laughed, to be sure; but at the same time he blushed all over. She had touched a tender place.—"It's all safe with me," she said, to reassure him.

"That was a secret," Brade told her. "That was a kind of unknown tongue;" but Mrs. Wadham, though (as she might have said) "very much the mother in her disposition," was a woman of observation and experience. She saw for herself his blushes; she saw his embarrassment. She might, perhaps, with some reason, think that she had the key in the very wards of the lock now.

If the reader will remember that these two words represented, in the private language which we saw undergoing its making, the beginning of a letter,—"Miss Ryan, I,"—he will not wonder at a little confusion, on the boy's part; but if he recalls that wish expressed when "The Language" was made, that the Postmaster-General, or some great person, might light upon it, he will believe that our young author must have felt a stir and glow of pleasurable mystery and importance at seeing Mrs. Wadham try her teeth upon the secret.

"Are we beginning to have a little confidence?" she asked; and then, applying the method which she had announced from the beginning, cemented the "confidence:"

"That'll do for the present. It's all perfectly safe with me;" and put him under her daughter's charge to look at flowers and books, and whatever he liked.

Then Mrs. Wadham had made a visit to the city. Her daughter cautioned her, beforehand, "not to make a fool of herself with that language," and was assured that she "would do just right about it, exactly,—no more and no less."

Mrs. Wadham had been away from home, day after day, for a good many days. No letters came from her; and it was thought at home, by Mr. Greenwood, who smiled over it, and Miss Minette, who assented with a smile, that "she must be pretty hard at work." "He thought the first one she met, with a Russian Bible and Dictionary under his arms, would satisfy her."

At length she had come back. "One thing," she said, "she had found out, at any rate: it wasn't Russian, — that was a clear case. It wasn't Russian."

"Well, let's see: how did the impression first get about that the boy was a Russian?" asked Mr. Greenwood, thoughtfully.

Mrs. Wadham was not easily stirred from her strong and solid standing, wherever she might have set herself.

"I hope you don't think I mean to give up every thing, when I say he ain't a Russian?" she said. "A boy may be a foreign nobleman, without being a Russian, I suppose."

"Oh, certainly!" said Mr. Greenwood, whose stores of education were always at his command, "a Livonian, Lithuanian, Esthonian, Tongusian" —

"Well, we'll take the rest for granted," said Mrs. Wadham. "He can be something besides Russian?"

"Why, he can be something else and Russian, too," said Mr. Greenwood. "He can be a *Finnish* gentleman, — that is, a gentleman from Finland, — or he may be a Kalmuc Tartar, that's harder to catch than a Parisian accent, or Greek, either. The Emperor's 'Emperor of All the Russias:' there are plenty of 'em. They all talk different tongues, and one can't understand a word the other says, and not more than every other word he says himself. I doubt if I could have understood the Russian Ambassador. It would depend upon what part of the country he came from, — it would be just as it happened."

"I thought you knew Russian?" said the lady, whose memory was good.

"Ah! I don't make myself clear," he said. "I was just saying that one Russian don't understand another, and he may be a Russian in every hair of his head. If you can't know 'em all, you take any one. I chose Old Muscovite, as central, including Cossack."

"I don't see much use in *having* Russians, at that rate," said Mrs. Wadham. — "Well, that doesn't any ways excuse the Russian Ambassador. My note was English; and there's only one English, I think."

What methods she had used in her research — whether she had shown her manuscript to some one in the peculiar guise of a Russian seafarer, as Mr. Greenwood thought likely, or had been in correspondence with men learned in languages — she carefully kept to herself. From her saying that "she had naturally, during her visit, met with several distinguished scholars," it might be thought that she had communicated with professors of the neighboring university.

One thing she was emphatic about: that "she herself was as near to that boy, and as near to his secret, as anybody was: she had touched a chord; she had opened an avenue."

Mr. Greenwood and Miss Minette were anxious about the party and the tableaux and the fun; but Mrs. Wadham set all apprehensions at rest. "The party," she assured them, "would go on. She should give a particular character to it. The boy might not be Russian; but that didn't matter. He was something. Mr. Parmenter had, most likely, thought it was pretty sharp, going to Mr. Bates. Who couldn't go to Mr. Bates? Anybody would think of that. Mr. Bates didn't know any thing. All Mr. Bates knew was the money was sent him, twice a year, as regular as the clock. If he wanted more, all he had to do was to say so. That was what Mr. Bates knew. The party was for her sons and their friends, and she should give a particular character to it."

Mrs. Wadham needed no long time to feel again the influences of home and habit; to be full of herself again and of her plans; to be well seated, and to get the reins of things well into her hands, and well-charged with electric sympathy between the driver and the animated and inanimate things that she controlled.

The eyes of Eastham had soon followed her progress on more than one errand to and from the pretty cottage in which Mrs. Ryan lived with Kate and one domestic. The general mind of Eastham, too, to which that of Eldridge contributed, and also that of Uncle Nat Borrows, who hobbled about Mrs. Ryan's out-door chores, exercised itself daily, at store or post-office, with these and other things. It knew that one of Mrs. Wadham's visits — and this, as it happened, on a very raw and chilly December's day — had been "to see the fruit-trees;" and recalled the fact that "there *wasn't* but about one old gnarled apple-tree and two-three damson-plums, *on* that place; and *they* couldn't be expected to be doing a dreadful sight, not at that season of the year." The general mind drew forth from its stores the fact that "there was some folks that wanted to make out that there was something underhand between the Ryans and that handsome-looking Brade boy, up there, to the School."

So, in discussing this visit, the general face of Eastham wore a smile of wonder; and it was "guessed them fruit-trees wa'n't all."

Much the same process was gone through with, in the discussion of another visit, "to taste Mrs. Ryan's water." The public said: "To be sure, there wa'n't no water in Eastham but what *was* good; but, if there was any water in Eastham that most gen'lly had a kind of a washy taste, spring and fall times, it was on that Farebrother place. Most likely Miss Wadham wanted something more'n that."

Therefore the public smiled at this also.

Then there was at least one other visit, "to ask Miss Kate to take part in a tableau at her house" (Mrs. Wadham's). "This," in the opinion of the same public, "looked all square and business-like; but it was well known to them (the public) she'd praised up the Roossians to Miss Ryan, and Miss Ryan told her she didn't know nothing about the Roossians. Now, what she wanted was to find out if there was any thing between that boy and them; and, if she'd only asked the neighbors, they could ha' told her fast enough that he'd been seen with one or t'other of 'em more'n once" ("yes, time an' time again," Jake Moody said) "'thout any smellin' round apples an' plums that wa'n't there, an' drinkin' water that wa'n't no great, no time o' year;" "an' *that* wouldn't show that he was a Roossian," added the public; "if any thing, jest the exact contrary, for the Ryans wasn't Roossians."

The public, therefore, felt reasonably hurt at Mrs. Wadham's taking such a method, without availing herself of the information already possessed by the public.

The lady had her own way of going on, and went her own way.

As for the coming festivity at her house, we know what amount of information she has shared with Mr. Don, and we remember how she enjoined secrecy upon Mr. Greenwood. Now Mrs. Wadham had given it to be understood that the forthcoming affair at her house "was not going to be a great climax of a party, — a ball, or any thing like that. It was just a pleasant little entertainment, — that's what you might call it, — an entertainment, pleasant and agreeable, of course (she couldn't have any thing that wasn't pleasant and agreeable). It was for her sons' friends, and to show a little attention to that young stranger in Albert's Form."

Now, to the Eastham circle that festivity, however it might rank in its relations to the great world of fashion, was not a small thing. It was an approaching event; and intimations had been fleeting through the community, keeping men's minds, and maiden's minds, astir.

As before the strong wind from the north comes down and possesses the lands, we see, up towards the pole, a flashing and glancing like that from icy scimitars and javelins of a dread spectral army of fleet Scythians, gathering from all the frozen seas and lands; or as, on or about the morning of the great St. Martin of Tours, the wise eyes that greet the earlier day see everywhere a staid, still-standing fog, and brighten with the hope of "Indian Summer," and, hoping, watch the hours until the sun, all things now being ready, sends off the fog, by this time thinned to mist, and lays all-open the smoky haunts of vales and woodlands where, never to be caught, if followed after, all things seem offering up their incense; or, as when beneath the league-deep and unlighted seas, while one or other continent is trembling with the shock of hosts, or feels the crash of rotten empire or of heart-eaten party going down, the Nereid or Triton, whose head is pillowed on the twisted cable, conscious, in sleep, of thrilling messages that are passing to and fro between the two halves of the world, turns on the other side, — so, before Mrs. Wadham's "entertainment," there were flashing intimations and waiting hopes and thrilling communications, and watching of signs and tokens.

The boys of St. Bartholomew's had caught an inkling of the preparations that "Wadham's mother was making for a jolly show;" and we are very sure that the lucky fellows, of the three upper forms, who, it was understood, were going, wished it might come, although they took the time between in comfort. Blake regretted that "he had an engagement for that afternoon, but he hoped to see part of it."

On the other hand, of the younger girls of Eastham, those who, under the self-adjusting machinery for in-taking and out-shutting the rising candidates for "society," might look forward to being present, some doubtless felt, as some good and pretty girls, elsewhere, that "they didn't want to see those nasty boys (or those great ugly boys)," while, to others, these youthful men were radiant with all that gelatinous and phosphorescent glory and beauty which, to the females of different degrees of age, dwelling in college towns, clothe the young forms of Juniors, Sophomores (shall we say Freshmen too?) preparing to be the hope and light of the world.

Mrs. Wadham had become all strong again, evenly weighted, equal to every thing.

The party came. Between the hours of half-past two and half-past five o'clock in the afternoon, all was to begin, go on, and be done.

The boys were early, and the elders were not late. The lady of the house was red and hot, in contrast to the wondrous coldness out of which her guests came in; for of the energetic atoms of her blood great numbers were rushing this way and that, and of these a great many were crowded behind the thick, but porous covering of her face, and busied themselves with putting forth, in countless beady drops, a dew like that upon the garden's broader leaves; but, hot or otherwise, she was Mrs. Wadham.

Miss Minette had on a gay company manner, and was very lively with the gentlemen from St. Bartholomew's, and with some of its boys.

The house was fragrant with sweet flowers, and warm as the balmiest days of spring; and so Mr. Parmenter, and so others, told the hostess.

Mr. Greenwood, bright and bustling, moved about the rooms with prompt and lively bow and recovery, making every one feel at home and curious for the pleasant little entertainment, which was to make one of the chief occupations of the afternoon.

Among the guests the city-gentlemen of the neighborhood, with their families, appeared, of course. Mr. Manson, with the Rector of the School and one or two of the Trustees (of course, Dr. Farwell, and his Committee), were there. There, too, of course, was Mr.

Parmenter. A select number of the younger Eastham people, including the young Misses Bemis and Miss Ryan, were there; and, not to be too particular, there was the estimable widow, Mrs. Osborn, sought out by all the more gallant gentlemen as very bright and chatty.

Brade was presented to Mrs. Osborn and some younger ladies, and satisfied all reasonable demands, in being neither pert nor sheepish. Remsen shared in the attention paid to his friend. Brade himself put forward Peters, and brought him out as much as he would bear.

Russell was there, and Lamson, and Gaston, and Meadows, and Hutchins, and Towne. Our friend Blake was missed.

Boys, with fresh-trimmed hair and careful neck-ties, in twos and threes and half-dozens, ready for fun, and more or less full of it, were everywhere.

The Russian Ambassador, "without," as Mrs. Wadham said, "affording any explanation — not the least" — was absent. "Mr. Greenwood," she said, "had done the best he could, under the circumstances;" and this information Mr. Greenwood supplemented by saying modestly that "he had told 'em to scare up the foreignest-looking fellow they could find, among those Russian consuls, and send him on."

This was Mr. Greenwood's information to the company; but to Mrs. Wadham he had given privately a much more important piece of intelligence: "He was sure, he told her, there was something between Brade and that Count Blakisoff."

"How do you mean something between 'em?" she asked, gravely, being not disposed to accept statements without sufficient examination, even when time was very pressing, and not disposed to have other people thread her mysteries for her, or get the start of her in finding information.

"Nearly connected," said Mr. Greenwood, feeling the pressure of time, — "family relation. That's why the Count's round here *incog.* He's under an assumed name."

"What do you mean by an assumed name?" she asked. "You mean that Blacksop isn't his name? What is his name?"

It was evident that, even if time pressed, she felt the importance of using time.

"I don't believe it's very far off, a little disguised. When there was a king of Naples, he travelled as Conte di Palermo; King of France, Comte de Versailles; Benjamin Thompson, Count Rumford. — Must have an eye to this fellow. Watch him with Brade."

"Ah!" said Mrs. Wadham, receiving his information without any formal acknowledgment, and reserving herself for her own judgment and guidance.

This hurried conversation had been snatched in the very midst of the throng of duties.

The Count Blakisoff's remarkable appearance more than confirmed Mr. Greenwood's account of the standard by which he had been picked out for a guest of Mrs. Wadham. Although, like many eminent men from other lands, he was not large, yet he had his sandy, northern hair brushed down over his forehead, and yet brushed out to right and left with such perfect soldierly smoothness, and on his face bore such an amount of sand-colored hairy clothing, trimmed to so great variety of ornamental shape, — as whiskers sweeping out over his shoulders; lip-locks drawn across each way so stiffly and so far as to seem to court collision and affront; his very eyebrows spreading out strongly to each side beyond his temples; beside these a chin-beard going down and tapering to a strong point; to say nothing of his yellow gloves and the "frogs" upon his queer-looking coat, enough to overrun half Lower Egypt, — that whoever lifted up his eyes in any direction could not fail to see this wondrous man. Many were looking at him almost all the time; and some of them, considering that he was a foreigner, took turns in staring at him and then facing about and making fun of him. The lady of the house herself talked of him at a short distance, much as she might talk of a horse or a lamp-post.

She carefully discharged the duties of a hostess by bringing up one and another with the address "Count —— (I don't remember his name), this is my friend (Dr. Farwell, or Mr. Parmenter, or Mr. Merritt, or Mr. Don)," and commending them (to herself) as they bowed and were bowed at with the brief words, half-aside, "That's it," as if both she and they had acquitted themselves well in a foreign language.

Of all the Russian nationalities, the general conclusion was that this gentleman was a Cossack; and most people were satisfied with Mr. Greenwood's assurance that "he himself was one of the few persons in this country, probably, to whom the Cossack language presented no difficulty whatever."

Now, foreigners are not insensible; and, where their honest ears have never been attuned to the jargon of our English speech, their eyes are delicate of intuition, and their hearts quick to feel, in a strange land. Mr.

Greenwood was not unmindful of the claims of hospitality, but came from time to time (of course his time was precious), and made a point of treating the well-bearded guest with marked attention. He told Mrs. Wadham, aside, on one of those excursions, that "he had not shown him Brade, till by and by; and this was the most extraordinary fellow, — Russian to the backbone, — not an English word in him."

To Mr. Greenwood's ceremonious attentions, the foreigner responded, mostly, by solemn inclinations of the body. His words were very few, although these few were often so effective as to amuse the only intelligent hearer (Mr. Greenwood) very much, and make him, before returning a sprightly answer, look round to see whether some little intelligence of the wit or wisdom might not make its way to others. "He's a Russian of the first water, — or rather ice," he assured the company, on leaving him. It added to the force of the Cossack gentleman's wit that he was never once seen to smile.

"But how's he going to do business at the Custom House," asked one of the city-men, "if he don't know any English?"

Antony Brade, of whom all the guests had doubtless heard more or less, not only had much made of him by the hostess, and was encouraged by Mrs. Osborn's amusing herself with him, and was introduced to the Misses Bemis and others, but also, we may be sure, exchanged a look or two (not many), and a word or two (under a little embarrassment) with Miss Kate Ryan, who was with them. As it was he, chiefly, with whom this "entertainment" of Mrs. Wadham's was associated, he was well looked at and admired, — mostly by the female part of the company, — while there were some, both male and female, who said that he looked much like any other boy. He certainly took things very quietly, and enjoyed himself simply and freely, as a boy with fresh clean blood in him ought to enjoy himself. The boys, generally, talked and laughed, among themselves, and moved about; and so did Brade.

Mr. Don confessed that he had two desires which he hoped, somehow, to have gratified, in the course of the evening; and these were to have a little communication with the Count Blakisoff, "who had to him," he said, "very much the appearance of the ideal Russian," and to bring young Brade into communication with that nobleman.

The hostess had arranged for the boys having a good feed, soon after they got to the house. "Boys like to eat," she said, "and I'd give 'em plenty. 'Taint as 'tis with grown-up people: after they've eaten, boys want to go right at something. We can put 'em to acting right away. My Edmund and Albert'll both be there, among 'em," she added.

This plan, therefore, was adopted; and while the elder guests, among themselves, talked of the last change of hours upon the Railway; of whether anybody could remember a year in which the Rock-crystal Ice Company had begun cutting so early as that year (having, as one of the city-men said, a heavy contract to fill); of the last demand of "The Welded Workingmen" (of whom Mr. Greenwood absurdly said that "he would rather hear of a few well-doing workingmen, than of any number that had well-did"); and while they handled the statuettes, and pulled some leaves of the geraniums, there came in to them such sounds as a crowd of boys make, when they are stuffing their mouths so fast and so full that the words have to climb over lumps of frozen cream or salad, and junks of cake, and yet are jabbering with every mouth of them all. These things, taken together, were appetizing to mouths and stomachs more advanced in years.

"Did you ever observe," asked Dr. Farwell of Mr. Manson, — and his eyes twinkled merrily, — "what a sympathy there is between people's stomachs? You may convince their heads" (emphatic, with an accompanying gesture of the shut hand, with the thumb on top, brought toward the breast), "you may persuade their hearts" (with like emphasis and gesture); "but give 'em roast turkey" (emphasis and gesture as before), "give 'em fried oysters, give 'em chicken salad, and you've got 'em '*ung rapaw!*'* (Now, Merritt, don't you be laughing at my French: it's very good French)."

Mr. Parmenter was mannerly and inclined to impressive conversation. His approach to Mrs. Osborn was particularly ceremonious and polite; Mr. Don, at the same time, retiring from her side with the remark that "he was glad to have his place so well occupied."

The din of boys began to slacken; and Mr. Greenwood, who had appeared and disappeared, continually, announced from the middle of the folding-doors, "An entertainment consisting of a piece of the life of a great foreign people, — the Russian." The word caught the general ear; and a little buzz of questioning, together with a looking round to see where the exhibition was or what place it was to come from, followed. Boys

* The French of our excellent divine is a little peculiar. Judged by the ear, this was probably meant for what some would pronounce "en rapport."

with marks of feeding on them began to come in; little Meadows, with his mouth still full and active, and with a piece of cake in his hand.

A most inspiriting strain from a French horn, which the boys all greeted, with subdued acclamation, as "Ned Prouty, from the village," stirred up the blood in an instant, and then stopped as suddenly, in the midst of a note, as if it had been killed. Then, at a side of one of the larger rooms, into what some of the gentlemen, who were not unintelligent, thought was surely the supper-room, but afterwards determined to be "that big library-room of Mrs. Wadham's," folding-doors were opened, and then silence crept over almost all the company. A movement took place to secure good stands for seeing; Mr. Parmenter gallantly helping Mrs. Osborn forward, and Hutchins and Remsen and Towne and Wadham First doing the same for the Misses Bemis and others. Kate Ryan, who, as Hutchins said, was, by all odds, the prettiest girl in the room, was not to be found.

The hostess, having seen her guests arranged, took the foreign nobleman, with words in English, and a wave of the hand in the language of nature, and stationed herself and him at a side door from the entry, in full view.

Mrs. Wadham announced that "all this was Mr. Greenwood's, she had left it all to him."

The room which had just been opened had been wondrously fitted up. An ice-hill, down which a host of capped and furred and mittened people were going on hand-sleds, as if for their lives, made a side scene. An icy plain stretched from this side to the other, with booths and tents, and a prospect of domes and towers beyond. At the left side was a throne, gorgeous to look at, and on it sat a royally-dressed young person, with a resplendent and far flashing diadem above his commanding brow. Over his head was a rich canopy, on whose front was an eagle, with a most imperial crown.

"The river Neva, in winter," said Mr. Greenwood. "St. Petersburg close by!"

It was a splendid scene of ice and snow.

"It makes you cold all over, doesn't it?" said a boy's voice. It was from Peters, whose fancy was lively, and whose speech was impulsive. He had not heeded the general stillness, and was abashed, when he found that he had made himself heard by the whole company.

"Wouldn't I like to be on one of those hand-sleds?" said Towne, with much less unconsciousness.

"Who's that king or whatever he is?" asked a good many of the company. "Is this Master Brade?" Mr. Parmenter asked.

The boys applauded; a buzz of approbation went over the whole room; while in a little louder voice, but not obtrusively, Mr. Parmenter called Mrs. Osborn's attention to "the happy effects of the various-colored booths;" and Mr. Don, to Miss Minette, admired the general gorgeousness of every thing. Mrs. Wadham announced that Mr. Greenwood would explain.

Mr. Greenwood, the Master of Ceremonies, spoke aloud: —

"It had been the purpose of his Majesty, the Emperor," said he, "in providing this entertainment, to have it accompanied by a series of Russian airs; but, as the Russian air is harsher than we are accustomed to breathe (and our own" — shrugging his shoulders — "is cold enough, just now, in all conscience), it was thought best to modify the programme. You have before you, ladies and gentlemen, in a compact form, 'the Heir of all the Russias.'"

Miss Minette made her part of the room very lively, — a little noisy, perhaps, but very lively.

There was a general good-nature, and everybody laughed, unless, perhaps, the Cossack gentleman; and then a dead silence came again, into which was uttered the last part of some pointed sentence which Mr. Merritt was uttering to Dr. Farwell, under cover of the general excitement.

"— the *air* of it, hasn't he?"

As soon as a new buzz of applause, at the Czarevitch's graceful salutation of the company, offered another "cover," the Doctor reciprocated (for wise men show their wisdom in nothing better than in their unbending) by saying, with his eyes twinkling, "He's an *air*rogant-looking fellow, certainly."

So the divines were evidently not without their share of the general hilarity.

The Master of Ceremonies continued: —

"The Czarevitch (vitch is the Czar that's going to be), on coming to his throne, takes it out with him, and seats himself upon it. The scene that follows is to exhibit to the world the fact that that which is supposed to be one of the strictest despotisms is consistent with the most absolute democracy. You will see the Russians exercise one of their dearest prerogatives, — that of shooting at the crown. This privilege is common to the lowest and the highest, and lasts three days. We shall let you off with two of them. The weather, you observe, is wintry; but it's warm work, as you may suppose; so the Czarevitch will be able to keep himself comfortable, in that respect."

Mr. Don, while the amateur Master of Ceremonies was giving this information, had, on his tiptoes, lightly found his way across, and taken his silent stand beside the Cossack, to whom, on approaching, he had gone through with a lavish dumb show, of bows and wavings of the hand; and pointing to himself and then to the floor, by way of implying, in the language of universal nature, that he intended to occupy that spot; while a third pointing, to the courteous foreigner, implied that its being near him gave the place its great attraction.

Mr. Don was not wrong in expecting to be met half-way, in the language of universal nature. The foreign gentleman talked it with shoulders and elbows, and hand laid to his frog-covered heart, wonderfully.

The performance divided the attention of a considerable part of the company, even with the lively Master of Ceremonies and the counterfeit presentment of the Czarevitch; and the sight of this intelligent foreigner engaged in a well-meant attempt to exchange courtesies with a polite American was too much for the self-control of most of the younger, and a good many of the older witnesses of it. It must be confessed that there was something extremely droll — at times, perhaps, to excitable spirits, overpoweringly droll — in the look of the distinguished guest.

Our young friend who represented Russian empire showed himself made of stuff like other mortals, when the man happened, while looking his very solemnest, to lay his foreign forefinger by his nose. The Cossack gentleman was again the object of thoughtless mirth. His own behavior, meanwhile, was exceedingly dignified, as he employed his hands on the abundant hair of his face.

The breach of good manners grieved those who had good manners most at heart. Mr. Parmenter had not been unobservant or indifferent; and, in behalf of propriety and hospitality, uttered aloud the statement that "he should be sorry to see any forgetfulness of the laws of courtesy, and was confident that nothing of that sort would take place."

The lady of the house was herself mistress of the occasion.

"Tell him," she said, "that we enjoy him" ("His appearance is certainly peculiar," she said, without much sinking of voice, to those about her, because she knew that he could not understand more than one person in the room, or, possibly, two), "and tell him there'll be refreshments after the play about his country. That goes to foreigners' hearts as quick as anybody's: everybody understands eating."

While Mr. Greenwood was giving this agreeable message to the noble foreigner, a voice was heard, in moderate but prevailing tones, from a corner in which a number of gentlemen were gathered: —

"That's singular, now. How can you account for that coincidence? That's the very thing I was saying a little while ago."

"Yes," said Mr. Manson, "and you observe she says there'll be '*ung repaw*' pretty soon, too."

"Not quite the Parisian accent, perhaps, but" —

"Pretty good!" said Mr. Merritt, who, as we have seen, can make some pretensions in the languages: "*un repas*, a feed."

Mr. Greenwood was quick-witted and ready enough to devote a little side attention to his Cossack nobleman. He interrupted himself: —

"My friend," he said, "the Count Ultrovian Blakisoff has the remarkable versatility and the wonderful facility for languages which make his countrymen so desirable to colleges and places of education. Entirely unacquainted with English, he can instantly master the phonetic signs, when written distinctly, which represent it on paper. While the Czarevitch is waiting impatiently, as you see him, for the performances of his dilatory subjects to begin, the Count may, perhaps, be persuaded to gratify us in a way that will astonish those to whom opportunities of witnessing such accomplishments are rare."

There was now a decent silence, and the faces of the company were generally smoothed. The representative of Muscovite majesty recovered himself. Mr. Greenwood, with an elegant stride, and placing the heel of his right foot in the hollow of his left, with such an air as almost to disturb again the general gravity, planted himself in front of the Count, and, drawing with a flourish from his pocket a paper on which were a few musical notes and some words, presented it with a low bow to the foreigner, and said something which was not English. He then hastened to the side of the scenes, and apparently gave a direction.

The Count took the paper with as much gesture as he had before bestowed upon Mr. Don, held it at arm's length, and suddenly burst forth in song: —

"Mee langguidge ees the Roosshin tongs:
Hi spake hit like a buck;"

And then, with the modesty and simplicity characteristic of accomplished foreigners when they have distinguished themselves, solemnly handed the paper back.

"Do they grow Cossacks in Ireland?" asked one of the city-men; and to more purpose was heard the wise voice of Dr. Farwell, asking whether a phenomenon of that sort — a man's singing right off, in a language that was perfectly strange to him — was to be explained in the same way that a stutterer could sing a thing that he couldn't read a word of.

This revelation was, as Mr. Greenwood had predicted, sufficiently astonishing; and the rooms were all in a flutter. It would be too much to say that all faces were serious; for there had been something a little peculiar, after all, in the pronunciation and accent, and the voice — for a voice coming out of such an ambush of hair — was rather slender; but just then Ned Prouty's all-enlivening horn took captive every ear, as it struck up "March to the Battle-field!"

Mr. Don was a man ready for occasions. With an intelligent look he presented to the eyes of the foreign linguist a soiled and crumpled bit of paper, like the "document" which we have seen, to which paper he pointed, and of which he asked, with a most expressive raising of the eyebrows and throwing of the head on one side, a question whose "waste" alone, like water from a mill-wheel, ran out in the words: "This? anything?" its strength having been spent in the face above.

The stranger, with his hand again upon his frog-enveloped heart, looked at the paper, and to the question in the universal language assented strongly with his head.

This scene had not been lost upon the eyes of Mrs. Wadham, who turned and watched it closely.

Suddenly a shot was heard, and the representative of

majesty put his hand to his head. Of course all eyes were fixed upon the stage, and all was still; a smell of gunpowder mingled itself with the sweet scents of flowers and pocket-handkerchiefs.

This time no harm had been done apparently.

Mrs. Wadham declared that "she supposed her time was come: she never could stand fire-arms." Some of the gentlemen jocosely asked "Champagne?"

The Manager assured the company that "probably few, if any, bullets of lead remained in the rifles, as he had employed a careful hand, with a No. 3 Faber's lead-pencil, to draw all the balls, and substitute something more comfortable."

The little descent from dignity in this about the pencil was probably intended for a certain class of minds. The boys appreciated it.

"I think I may safely assure the ladies, on Mr. Greenwood's authority," said Mr. Parmenter, "there is not the slightest danger."

A voice from the group of Trustees in the corner, which our readers may be able to assign to its owner, said, "I think I should *bawl* if I was that chap on the throne."

The ladies moved uneasily. Some of the gentlemen, laughingly, thought it was time to adjourn. A lovely female figure rushed upon the stage, in splendid robes that matched the Czarevitch's. "That's Miss Ryan!" said the Bemises; and then a Russian of the Russians, with sheepskin hat, coat, trousers, mittens, and boots, and a beard of much the same general character, appeared. He and his wife and seven children, in a line, bore his formidable weapon. He kneeled upon his knees, first took off his hat in obeisance to his liege lord, and then, resuming it, he and his family arranged the gun upon their shoulders, in a slope up to the wife! and so it reached from him, squatting at one side of the stage, close up to the princely potentate's crown, with his head inside, at the other.

"Your scene is very well got up indeed, sir," said Mr. Don; "but I hardly think they would let the man get quite so close."

"True, sir," said the Master of Ceremonies. "In point of fact they do not allow such dangerous proximity. It's only the exigency of circumstances. Our room is so narrow that we have to crowd a little. You see a gun fifteen feet long (the usual length of the weapons used on these occasions), in a room eighteen or twenty feet wide, crowds us."

This was a mere mimic scene; and yet, when this long, dreadful-looking weapon reached to such fatal neighborhood of the boy's head, the Count, clasping his hands, threw himself into a marvellous foreign attitude of despair. This Mr. Don, as we should expect, appreciated; while the boys, and many beside them, seemed not at all touched by the gravity of the situation. Mrs. Wadham, almost pale at the appearance of the gun, but bravely keeping her ground, at the crisis, turned away from the threatening weapon; but did not forget to see what the Count was doing.

Mr. Parmenter gallantly advanced Mrs. Osborn nearer to the scene, remarking that "there was a great deal of merit in it, — it would bear inspection." He delicately replaced her light shawl which had fallen from one shoulder.

"The Grand Duchess Alexandrovna" (explained Mr. Greenwood) "interposes her efforts (which the law of

Russia provides for) to persuade this resolute Muscovite to forego his privilege. You see her appealing to his veneration for the sacred person on the throne: he squats unmoved: to his humanity: he puts tobacco in his cheek, and lays his finger — I should say his mitten — on the trigger!"

Here Mr. Greenwood made what might be called a rhetorical pause, to let the scene take its full effect.

"That fellow with the gun's Gaston — or Lamson: where's Lamson?" said Tom Hutchins. — "Ain't Brade good?" said Peters.

The Czarevitch sat with a lofty indifference to danger becoming his high blood: his look of disgust, as he saw the death-dealing muzzle so near, and glanced down the sloping backs of the enterprising family which bore it, and as he shook out his dainty pocket-handkerchief and held it between the frightful instrument and himself, called forth immediate and universal applause.

"A good deal of the dramatic gift there," said Mr. Parmenter, who generally spoke well. "That fellow's got it in him." "There's fun in that boy," said the city-gentlemen: and indeed he was excellent, and handsome, too. The Grand-duchess, who at the applause had glanced that way, seemed struck, and apparently forgot herself; and then came back with a little start.

While this was going on, the Count (not unobserved by that considerate man, Mr. Don) was restless, and seemed about to go forward. The mind of Mr. Don was active, and doubtless weighed the emotions by which the bosom of the foreigner was agitated.

Did he understand that this was only "acting"?

Perhaps he was a partner in the scene. Mr. Don humanely and politely (whatever might be the case with the Count) addressed him, and accompanied the address with lucid gesture. He smiled also, at the same time, as if to show that he knew perfectly how intelligent the Count was.

"Of course, sir, there's no danger," he said; "they've taken all precautions," shaking his head vehemently, and throwing his hands asunder, rapidly, several times. "Ha! I can't make him understand. I suppose he knows." Then to the stranger again, with new energy, "Of course it's all make-believe!" and he shook his head vehemently again. "Nothing in it, sir." Then he smiled strongly, and said, "You understand, of course."

Mrs. Wadham, divided between alarm for the issue of the Princess's entreaties to stay the deadly firearm, and her interest in the secret whose development was, perhaps, to be hastened by the progress of the play, held up her fan between herself and the actors, and from time to time looked over it. Mr. Greenwood went on: —

"The Princess having failed in her appeal to his veneration, and to his humanity, now addresses the father of a family with another argument. See how she lays her hand first upon the bending wife, looking appealingly to him; and then upon each successive bearer of that frightful weapon, from the first-born daughter, down through alternate sons and daughters to the last, the joy of his father's eyes, whom you see innocently occupied and amused with his own small nose. At each she utters a few heart-moving words, and casts the same pathetic and appealing glance to the father. She is urging upon him the likelihood (too often warranted by melancholy facts, in that country) that his gun will burst, and so kill every member of his household. He is unmoved. Now, having, with the instinctive sagacity of a woman, reserved her crowning argument for the last, she shows him that, in all probability, it will kill him, too. He wavers. He might get along without his family; how could he get along without himself? Now she lays her gentle hand upon the instrument of death, to draw it from its fatal aim."

The "Princess Alexandrovna," of this little stage, was certainly a lovely being. If royal or imperial houses have so fair daughters often, they are happy; and so the company seemed to think; for, led by Mr. Parmenter, there was a general round of applause, in which Tom Hutchins and the boys helped, to the echo. Even the Count joined the prevailing enthusiasm; but, in his foreign way, checked himself, after a few most hearty clappings of his yellow-gloved hands, while all the rest were going on, and stood mute and wonderful to look at as before; but every one, unless the Czarevitch, was looking at the stage. No one seemed to enjoy himself with more quiet thoroughness than the Rector of the School, to whom Mr. Manson called his neighbors' attention.

The Czarovna Alexandrovna was drawing the gun with a gentle energy, by its barrel, at a point somewhere between the second son and third daughter, when the extraordinary weapon gave way in the middle, and, at the same time, the catastrophe against which she had warned the unreflecting Muscovite took place: there was an explosion, — not loud, but effectual, — and the whole family, father, seven children, mother, struck with a marvellous accuracy, fell at once to the ground, and lay motionless. The Princess, to the joy of the audience, shown by much clapping of hands and waving of handkerchiefs (from Mrs. Osborn first, and then from all the ladies), in this happy administration of poetical justice, stood unharmed, and, of course, lovelier than before. She was very modest, and yet became her part extremely well.

"There ought to be a patent for that powder," said one of the city-gentlemen.

"Very moderate cost of ammunition," said Mr. Parmenter.

"How are we meant to account for it," said a sagacious-sounding voice from the corner, which, though doubtless addressed to some particular neighbor, was permitted by the speaker, in a friendly way, to pervade the several rooms, "that a whole family — a whole Russian family, or, you may say, any other family, can be put out of existence by a puff — by a flash" —

"I am glad that firin's over," said Mrs. Wadham, "and no more harm done."

The Count with an animated action of the foot showed that he would like to kick the prostrate father of a family.

"The accident which has just occurred, such as very often happens on these occasions," said the gentleman manager, "will release the Czarevitch and give him command of his time. He attends the funeral, in state, accompanied by the nation at large. ("Neighborly people!" said Mr Merritt.) "The Princess and the Czarevitch," continued Mr. Greenwood, "congratulate one another; and presently, with your permission, ladies and gentlemen, our little play will come to an end."

"I don't see as we've discovered much," said Mrs.

Wadham, without much reserve, "unless you can make something out of that Count."

"Well, keep an eye to the Count," said Mr. Greenwood, privately.

A lovely blush suffused the cheek of the representative of the Princess Alexandrovna, as also those of the young representative of imperial majesty, who now descended from his throne and took her by the hand. The reigning house of Romanoff is counted handsome, but we doubt whether it ever appeared to better advantage in any two of its members, than here. One thing distinguished these young persons from many others: they were very delicate and distant in their intercourse with each other. "Make a handsome couple, — that boy and girl, wouldn't they? eh! Mrs. Osborn," said a city-gentleman.

Mrs. Osborn, who carried on a lively conversation with three or four gentlemen at once, as well as with Mr. Parmenter, remarked pleasantly that "she liked Mr. Greenwood's disposal of his characters better than Shakespeare's; for here he killed off only just those that were wanted out of the way." Mr. Greenwood bowed, with much flourish. Mrs. Wadham was not a person to lose sight of a great purpose.

"What did you make out of that Count?" she asked, turning promptly to the intelligent inquirer, Mr. Don. "Did he understand that paper?"

"Well, ma'am, I can judge only by the eye, you know," he answered, "as I unfortunately cannot talk Cossack. He *seemed* to recognize it, instantly, and to be quite struck by it. The impression upon my mind was a strong one; though, as I say, I couldn't hold conversation with him."

"Mother," said Miss Minette, behind her fan, having worked her way to the neighborhood, "I'd let that language go."

"I'll do what's right;" said the mother. — "Who's found out most about it, so far?"

Instead of being ready to dismiss the pretty pageant at the end, the public, if it might be judged by its uproarious and long-kept-up applause, would gladly have had the whole thing over again; but the good sense of the elders was convinced, and yielded. The folding doors were slowly closing on the imperial pair; and Ned Prouty, who had a soul of music in him, and a sure taste which came of no passing fashion, sounded, with really delicate feeling and tenderness, an Irish air, which was lost, perhaps, on most of the company, but to which Mrs. Osborn at once gave its name, and a little more, — "Though 'twas all but a dream at the best, And still, when happiest, soonest o'er."

Mr. Parmenter assured her that "her way of uttering the words (certainly very clear and graceful) gave them a charm."

Everybody called for keeping the doors open till it was done, and for the Czarevitch and Czarovna to stay before admiring eyes; but things in this world march with inexorable steadiness toward their endings; and so, while Prouty's bright coil of brass was making all the unseen air musical, certain young fellows in the attire of pages rushed in upon the stage and set themselves to the dragging off of the lifeless bodies of the Muscovite family sacrificed in the exercise of their prerogative. The jolting shook out from the father some words which had, perhaps, lodged in his throat: "Heu, me mis —." To which of the many tongues of the Great

Empire they belong, our young readers must find out.

In the hasty and rather rough handling which these remains received, a mitten worked off from the hand of the youngest born and fell near Mrs. Osborn's feet. She picked it up, smiling, and examined it; while Mr. Greenwood, whose eyes were quick, begged her to keep it as a little token of the afternoon's amusement.

Mr. Parmenter suggested that *a mitten* was an awkward present to receive; and Mrs. Osborn, in her prettiest way, told him that "she must ask him to relieve her of it;" and persisted, prettily, in making over to him all her property in it.

At this the city-men made some pleasant remarks among themselves; and, as good jokes always bear repetition, one of them good-humoredly told Mr. Parmenter "they were just saying Mrs. Osborn had given him the mitten."

"We'll call it a glove," said Mr. Parmenter, gallantly, and putting it in his bosom: "any thing from Mrs. Osborn is worth keeping."

While this lively scene was going on, the hostess was expressing to the two chief actors her solid approval and thanks for their performance. The Czarevitch was in good spirits, but not inclined to accept any praise "for just sitting still. Gaston and the rest had done something." The Princess Alexandrovna was a good deal excited at what she had been through.

"I hear the Count understands that unknown language we talked about the other day," said Mrs. Wadham to the former. The Czarevitch looked embarrassed. The two young authors and owners of "The Language" glanced at each other, but said nothing.

Mrs. Wadham went on: "Mr. Don showed it to him.— Don't go, Miss Ryan: we ain't going to talk any secrets;" and when Kate, like a simple girl, expressed her anxiety "to change those things for her own," Mrs. Wadham assured her strongly:—

"They're monstrously becoming, though, let me tell you, young lady."

As Kate Ryan disappeared, the representative of the Czarevitch, whom we may now, we suppose, call Antony Brade, hastened to tell Mrs. Wadham, like an ingenuous boy, something to which she listened, very gravely, looking him steadily in the face, in such a way as almost to disconcert him. A sort of working seemed to be going on in her, as palpably as that of swallowing goes on: the whole Wadhamic system seemed to be engaged in appropriating the communication.

"Yes," she said, taking a breath, when he had done; then, after looking at him another moment, to see if he had any thing more to say, "Of course that's what it was,—of course it was. It was fun.—Now we'll have something else! Yes."

The boys' time was not up, nor were Mr. Greenwood's resources for their amusement exhausted.

"It was our intention," said Mr. Greenwood, "to give you a list of all the passages from history which we have omitted to represent to-day, and which are, of course, reserved; but the list was rather long" (here he showed a monstrous roll. At which some shrewd observer said, "Have you got 'em all there? No, you don't, then!") Mr. Greenwood went on: "The reading will therefore be dispensed with."

The party was chiefly for the boys: the Muse of History must therefore condescend with a good grace in speaking of the entertainment. Charades were acted, in which "buff-fell-oh!" and "hip-hop-pop-what-a-muss," and "blunder-buss," and "mag-pie" and "file-and-throw-pie," and others, were spelled out, with great energy; but they have no special bearing upon our story, and we shall therefore ask the reader to fancy and act them over for himself.

When the boys went away, Brade, at Mrs. Wadham's solicitation, had special leave (considering his part, considering, also, his yet undiscovered relationship to the Count) to stay an hour longer. Mr. Parmenter, who was not now confining himself to any one person, but taking a general interest in things, congratulated Brade, with dignity, upon this privilege, as well as upon his acting; of which the boy, like an intelligent and ingenuous fellow, as before, said that "being dressed up and keeping still wasn't any thing." He looked pleased, of course, at having succeeded.

"It's a great part of king-craft, though;" said Mr. Manson, going into high thought.

"The effect of blood, I suppose;" said Mr. Parmenter, partly but not wholly aside, and with a bow.

CHAPTER XXXIII.

WHAT THE COUNT IS TO BRADE.

A LITTLE ceremony was to be used in going to the dining-room. It was understood that the late Czarevitch should lead in the late Princess Alexandrovna; the Cossack Count, of course, conducting the lady of the house.

Mr. Don, before this took place, was apprised of a discovery which Mrs. Wadham had made, nearly affecting his document: "I suppose you know that strange language everybody was puzzled about was all made up. Oh, yes! entirely, — altogether. A pretty good language to be made up for fun?"

"You surprise me, ma'am!" Mr. Don said, a good deal astonished. "Well, I think with you it was worthy of a better fate."

He at once explained the state of things to the Rev. Mr. Merritt.

"Then my Anglo-Saxon goes to the bottom;" Mr. Merritt said good-naturedly, as if a great part of the world was still standing.

The Count seemed not quite to understand the duty expected of him.

Mr. Greenwood was for the moment not to be found. Thereupon, the lady, in a very purpose-like way, walked up to the eminent foreigner, and showed, in the same way in which Robinson Crusoe expressed himself to the savages, that she would take his arm, and they would go yonder, and, as she explained by forcible action of the jaws, would there put their mouths to the best use that most mouths are capable of. The Count, with his facility at language, caught the meaning readily; and having gone through with the same symbolic representation in his turn, and occasioned another breach of good manners on the part of the impulsive young people and others, he made a profound bow and gave the hostess his arm.

It was a disappointment to the company that Brade and Kate Ryan had abandoned their splendid dresses (for the boy had been as much in a hurry to get back to his own, as the girl had shown herself); but it was still generally agreed that they were an uncommonly good-looking couple, and well matched.

They were not at all upon the easy and familiar footing with each other that we once saw, but rather on that which Kate made a condition of their correspondence in "The Language." He addressed her as "Miss Ryan;" and she (we believe) called him "Mr. Brade." They talked together with plenty of reserve and courteous distance.

The mysterious link of relationship between the Count and Brade had not been broken when the unknown tongue was stripped of all mystery; and it was arranged that they should come next each other, in the dining-room. The clerical party were not far off; and Dr. Farwell, very happily, as usual, hit the feeling of the guests by saying, in his pleasant way, —

"Now here's a place where action is better than speech."

The Count's formal salutation of his young kinsman (if Brade was his kinsman), and the look with which it was accompanied, had a strangely exhilarating effect upon the boy and those near, although Brade, as we know, was no giggling fellow, to be carried off his gravity by every trifle.

Mr. Merritt saw the state of the case, and considerately came in: —

"The foreign Count will be too much for that youngster," he said: "some of us older people better take him."

Meantime the foreigner, unwilling to remain a stranger, and wishing to tighten the cords of human brotherhood, had adopted the readiest way he knew to that end; and forgetting even, for an instant, the immediate claims of the lady of the house, whom he had had the honor to bring in, presented Brade ceremoniously with a card. But this was only for a moment: then he turned diligently to the discharge of his duties, and showed himself more practised in the arts of civilization and usages of the table than many of his titled brethren have appeared in this country.

It has been already said that the Rev. Mr. Merritt professed to have kept by him a good deal of his school-boy associations; in like manner he had not forgotten his school-boy manners. He now beckoned for a sight of this paper, much as any of Brade's comrades might have done. Brade, smiling, handed him the card; and Mr. Merritt, turning his back and drawing some of his neighbors to do the same, evidently enjoyed himself heartily. The Count, getting no answer, devoted himself the more strenuously to the comfort and refreshment of the hostess.

"This is about as good as my unknown tongue — Anglo-Saxon and all," Mr. Merritt said.

"'Kollidg tis kontra gif digri tu mi on languidg?'"

"'Give degree,' sir, is what he means evidently;" said Mr. Don, good-naturedly giving his help.

"That's plain enough," said Mr. Merritt; "but what does the rest of it mean? Will a college in this country give a degree in his language, or to a man of his language? I should say he ought to be encouraged, somehow, to go on. — I thought," he said, showing the card to Mr. Greenwood, who happened to pass, "you told us he didn't know a word of English."

"I said 'there wasn't an English word in him:' well, I don't see any thing there against it."

Dr. Farwell's wisdom was close at hand, and came to the rescue: —

"But these," said he, "are the phonetic signs: he sings by the phonetic signs; he spells by the phonetic signs. 'K-o-l-l-i-d-g' isn't according to our spelling-books; but isn't it according to another principle, — perhaps a better principle? The American child says 'B'e'd,' when he's hungry; and 'Bed,' when he's sleepy. Now may not that sound — I put the question as a question in science — may not that sound represent to that child — be associated in that child's mind — with the general idea of comfort? — comfort?"

While this thoughtful speculation was going on, emphasized, at emphatic points, with the peacefully-shut fist, across the chest, the great order of things had also been going on. Ices, salads, jellies, oysters, confectioneries, in many a tempting form, were carried about; and trustees and clergymen could not keep their backs set against them. It happened ill for science that this strong diversion came just as the Reverend Doctor had been called upon by Mr. Pettie or some one, to explain "how the Cossack Count could spell 'college,' or 'give,' or any of his other words, in 'phonetic signs,' if he hadn't first got the words that he wanted to spell." The answer was lost in the general occupation that followed.

The Count by no means confined himself in his attentions to his young relative, nor to the lady of the house; but in active dumb show, with a noble flourish of manner, he helped half the young ladies near him, before their attendant gentlemen knew where they were, — to the amused fright of the young ladies themselves.

Mr. Merritt's wit was alive, and found vent, confidentially, but in a pretty loud confidence, to his friend the Doctor (and a few others): —

"Though the Count don't understand English, I think, looking at his performances, we should hold him a-count-able, shouldn't we?"

"I was expecting to make two or three very good jokes out of that word," said Dr. Farwell; "and now here's Merritt spoiled one of 'em, right off."

The Count, who, of course, heard but a confused jargon of speech all about him, unless when, like a warble from his native woods, or a strain from his own ancestral halls, or, in short, like just what it was, a word or two came to him from Mr. Greenwood, did not despair of communicating, in his own way, with the intelligent life around him. Again he presented a card to Brade, and accompanied it with a look of inquiry, and an inquiring attitude of the different members of the body, eminently foreign. The card this time bore upon its face the words: —

"Konow Russik?"

The Trustees happened at the moment to be engaged in discussing the arrangement for "Benefactors' Day,"—the "Triumphal Arch," or the "Arch of Welcome," or whatever it should be called; the Latin speech, to be in two parts, for Gaston and Brade, but very short, so as to be fitted for out-door delivery, if the weather should not be too cold or stormy. Dr. Farwell was just settling things in their places, as they ought to be settled,—"that seems conclusive as to that *thing*, at that *point*,"—when Mr. Merritt nudged his elbow, and it was astonishing, considering the speed and force with which he moved, how soon he checked himself to see what Mr. Merritt wished him to see.

Brade, not thinking himself seen, was answering Count Blakisoff's card as well as he could; showing, in his eyes, a feeling of the drollness of his own appearance, and that of the Count, who was gesticulating in sympathy, and with that gravity which belongs to well-bred foreigners. Catching sight of the clerical party, Brade politely presented them with the card, and, leaving them busy, took the opportunity to make his modest leave-taking and get away. A more conspicuous part was played by the Count, who hastily followed him, after a very low bow to the hostess, and another to the company; Mr. Greenwood explaining that "he was drawn by strong ties."

The air was sharp and biting, as Brade, followed closely by the noble foreigner, left behind the house full of pleasant warmth, and sounds of mirth.

"Brade!" said the Count, in a strange accent; and, as Antony turned, he could see that some change had taken place in the stranger.

"Ha!" said the Count, in the cold air, but speaking as good English as Russian, and putting his hand to his face.

Antony waited to join him; and, as the Count withdrew his hand, a great part of the hair of his face came with it.

"'Kollidg gif digri tu mi on languidge,'" said the Count, making out pretty well to repeat the words on his first card.

Brade laughed. "Ulterior College might do it, I suppose," he said.

"Didn't you find me out before?" asked Blake, — for Blake it was, rid of his hair, but still wearing his frogged coat. "Really? — The trouble about getting an 'honorary' from Ulterior," said he, running on, in his old way, "is, if you haven't been there four years, you've got to prove you wa'n't bright enough to get through College; or you want to preach or teach, and people think you don't know enough."

Some boys, who were out with their sleds, espied the two, and, after gazing at them, broke forth in shouts: "Hooraw for Count Blakisoff!" — "Hooray!" "Hooraw for Imperial Highness!" and escorted them home in triumph.

CHAPTER XXXIV.

BENEFACTORS' DAY.

Mr. Parmenter's "evening," after Mrs. Wadham, was handsome and costly. Except the boys, he had most of her guests, and some others. The weather had grown still colder; but there was to be a full moon; and, as snow already covered the ground, the night would be a fine one, and everybody was in good spirits. Mrs. Osborn was not there, and there were those who said that "that *giving of the mitten* was a genuine thing;" others "didn't believe it: it was only fun before people." But she was not there.

Mrs. Wadham was at Mr. Parmenter's, and gave a good deal of tone to things, in whatever part of the house she was. The rumor of Blake's transformation, and changing-back, had found its way up; and the city-gentlemen, having got an inkling of the supposed relationship to Brade, laughed heartily, and said a good many funny things about "the other boy's Cossack uncle," and called him "a first-rate actor."

Mrs. Wadham, when the intelligence first reached her, treated it as a deliberative body treats a report from a committee, and "accepted" it, as it were, for her own consideration, by saying "Yes." She changed color a little, to be sure; and then was silent over it, until she had disposed of it within herself, and, as it were, "adopted" it. This all took place at Mr. Parmenter's; and Mr. Greenwood had been so occupied with different gentlemen as not to have been able to exchange any conversation with her, further than a hurried exclamation, in passing: "How that chap did impose upon us!"

Mrs. Wadham made her answer, in the hearing of those who were near: "I'm sure I gave 'em chance enough to find him out. I introduced Dr. Farwell to him; and I introduced Mr. Parmenter, and Mr. Merritt, and Mr. Don. They had *chance* enough."

The buzzing of animated conversation; the admiring exclamations; the compliments paid to the host; the moral reflections and sagacious observations made about him and his fortunes; the arrangement of lights, so as to "bring out" the pictures; the glances of eyes and of speech, — all this would make a very good subject for the pen; but we pass it, and even the talk about Benefactors' Day, and the boys' coming match on the ice, as not necessary to our story. One happening we describe, as connected with Brade and with what is coming.

It had become known throughout the company that Mr. Parmenter was looking for a very distinguished guest; the wiser ones said, "for an eminent musician." An hour or two late, there was a stir outside, and a busy-looking movement on the part of the host, and little eagernesses among the guests; and a man with a military cloak thrown over his cap, and high boots, with fur tops, meeting the cloak, was brought through the rooms, with much ceremony on Mr. Parmenter's part and very little on his own, and taken into a room beyond, where, as some of the gentlemen remarked, "that foreign fellow was getting some grub, after his sleigh-ride." "He ain't another Cossack Count, is he?"

After a while he came out, having his cloak now hanging from his shoulders (his boots still on), and was wiping his chops and beard with his fingers. Mr. Parmenter made it to be understood that this was "The MAESTRO!" (with much accent: it was repeated as "the Maelstrom!" by one of the ready wits) "VOLKOV, the great composer!" In that character, he was looked at and commented upon, as he stood with his back to the piano, uttering occasional very "basso" words and laughs. "Queer-looking '*company*'-rig," some said. "Becoming, though," others thought. "Genius does so," was a third opinion. A crashing sound, from the heavy cords of the piano behind him, brought a sudden stillness, during which Mr. Volkov, without heeding either sound or stillness, kept on, at intervals, uttering his deep-toned speech and laughter. A tinkling, as of fairy sheep-bells, but rhythmical and melodious, came from the piano (so Mr. Manson enthusiastically described it): all ears were strained to catch it. A sound, as of a fairy people dancing to the pipe and tabor, followed; then a march; then a dirge; and while all ears, except of the artist, were strained to hear, he stood with his back to the piano, asking questions about the snow in different winters, — how deep, how early, how late.

"Why don't Parmenter show him his fiddle?" some asked; and in a moment were answered. There was a sudden blaze of light thrown on the Stradivarius. The host had been standing near the artist, and listening, with bowed head. He now ceremoniously spoke: —

"I'm very sorry to interrupt you, sir, and to deprive us of the treat we're enjoying; but many of my friends are a little impatient to have you see a very precious relic in my possession, — a genuine *Stradivarius!*"

"Stradivarius!" said the Maestro, leaving the piano, and following. (Of course the golden thread of music broke, when he walked away.)

The Stradivarius of Mr. T. Parmenter, as Mr. T. "Parmenter's fiddle," was as well known, almost, as the regalia in Edinburgh Castle, or elsewhere, and the company flocked over to its stand.

Here, having allowed a little time for things to settle, Mr. Parmenter drew from his pocket a package of worn and yellow papers; and, holding them in his hand, smiling, made a little speech: —

"You know, better than I can tell you, sir, that the violin of Cremona is very famous and very rare. I think there were three houses most eminent for making them. They are so scarce as to command a fabulous price. — I suppose I ought to be ashamed," he added, bashfully, "to confess what I paid for this; but the evidence" —

The great artist looked glum at the sight of the papers, as if he feared the having to read them all through, and proceeded to his own line of evidence. Taking the "Cremona" from its cushion, he tightened up the old strings, whose fibre had been toughened by the goat's milk and mutton of Padan fields, and first attuned to music in the open night-air of Cathedral-leads or humbler roofs, or in the little-frequented and much-resounding halls of the University. The Maestro ran his fingers up and down and across the tightened strings, faster than common ears could follow; then rapped hard on the back of the instrument with his knuckles; then squeezed with his two thumbs the front, as if he would break it in, like the breast of a chicken; then, with a nail of one of his many-ringed fingers, scraped at the dark crust; and then loosened the strings, and laid down the Stradivarius, saying that "he was yoost so goot als how he ever was. He never was goot for nodsing, 't all. — They had sheeted the goot friend, Parmenter."

At this candid announcement, the sudden expressions in the many faces gathered about were worth a painter's study. Many glances were interchanged; some mouths were pursed up, and eyelids rounded; some tongues were thrust into cheeks; a back was significantly scratched; shoulders were shrugged to the ears. One face, staring with all its eyes, hearing with all its ears, was particularly amusing: it was that of Mrs. Wadham's man, Eldridge, who, somehow, happened to be among the foremost by-standers. The lady herself had not observed him. She had received the artist's words with silent, open mouth, and had closed upon it with a deep "Um!"

Mr. Parmenter took the event gallantly: —

"I suppose, sir," he said, smiling, though very red, "you would hardly care to read these vouchers," and he put them back in his pocket. "We must accept the verdict — unless" (looking round at his guests) "we can get it amended." Then, spying Eldridge, now engaged in searching the faces of the on-lookers, he said: "You were looking for Mrs. Wadham, I suppose;" and having recalled that intelligent observer to himself and his business, he said, pointing to the Cremona, "This needs a taste for antiquity to appreciate it. Perhaps, sir, you'll favor us with a little music from an instrument of to-day, which, you have shown us, can '*discourse*' very sweet sounds."

So, with this pretty speech, Mr. Parmenter turned off his disappointment. Mr. Don said, "I think he didn't make allowance for the age of the fiddle, sir. I think you told me it was three hundred years old." Mrs. Wadham asked, "You've kept your vouchers, I suppose?" much as she might ask if his securities had escaped a fire.

Mr. Parmenter devoted himself to his guests. The Maestro, after bestowing an hour or more on this social gathering, out of his way, was whirled off again to a railroad station, and in due time the guests were scattered.

The public, in its informal assemblings at the store and the post-office, did its duty by all parties, — the host, the great musician, and the fiddle. We have seen that one of its channels of information lay through Eldridge; and Eldridge had had special advantages. Several intelligent persons had also questioned Mr. Parmenter, before twenty-four hours had gone by, whether "it was true that that musical man had knocked the old fiddle all to smash?" and whether "that foreigner hadn't ben ruther aggravatin'?" and Mr. Parmenter had taken every thing very quietly, saying that "the fiddle was safe in its place, where he should be glad to have any of his neighbors come and see it;" and that "VOLKOV was considered the greatest living authority in music."

Now, the public, taking the whole thing in hand, sifting and weighing, came to the conclusion that "Parmenter was awful cut up, when the Dutchman spoke up, as pert as *could be*, and said 'his fiddle wa'n't wuth a snap, then, nor wouldn't be, if he kep' it a thousand year.'"

All now was looking forward to the new "Benefactors' Day," and working for it: the great doings of the forenoon and the great match on the ice. "An arch was to be made by Mr. Chambers, the carpenter, and decorated by the boys, and then set up on one of the school-roads or paths, and somewhere where it would be sheltered, because it would have to be all covered up till it was unveiled, and, if the winds should get at it, they'd make short work of it." So ran the talk of the School; and accordingly Mr. Chambers built it on the large barn-floor, and Lawrence and Lamson and Mason were busy for all the spare time of three days, in illuminating the front with the words "*Hail, Benefactors!*" in beautiful Church-text.

A steady, soaking rain set in during this time, threatening a thaw; but it cleared off, and cold came steadily on again.

The arch, as decorated, and covered three or four feet down by canvas which was to be drawn away at "The Unveiling," was set where no wind could reach it, and neatly held up at the back by shores let into the ice-covered ground. The monitors undertook the charge of it, in high hope; for all was ready, and the evening promised a fair morrow. It was dark when the last cluster of boys broke up; and Brade, in a sudden freak of liveliness and nimbleness, as soon as the rest were gone, set out to climb the arch, and climbed it safely, in spite of Peters's earnest remonstrances, urging what a risk and how needless a risk he was taking, "with that canvas on it," and that he himself "could not bear to see it."

As Brade sat astride at the top, and waved his hat in the faint light of the rising moon, with one hurrah, Mr. Parmenter, unseen, wished him "Good evening!" and complimented him as "an aspiring genius;" advising, however, his speedy coming down, for his own sake and that of the arch. So Brade made his harmless boy-brag that he was not afraid, and came down; receiving the benefactor's very courteous expression of "hope to see him to-morrow in an honorable position." Then, with Peters, who "was glad to see him on dry land again," at which blunder both laughed, he went into the house.

The next dawn rose over the earth as if all things above and around were ready to make a fine winter's day for the new holiday.

The younger boys were astir early, their blood all bustling; and the elders were full also of the great match and the doings at the arch beforehand, and talked them over. Gaston and Brade, as we know, were to come out in Latin; and each had contrived a little joke to give point to his short speech. One was going to wish that "it might hail benefactors," and the other that "the benefactors might be hale and hearty." This latter, being hard to make telling in Latin, was to be clapped till hands were sore. Some of the Trustees were to speak, — not too many, the boys hoped.

At ten of the clock in the forenoon, Rector Warren was at the arch, with his boys: Gaston and Brade wearing badges of red and blue ribbon. At ten of the clock, a handsome open sleigh, bearing Mr. Parmenter, handsomely furred, and Dr. Farwell in a skull-cap and muffled thoroughly, and Mr. Merritt, and Mr. Don, drew up. Sleighs full of neighbors, and a small crowd of neighbors on foot, had gathered, and were gathering.

Mr. Parmenter sat combining a look of dignified indifference with a look of modest consciousness.

Dr. Farwell rose, and, on a hint from Mr. Merritt, stood upon the seat.

"I am called upon," he said, his eyes twinkling from beside his nose, and from among his mufflings, "to make a speech. It seems to be thought that I know how to *do* that thing which is called *a speech*." (His hands being in his coat-pockets, the gestures were chiefly made with the shoulders, and by a flapping of the arms against the sides; and in this way, considering his greatness of manner, he was stately and emphatic.) "Have any of the boys who hear me thought what an *occasion* is? An 'occasion' is a time. If I act at the proper time, I act on the proper occasion. Now an occasion may be a *great* occasion; and men are said to rise" (here the gesture was easy, — a going up upon the toes, and down again) "to the greatness of the occasion. — *This* is a great *occasion!* — Perhaps benefactors need institutions: institutions also need benefactors. This occasion brings the two together: the institution welcomes its benefactors with a simple and significant display" (Mr. Parmenter was moved, and lifted his hat). "The taste and judgment of teachers, the zeal and skill of pupils." — Here, bowing his head, he gave the signal for withdrawing the canvas. Russell and Lamson ran it off; and the arch, with its illuminated inscription, was left bare. The orator started: everybody was astonished: there was the illumination; but there was, moreover, dangling below by a bit of tarred cord, the wreck of a junk bottle, to which was fastened a great sprawling inscription, "MELLO TRICK;" and, furthermore, there was a strange-looking black fiddle, with "STRADLE VARIOUS" upon it, hanging by another bit of tarred string.

The orator paused; but the intelligent neighbors began to question: "What d'ye s'pose that's for?" "'S he goin' to read his dokyments 'n public?"—"You'd better get a little nearer, Eldridge," said a resolute female voice in one of the sleighs.

The reader knows that boys are boys, but will believe that the St. Bart's boys kept pretty steady.

Meantime, the combined expression of Mr. Parmenter's face had become simplified and more intense. He was standing, now, in his sleigh, handsomely furred, as he was, and spoke with a hastiness unwonted in him:—

"Any thing like good discipline in the School," he said, "would have prevented"—

The orator spoke again:—

"It is hardly to be supposed that boys of Saint Bartholomew's School"—

Mr. Don also opened his mouth:—

"I can hardly conceive"—

"I saw *one* young gentleman on top of the arch after it was set up last night," said Mr. Parmenter, still not using his self-control.

"Of course you don't think *I* did that," said Brade, as hastily.

Peters stood forth like a born champion:—

"Brade only climbed up for fun," he said: "I was there."

Mr. Parmenter was either too angry or too much occupied to answer; and Brade walked straight over to Rector Warren, who was just coming forward, and said, "I hope you'll excuse me, sir: I can't speak this!"

Rector Warren, also, seemed too much occupied to give him much heed, and came forward in a hasty mood, like the rest, and said: —

"This is some mischievous prank. Of course no boy in School"—

The orator, who had kept his stand on the seat, here began again: —

"I can hardly suppose that any one of those" (from the rhyme he seemed unconsciously to take strength) "imbued with the spirit of St. Bartholomew's School would insult *this solemnity* — I speak advisedly — *this solemnity*" —

"If he did, he ought to smoke for it! that's all I've got to say," said Mr. Merritt.

By this time Russell, with help from Blake and others, had rid the arch of its incongruous hangings. The fiddle (a very rough thing) was handed about among the boys with some laughter, — Will Hirsett, with a grin, trying to play upon it like a banjo. Mr. Parmenter had recovered himself.

"We've had our little interruption," he said, smiling. "One of the poets assures us that 'the wisest plans of mice and men often go wrong.' Our young orators won't be in the mood for speaking. I've just got from town a quantity of West India fruit. With the consent of the Trustees and the Rector of the School, I will ask the Rector's acceptance of it, for the boys, and propose to adjourn till the great match on the ice, with three cheers for St. Bartholomew's School."

"I'd sooner break up the fiddle than break up the meeting," said Mrs. Wadham.

Mr. Parmenter's proposition was at once adopted by everybody, and, after three huzzas, in which the bottleneck and the fiddle bore a conspicuous part, the gathering broke up.

"How strangely we are made!" said Dr. Farwell comfortably, having sunk down in a corner of the sleigh and drawn up the robes. "Sometimes it seems as if we had the wrong parts: my heart was meant for a soldier,—a Cæsar or a Bonaparte. If there'd been a concealed rebellion under that bottle and that violin, I felt when I was speaking as if I wanted to face it, to put it down!" His hands being still in his coat-pockets, he emphasized by setting his lips firmly together, and flapping his elbows against his sides.

"It won't do to let that stop here," said Mr. Merritt.

CHAPTER XXXV.

THE MATCH ON THE ICE.

"The Great Middle Class," the self-confident Third Form, had got the Fourth to join them, and had challenged the rest of the School, at hockey, on Lake Thrash; and the school was eager to "stop the bragging of those everlasting Thirds." Stores of hockey-sticks had been laid in; Blake making much fun with his queer-looking set, and Towne much show of his, while Gaston bragged of one favorite that it was "tough as the oak on Alpine heights, that wrestles with the winds, this way and that, *at ipsa hæret scopulis.*"

The boys had not been to the lake since the beginning of the rain; but there had been a day or two of steady freezing.

The day, as we have seen, was splendid; and nothing that had happened, or "might, could, would, or should" happen, was to hinder or hamper the sport of that afternoon. All day the flags were flying on the boat-houses at the lake. All day the whole landscape — beautiful as it was, with ups and downs, and sweeping, wooded dales — was sending back to the sun, from its smooth, icy crust, a dazzling splendor. No wind was blowing, and the steady cold seemed breaking again.

The match was to come off at two o'clock, precisely.

Russell was to call the game at that hour; and, after that, "whoever was not on the spot, it was his own loss." Dinner was hurried, as we may suppose, and but half eaten, and then, in troops, the boys went down, the smallest ones, of course, leading the rest. All were merry as kids and kittens.

One company, in which are Will Hirsett, Wilkins, Dover, Ransom, and Wadham, Second, are rehearsing the more eminent attractions.

"Ned Prouty is to be there with his French horn;" and "there's to be the biggest bonfire that was ever seen, — Mr. Stout has carried down ever so much cord-wood;" and "there's to be coffee, and chocolate, and lemonade, just as people like." "Do you hear that? There's Prouty! There ain't a man in the United States can beat him!"

Our readers, to have the scene well before them, must remember that one of the chief beauties of this lake abounding in beauties (may ruthless and tasteless road-makers never spoil it!) is St. Bart's Bay. To make this, the western shore, at less than half a mile's distance from the northern, trends away, rounding Crystal Point; and then the bay, or cove, sets in for three-quarters of a mile to the westward. The southern or further shore of this bay is winding and wooded, with granite cliffs half-way toward the west, and then a beach. The northern shore winds less. On this, and about as far from the west as Crystal Point, stand the boys' boat-houses.

The scene now lies before us. Yonder up the bay, and over, near the southern shore, are people gathering. On the road, along the western end, can be descried horses and sleigh-loads of people; and there are janglings and tinklings of sleigh-bells on the way. From the lake a blue smoke is beginning to curl upward in the still air; and there are boys, we may be sure, busy as ants, feeding and fanning the flames.

A line of flags, on short staves, stretches across from inside of Boat-house-pier to the shore inside of Crystal Point.

From the far gathering comes, now and then, a single living note or two of Prouty's French horn, as if thrown out to stir and waken, as they do, the merriment and happiness of every thing about.

"What flag is that?" asked Russell, as soon as the turn on the lake-path brought the boat-houses into sight. "There's the Caput, already!"

"Why, that's the old Admiral's bunting!" said Blake. "Don't you see the S. B. and the dagger?"

"No, no," said Russell. "I don't mean that: what's that one over the 'eight-oar'? I never saw it before. It wasn't there this morning."

"That's Peters's," said Meadows, who was within hearing. "His mother made it for the Rosicrucian Nine; and they're going to wear their red-cross shirts to-day. It's all silk."

Russell spoke again: —

"Now, see here, fellows! just at this turn, where nobody can help seeing, we've got a sign up, 'WARNING! LOOK OUT AND DON'T GO EAST OF THE FLAGS, FOR YOUR LIFE!' Mr. Folsom made us ten of 'em, and we've got some on the flag-staffs, and some all round. There's been notice given twice in school, and we've got to do it again down here. Has Brade come down yet? He's got the ball."

"Maybe he feels badly about this morning, and won't come," said Hutchins.

"Poh! That isn't the stuff he's made of, let me tell you," answered Blake. "Mr. Parmenter don't get over it so easy, I bet you! Wa'n't the Caput wrathy?"

"Brade was mad: who wouldn't be?" said Russell. "But when he found everybody knew he was right, he didn't care. Now, fellows, the sun lies too much on our side of the bay; we've got to work over toward the other shore, so we've had the floats* from the boat-houses, and any thing else we could get, carried over that way for seats and standing. Look at the spectators! All Eastham 'll be down, you see if they don't. Call all the fellows up here, will you? Where's Prouty?"

Straightway began all manner of calls and cries, for Prouty was over near the other side; but the boys gathered as dutifully as bees to kindred music.

"There's a squad of fellows coasting down that bank! call 'em, Walters, will you?" said Russell, whose eye was, as it ought to be, over the whole field of sight. "The Caput's there, and Mr. Bruce and Mr. Hamersley; and there's Mr. Manson; and there are the Wadhams, and Mr. Parmenter, and Dr. Farwell, and lots of 'em. Now, fellows, look here!" he said, as the boys on this side of the lake gathered, "there isn't any safety outside of the line from here to Crystal Point, because they've been cutting ice. The place is all up in our bay; and then we've got to go away over to the other side to get out of the sun. (Wilkins! don't make such a noise, please, we're laying down the rules again, and the lives of some fellows may depend upon it. Everybody's got to listen.) Now, we've got four base-ball

* So the landing-bridges were called at St. Bart's; rafts hinged-up to the boat-houses, and with the lower ends floating freely on timbers.

flags set right across, clear of all danger. (You see where Lamson's looking at 'em.) Nobody's to go *outside of that line* to the eastward; *inside* there's no danger. If you see anybody undertaking to pass that line, knock him down! Now we've got seven minutes to get over there and begin."

A shout followed Russell's laying down of the law, showing the School's acquiescence in the requirements of recognized authority. The sound of Ned Prouty's horn came, smooth, and clear, and inspiring, across the ice. A Scots tune, — "Come through the heather! Around him gather! Ye're a' the welcomer early," and so on, Prouty was playing; and away the boys went, large and small, Russell, and Blake, and Walters, no less than Hirsett, and Wilkins, and Meadows, and lesser ones, to the edge of the ice, and put on their skates, and were off to see which would come first to the ground. Prouty was beginning Yankee Doodle.

"There's Brade, now!" cried some of the hindmost, who began beckoning with hands, and arms, and hats, and caps, to hurry the loiterers, — two or three boys who were now doing their best to make up for lost time.

Yankee Doodle, well played, is enough, almost, to set the very trees off their standing. The boys from the edge of the lake were all scampering over the ice toward the further side, after giving their last shout to Brade and his friends to hurry; and, hurry-scurry down the hill, come the three laggards.

They near the bend in the boat-house path, by which the warning-board is set, in full sight; and Peters cries out, in triumph, —

"There she is! Look at her! Isn't the red cross a beauty!"

They all look over at the flags.

Peters was strongly inclined to linger and admire; but there was no time. Panting, they all agreed, as they ran, that the red cross was the handsomest flag in the School.

"There's the Caput, and everybody!" cried Brade, panting. "Down with us!"

Ned Prouty's music came as fresh and clear across the lake as if on its way it had gathered sparkle and tinkle from the frozen water; and it seemed to be joined by accordant notes from hill and dale.

The three late-comers are at the bank. An inarticulate noise of voices from the further side comes to their ears, and they can understand it, without distinguishing a word, to be a call, from fifty tongues, to hurry. One or two boys set off from the crowd to meet them.

"If it hadn't been for this ball!" said Brade; and he held up to be seen, if it might, at the other side, the ball which he had in charge.

"Plaguy thing!" said Peters. "Long enough we looked for it!"

"Play's called! They're at it now! Those fellows are going back!" cried Remsen; and, in an instant, the three were on the lake.

The French horn had ceased to play.

"There it goes!" said Brade, who tripped at the edge of the ice, and lost the ball from his hand. The ball skimmed over the smooth surface, and the loser started after it. Remsen, as he put on his skates, called out, —

"Look out for thin ice!"

Peters started up. "*Where's the line?*" he cried, frightened, and set off, without his skates, as Brade was, to follow. Already Brade had come so near the ball as to have touched it with his hockey-stick, but, failing to catch it, he had, of course, given it a new start.

Now, from the other side, came one far shout, whose words were indistinguishable. Then arose an inarticulate din, and a rush. Peters called to Brade to stop, but followed on himself as fast as he could run on the glossy level, still shouting. The din from the crowd became an uproar.

"I've got it!" cried Brade; and at the very instant there was a sound of rending of the ice in all directions, and a dreadful plunge, and the boy was in the lake, where the water was deep enough to float a ship of the line like a leaf.

The din, which had been continually drawing nearer, suddenly became an utter stillness, as if the splash in the deadly water had swallowed up every living soul, except one figure not far away from the frightful scene, and one among the on-lookers afar.

Peters uttered a shriek, and for an instant faltered. A terrible cry of agony, in a girl's voice, clear as the track of lightning through the air, and leaving a stillness as utter as is the blackness after the flash, came from the bay.

"Stop, Peters!" shouted the Caput's voice; "and everybody that can't help, do keep away! Keep back! Keep back! Where are the floats?"

Mr. Parmenter appeared at his best here, and was quick and business-like. He sent for medical men; he sent for ropes. Everybody was eager to help, — to go or stay. Horses and sleighs were ready; lives, — every thing.

Peters half turned his head; but all along now he

guided himself by some rule of his own. He did not rush headlong a single heedless step, and yet he hurried forward, bending over, steadied by his hockey-stick, and peering at the ice as he went, and never taking off his eyes from the faithless and dangerous ground on which he was setting his feet.

Shouts that he could not have failed to hear called him by name. He never turned; he never gave the least heed. Every thought, and all his life, seemed to be given to the one thing that he was doing.

A gasping, choking cry came from the drowning boy; and the noise of ice breaking again and again, as Brade, in his struggle to save himself out of death, in which he was already, clutched again and again the treacherous water's crust. Peters groaned.

"Keep up! keep up!" he shouted. "I'll help" (the word he was so fond of), and, never lifting his eyes from the ice, he went on.

Now, suddenly, he changes his way; and, never stopping, goes down, full length, upon the ice, and pushing his hockey-stick before him, works himself forward with his left hand, slowly perhaps, but he has not far to go.

"Catch hold of me! Remsen! some one!" he cried, working himself forward.

By this time the noise from all sides had gathered, till it had become like the roar of the sea. Some sounds might be distinguished; but there was one that made itself felt, as if it were from the very soul of the scene, — a pleading cry from that girl's voice, which had been heard before.

Meantime, and all the while, the mass of human life that was near this struggle with sudden death was hurriedly bringing all it had, of strength and wisdom, to the rescue. Dr. Evans and Dr. Mott, of Weston, had been sent for by Mr. Parmenter. It seemed long, long; but it was only two or three minutes since the boy had broken through. There had been a half mile to come over; but the rush to the rescue had begun the moment that Brade started the wrong way from the shore.

"Catch hold!" cried one of the foremost of those who were running upon the ice, but still a little way off. He seemed to be repeating Peters's call.

It was the new tutor, Mr. Hamersley, deathly pale. He stripped himself of his outer coat, as he ran, and let it fall.

"Make a line of men, right here, at these flags!" said Rector Warren, assisted by Mr. Parmenter and others, who all were near enough now to help.

"The ropes are coming," said Mr. Parmenter, beckoning to bring them.

There was a hurried sound of trampling and of sleigh-bells close at hand, and a confused shout, and the line opened. A horse came through, and behind him, on a large boat-house-float, to which he was harnessed, was Mr. Stout, with three or four boys. Others of the Tutors, too, were close by to give their help.

Mr. Hamersley, following Peters's plan, had already gone down flat upon the ice, and was working himself forward, as Peters had done; but the leader was still many yards ahead, and working on.

Oh, what a sight it was! Amid the broken floes of ice, Brade's head could be descried, and his arms, laying themselves on one support after another, which gave way as he tried it. A sort of drowning moan came from him.

"Here! Here!" cried Peters; and Brade struck out for him. The hooked stick, thrust out ahead, was nearing the water; but the ice broke, as Brade put up his arms upon it. The haggard boy already looked like one belonging to The Dead.

"I'm coming, Peters, — brave boy!" said Mr. Hamersley.

Without a single word, but with his lips set fast together, Mr. Stout had unhitched his horse, as soon as he got a little way clear of the throng, and had given him in charge to Lamson, to lead back. Between the silent man and the three silent boys who stayed with him (Remsen was one, and Blake was one, and Towne was one), there seemed a perfect understanding. All four worked together as instantly as if they had a single will, and had done this same work many a time before. The Rector of the School came up. He saw that all was going well, and, saying nothing, joined himself to the party, looking agonizingly towards the fatal struggle, and laying hold, with the foremost, of one of the fasts of the float, to urge it forward.

"One o' them ropes! from Prouty!" said Mr. Stout, briefly, to Blake; "and follow right up!" The kindly French-horn-player was already near.

Before the words could have been understood, the Rector had rushed toward the advancing messengers, and in another moment was back again, close upon the light raft of boards now sliding fast over the glossy ice to the danger, and had flung a coil of rope upon the middle of it.

There was a great noise of men's and women's voices, and yet there were those who marked the frightful, haggard face of Kate Ryan, as, yielding and trusting to

Mr. Manson, she was led and half borne away by him.

But a cry suddenly goes up, — "He's got him!" and a sort of unthinking start forward was made by the crowd, but instantly checked.

Peters's hook seemed to have caught Brade's clothing, or to have been grappled by the drowning boy. Some sound was made by Peters, as if he would speak; but no words were heard. Mr. Hamersley pushed himself forward.

"Hold on! hold on, Peters!" he said, — "hold on!"

"That other boy ought to be stopped!" the crowd shouted; but Peters heeded nothing but his purpose.

Mr. Stout, with his crew, had never halted or hesitated for the twinkling of an eye.

"Now, Blake, there's new ice," he said. "You and I stay back" (all the while he was fastening a rope with a long free end to the front part of the float, then going to the back and making a running noose there). "Towne!" — he began.

Another of the fatal crackings of the ice was heard, and Peters was in the ice-cold water! A shout of horror went up from those who were looking on and could not help. Again a start was made by the crowd; but it was checked.

Mr. Stout cast one glance. "Be we all going in?" he said; but his hands kept about their business all the time.

"Stop that man! Don't let anybody else be drowned!" shouted the crowd.

"Bring on your raft!" called Mr. Hamersley, now rising to hands and knees, and so still making his way forward, almost as if he were running.

"O great and loving God! Help! help! for Jesus's sake!" cried Rector Warren, baring his head, and flinging his arms forth.

"Amen! Lord! Lord!" cried many a voice.

"Where's that other float?" Mr. Stout called, as he finished with the first. "Towne, you and Remsen must do it now. Down on your bellies!" (it was done before it was said) "I won't tie you; trust to your grip, if *the world* goes, and look to God!" said Mr. Stout.

The boys were off, shoving the raft from behind, while Mr. Stout and Blake "paid out" the rope, flinging the end back to be grasped by those behind, — the first of whom, of course, was the most interested, Rector Warren. "Wait, Hamersley!" he shouted.

A crash, and Tutor Hamersley was in the icy water, as if of his own will. He did not sink, and, to the horror of the lookers-on, his was the only head to be seen among the floes.

"Keep your fast grip!" said Mr. Stout, in a clear, low voice. "Cling to your raft!" and so the boys pushed forward, and the rope slid through his hand.

Already Mr. Wilson and others had brought a second float, and made it ready. The Rector seized and helped it forward. Mr. Parmenter expostulated against his running needless risks; but, with his hired men, helped.

The Tutor struck out among the floating ice, and grappled something.

"Now, now!" he cried.

"Now!" said the crowd, "on with your raft!"

Remsen and Towne pushed forward bravely. Mr. Hamersley seized their raft, and got one elbow up upon it. Instantly Mr. Stout called to his boys to back away, and they came safely out.

Meanwhile, with both hands and his one free arm, Mr. Hamersley strove to heave a senseless, heavy mass out of the water. The second raft went forward, a little way off.

"Here, boys!" said Mr. Stout, shoving with his foot a piece of scantling. "Tilt your float up with this, and while you're doing it keep tight hold to your raft!"

Even while he was speaking to them, he flung a rope to Mr. Hamersley. Then to the boys, again: "Now prize it up, further along; but look out and hold tight!" he added.

The work went on as fast as speech almost, and yet the time seemed to be wasting.

"Quick! quick! can't anybody help him?" said the crowd.

Beloved and esteemed as Brade was, the persevering heroism of the boy who had fearlessly, and not at all unwisely, but thoughtfully, bestowed his life to save the other, had so impressed all witnesses that a cry went up, "Have you got Peters? Is it Peters?"

The lifting and sloping of the raft was not all that was wanted; but yet it helped the faithful worker in that chilling water.

"Haul! haul!" he cried out, huskily.

There seemed a great throb in the air from the crowd, and a low sobbing, as from one man, while the soaked, heavy, lifeless mass was dragged over the cracking ice.

"Brade! Brade!" said the crowd.

"Now one tremendous shove! with all your might!" cried Rector Warren, whose movements had been little noticed, but who was working in a sort of frenzy. As the new float darted forward, he flung himself at full length on it, and went out. The ice cracked, but did not give way.

"Who's saving that man?" cried the crowd. "He can't live there."

"Get Hamersley out!" said Dr. Evans, who had just come, "or you'll have another patient for me. Take this boy carefully, and carry him gently. Don't jolt him. As fast as you can go, and go gently. The School's the nearest place."

Ned Prouty took the heavy, dripping mass like a baby, and bore it tenderly. Remsen and others followed.

Mr. Stout kept steadily at his work, without a word; and, before the poor boy's body had been taken off, its rescuer had been dragged to solid ice, sinking, and shivering, and shaking, livid and nearly dead, but mindful enough to gasp a single word, "Peters!"

Two of his brother-tutors bore him off.

Now all thoughts were turned to Peters.

The Rector of the School, on hands and knees, peered for an instant from the float, which had been checked just as it reached the edge, and then threw himself in among the floating cakes of ice and struck out definitely.

"He sees the other!" was the cry of strangers. Many said, "He's after Peters!"

He had got something, and among cakes of ice made his way back and got the rope in some way fastened round his burden, then helped it up.

"Remember bones and flesh, men! pull easy!" said Mr. Stout; and the neighbors were gentle and tender enough. It was drawn out as fast as a heavy and jointed body could be drawn out of the water, and over the breaking, thin ice. Once on the float, and it was in their hands in a moment.

There was no crowding or rudeness. There was no cry, as there had been before. The crowd of neighbors held themselves back; the boys kept a little aloof.

"There's a hero, if ever anybody was!" said Mr. Stout, still working. No one else spoke; but there was a reverent and tender way about all, which showed that they all thought one thing.

"It isn't the first brave thing he's done," said Blake, with tears in his eyes.

Mr. Stout's float was shoved out to the Rector without an instant's delay.

As the Red Cross came to sight, on Peters's bosom, Towne said, kindly, "Those flags ought to be half-mast!" but Blake said, "I wouldn't fuss with 'em; I believe that's death!" Russell approved.

As they bore off the body, tenderly and reverently, the Rector, with help, followed. Mr. Parmenter's sleigh was ready for him; but it seemed best that he should walk; and so, with help, he followed the bearers up the hill.

The crowd broke up. Many followed; many lingered; many went sadly from the gloomy spot, in different directions across the ice.

Mr. Stout steadily gathered up the ropes; gave to some of the men, who offered themselves freely, a few directions about gathering the property together and putting it back; then glanced at the fire, blazing alone upon the ice, and the flags flying for the holiday, and turned to go.

"It's my opinion," said he, "if there'd ben another

18

boy to follow Peters and hang on to him, they'd all have been here alive."

"You mean Remsen?" asked Towne, who had waited, silently.

"I don't say that, but if there'd been *somebody* to follow up. *But*—'tis so, and I suppose 'twas meant to *be* so."

CHAPTER XXXVI.

OUR STORY IS ENDED.

THIS great happening will bring the end to our story.

A telegraphic message was at once sent to a friend of Mrs. Peters, to be conveyed to the widow.

Almost as soon as Prouty had borne Brade's body in, came Mrs. Ryan, agonized with grief and fear, and insisted upon being "let go in to the child." Mrs. Wadham, who during that dreadful time had planted herself in the house, and was anywhere at any moment, to be of use, was at that moment within sight and hearing, and tried to take charge of her and prevent her intrusion upon Dr. Evans and his helpers.

"Bring me to the Rector! — Mr. Warren!" cried the other, almost frenzied.

"But Mr. Warren's in the water himself, or drowned, by this time," answered Mrs. Wadham, solemnly.

The sad procession with Peters's body struck all dumb; but Rector Warren, who followed, weak and shivering, called Mrs. Wadham, and begged her to tell the doctor that "Mrs. Ryan had a right to be in the room, if any one."

Mr. Parmenter, who had come up with him, asked "whether that would be entirely wise," but did not press his obiection; and Mrs. Wadham undertook the charge, following close upon the bearers. Philip Rainor, who, with a strange pertinacity, tried to force himself in, Mr. Parmenter effectually kept out.

"*Nobody* has any right here but my helpers," said Dr. Evans when the message was delivered to him: "we cannot be hindered."

"Try me, only! Try me!" Mrs. Ryan said, with hands clasped, and was let in.

There was one short outburst; but she only threw herself on her knees against the wall, without hindering the work which, under quick orders of Dr. Evans, went on. Then she found herself a place among the workers, and was most ready.

How skill and hopefulness and untiring effort were used to set in motion again in these young bodies the many-working powers of life before they should be once for ever set fast in stillness, we need not tell. Before fairly recovering himself, Mr. Hamersley sent an urgent request to be allowed to help, but was enjoined to keep his bed. Mr. Bruce was there at work.

Slowly and painfully, but like true life, the life came back to Brade, and instantly Mrs. Ryan, who had already not failed to give tender help to those who were working upon the other body, left him entirely for the other. But here all warm chafing, all gentle forcing in and out of the life-feeding air, all scourging of the water-soaked soles and palms of feet and hands, showed only that the life which Peters had without fear risked was lost out of this world for ever.

Brade was taken away in warm blankets to a bed elsewhere; and the faithful, loving work upon the body of his true-hearted friend went on untired far into the night through six or seven long, slow hours. The last who left it were Mrs. Ryan and the Tutor. But all had long been done: life was not to come back, and it was left for dead. As these two were folding carefully the clothes which had been stripped off Peters, there fell out a small plate of silver, on which was rude, boyish engraving. Mr. Bruce read it aloud:—

"'B. R. C.—Rosicrucians.—Inst. Oct. 8, 18—, by me, A. P.'"

"Poor fellow! So he was the whole of that 'secret society'!" he said.

"The poor, dear child, indeed!" said Mrs. Ryan, kissing his forehead.

Meantime the hours and bells went on, and the Rector made a point of having all in their places at tea; but the house was still, as if no boys were in it but two,—the half-living and the dead,—save for the noise of doors, as many neighbors came and went, or of voices, as when Mrs. Wadham asked, and perhaps asked again, a question of some one passing the room in which she sat. She had sent often to her own house for whatever she thought might be of service, and kept Eldridge waiting at call. She explained that "she had scarcely seen Mrs. Warren; but that wasn't strange.—That Mrs. Ryan's the mother of him,—that's plain enough!" she said.

"I hope it's something as creditable as that," said Mr. Parmenter.

The boys were cheered by knowing that Brade was saved, and some of them reasoned that Peters had been less time in the water. Among the guests in the sitting-room more was known, and the evening was gloomy. Mrs. Wadham meant to spend the night; Mr. Parmenter, and Dr. Farwell and Mr. Don, who were his guests, stayed late. All talked in lowered voices of the sad things which had made the afternoon so long as seemingly to sunder them by many a day from its own forenoon. Late in the evening Mr. Manson came, having made an arrangement with the Rector of the School to watch with Antony Brade.

"The mystery about him seems to be clearing off," said Mr. Parmenter.

"What's a mystery for, if it *ain't* to be cleared up?" asked Mrs. Wadham.

"I take it," said Dr. Farwell, his elbows resting on his chair, and his hands spread open, "that mysteries may sometimes *baffle investigation* or *elude investigation.* On the other hand, there are times" —

"This seems to have been a very harmless mystery," said Mr. Manson.

"If it *proves* altogether harmless to the character of the School," said Mr. Parmenter, gravely.

"Exactly, sir! I hope it'll prove so," said Mr. Don.

"I don't see how the character of the School is concerned. He's an orphan, and Mrs. Ryan's his aunt. That's all. She's an Irishwoman, and made a secret of it."

"*It may not be quite so harmless,*" said Mr. Parmenter.

"Possibly not, sir," said Mr. Don.

"*People sometimes have reasons,*" said Mrs. Wadham, with quiet authority.

"You shall judge for yourselves. Mr. Warren has known her for years, and knows all about her. Brade, her brother, looked high for his ancestors, among 'Macs' or 'O's.' But then *he* made his living and a good deal of money, with job-wagons or some such business.

Just then the family, every one, died off by fever, except this boy; and his aunt brought him up, and, in due time, put him here under Mr. Warren, and kept the relationship to herself."

There was a silence, which Mrs. Wadham broke by saying, —

"I should think that was a very likely explanation: yes."

"It might explain some things about the boy," said Mr. Parmenter. "Well, I suppose when arrangements are made, we'd better go."

"Mr. Stout *will* sit up with poor Peters; but he's willing to let Rainor stay with him," said Mr. Manson.

"Why, I've told that Rainor we didn't want him round here," Mr. Parmenter said hastily.

"Now," said Mr. Manson, "he's not so bad: you didn't give yourself a chance to hear what he came for. He came to say he put those things on the arch."

"That shows some degree of grace, now," said Dr. Farwell.

CHAPTER XXXVII.

A PURPOSE FOR LIFE.

BRADE gained; but he gained slowly. He had not asked about Peters since the first day that he spoke, although he constantly talked of him. At length Mr. Manson sat down, and tenderly and freely told him all: that "Peters had ended his life well, and entered into his rest in Him who gave His life a ransom for many." Mrs. Peters was in the room, — looking like her son. She heard the words and said, "Yes: he had ended his life well. She had often feared for him in the world: now she should be at peace. But she must look to the boy for whom" —

"I can't stay here, after Peters," said Brade, trying to lift himself; "but, if I live, I'll never forget Peters, and I'll try to do as he said, and *help*."

"God give you grace to do it, dear Antony!" said his aunt.

Mrs. Peters took the boy's hand, and kneeled, with her face bowed upon the bed, as if she prayed the same thing in secret.

Mr. Manson, standing, said, —

"AMEN!"

Cambridge: Press of John Wilson and Son.

"MISS ALCOTT IS REALLY A BENEFACTOR OF HOUSEHOLDS." — *H. H.*

LITTLE MEN: Life at Plumfield with Jo's Boys. By LOUISA M. ALCOTT. With Illustrations. Price $1.50.

"The gods are to be congratulated upon the success of the Alcott experiment as well as all childhood, young and old, upon the singular charm of the little men and little women who have run forth from the Alcott cottage, children of a maiden whose genius is beautiful motherhood." — *The Examiner.*

"No true-hearted boy or girl can read this book without deriving benefit from the perusal; nor, for that matter, will it the least injure children of a larger growth to endeavor to profit by the examples of gentleness and honesty set before them in its pages. What a delightful school 'Jo' did keep! Why, it makes us want to live our childhood's days over again, in the hope that we might induce some kind-hearted female to establish just such a school, and might prevail upon our parents to send us, 'because it was cheap.' . . . We wish the genial authoress a long life in which to enjoy the fruits of her labor, and cordially thank her, in the name of our young people, for her efforts in their behalf." — *Waterbury American.*

"Miss Alcott, whose name has already become a household word among little people, will gain a new hold upon their love and admiration by this little book. It forms a fitting sequel to 'Little Women,' and contains the same elements of popularity. . . . We expect to see it even more popular than its predecessor, and shall heartily rejoice at the success of an author whose works afford so much hearty and innocent enjoyment to the family circle, and teach such pleasant and wholesome lessons to old and young." — *N. Y. Times.*

"Suggestive, truthful, amusing, and racy, in a certain simplicity of style which very few are capable of producing. It is the history of only six months' school-life of a dozen boys, but is full of variety and vitality, and the having girls with the boys is a charming novelty, too. To be very candid, this book is so thoroughly good that we hope Miss Alcott will give us another in the same genial vein, for she understands children and their ways." — *Phil. Press.*

A specimen letter from a little woman to the author of "Little Men."

June 17, 1871.

DEAR MISS ALCOTT, — We have just finished "Little Men," and like it so much that we thought we would write and ask you to write another book sequel to "Little Men," and have more about Laurie and Amy, as we like them the best. We are the Literary Club, and we got the idea from "Little Women." We have a paper two sheets of foolscap and a half. There are four of us, two cousins and my sister and myself. Our assumed names are: Horace Greeley, President; Susan B. Anthony, Editor; Harriet B. Stowe, Vice-President; and myself, Anna C. Ritchie, Secretary. We call our paper the "Saturday Night," and we all write stories and have reports of sermons and of our meetings, and write about the queens of England. We did not know but you would like to hear this, as the idea sprang from your book; and we thought we would write, as we liked your book *so* much. And now, if it is not too much to ask of you, I wish you would answer this, as we are very impatient to know if you will write another book; and please answer soon, as Miss Anthony is going away, and she wishes very much to hear from you before she does. If you write, please direct to —— Street, Brooklyn, N.Y.

Yours truly,

ALICE ——

Mailed to any address, postpaid, on receipt of the advertised price, by the Publishers,

ROBERTS BROTHERS, BOSTON

AUNT JO'S SCRAP-BAG.

BY LOUISA M. ALCOTT.

Vol. II., comprising "Shawl-Straps."

16mo. Cloth, gilt. Price $1.00.

From the Morning Star.

Nobody expects from Miss Alcott any thing but books of the raciest qualities and the choicest flavors. This story of her foreign travel, in company with two female friends, is just as vivacious and unique as any thing previously issued with her name on the title-page. One may have read the narratives and notes of forty tourists over the same field, but he cannot afford to neglect this story. He will find nothing repeated either in substance or form. It is a new vein that is here worked, and the products are all singularly fresh. It is a rare literary bundle which these shawl-straps enclose.

Mr. Whipple, in the Boston Globe.

Roberts Brothers have published a small volume the mere announcement of which is enough to insure its circulation. This volume is "Shawl-Straps," a second part of "Aunt Jo's Scrap-Bag," by Louisa M. Alcott, — a name well known to all "little men," and "little women," and "old-fashioned girls," now inhabiting the country. The book is a racy, almost rollicking account of the personal experiences of three American women travelling in France, Switzerland, Italy, and England.

Miss Alcott carefully abstains from writing what is called a book of travels, and confines herself to giving an amusing account of what really occurred to herself and her two companions. Thus, in London, the party devoted much more time in hunting up Dickens's characters than in visiting "leading objects of interest." They nearly succeeded in finding Mrs. Gamp, and actually took "weal pie and porter" at Mrs. Todger's. The description of Spurgeon and his congregation is the most life-like we have ever read. Indeed the whole tone of the book is that of conversation, in which the familiarity of ordinary talk is accompanied with more than ordinary certainty of phrase, so that her readers may, in some sense, be said to join the party and become "Shawl-Strappists" themselves. It may be added that one is never tired of any record of a foreign tour which makes him or her a companion of the journey; and, as Miss Alcott succeeds in doing this, the principal objection which will be made to her book is its shortness.

Sold everywhere. Mailed, postpaid, by the Publishers,

ROBERTS BROTHERS, BOSTON.

WORK:

A STORY OF EXPERIENCE.

BY LOUISA M. ALCOTT,

Author of "Little Women," "An Old-Fashioned Gi l, "Little Men."

With Character Illustrations by Sol Eytinge.

16mo, cloth, gilt. Price $1.75.

Rev. H. W. BEECHER, the Editor of the "Christian Union," says: —

"This week our columns witness a parting which, we believe, will be matter of regret to thousands of our readers, — between 'Christie' and all who have followed her fortunes in Miss Alcott's serial. We owe to the author our hearty editorial acknowledgment for the great pleasure, and the something more than pleasure, which she has furnished to our wide-spread family of readers. With most of them, we doubt not, her heroine has been 'first favorite,' since her appearance, six months ago. Right well we know that our solemn editorial preachments, nay, our very best editorial attempts at being wise and witty together, — with all the learning, poetry, orthodoxy, and heresy of the other departments, — have been utterly slighted by most readers of the 'Christian Union' until they had eagerly followed the fortunes of Christie and her friends down to the unwelcome 'To be Continued,' until, this week, is reached the still more unwelcome 'The End.'"

The New Bedford "Standard" says: —

"*It is seldom that an author can achieve four successive triumphs such as Miss Alcott has in 'Little Women,' 'Little Men,' 'Old-Fashioned Girl,' and now in this new candidate for public favor.*"

The New York "Mail" says: —

"No novel can be purposeless which brings sunshine into the home or the heart, and to say that Miss Alcott's books hitherto have been without purpose is to use the word in very limited meaning. She has done a vast deal of good. But now she has reached that higher stage of development in which purpose is not simply a factor, but the chief factor of writing. She would do something more than entertain, however blessed that in itself be; she would exert her utmost powers directly in uplifting. That is good for her and for her readers. She is proving herself even a greater writer than her admirable 'Little Women' series asserts. For that canon of art which rules out work because it is purposeful restrains the scope of art within too narrow bounds. Purpose is the inspiration of the highest art."

Sold by all Bookseller. Mailed, postpaid, by the Publishers,

ROBERTS BROTHERS, BOSTON.

"As there was nobody to see, he just sat down and cried as hard as Dotty herself."

www.ingramcontent.com/pod-product-compliance
Lightning Source LLC
LaVergne TN
LVHW021147110826
845150LV00005B/1150

* 9 7 8 1 4 2 5 5 4 6 9 2 2 *